19.95

D0220279

Homosexuality and Sexuality

Dialogues of the Sexual Revolution

Volume I

Homosexuality and Sexuality

Dialogues of the Sexual Revolution

Volume I

Lawrence Mass

Harrington Park Press
New York • London

ISBN 0-918393-89-2

Published by

Harrington Park Press, 10 Alice Street, Binghamton, NY 13904-1580
EUROSPAN/Harrington, 3 Henrietta Street, London WC2E 8LU England

Harrington Park Press is a subsidiary of The Haworth Press, Inc., 10 Alice Street, Binghamton, NY 13904-1580.

Cover design by Marshall Andrews.

Library of Congress Cataloging-in-Publication Data

Mass, Lawrence, 1946–
Homosexuality and sexuality : dialogues of the sexual revolution / Lawrence Mass.
    p. cm.
    Includes bibliographical references and index.
    ISBN 0-918393-89-2 (v. 1)
    1. Homosexuality—United States. 2. Gay liberation movement—United States. 3. AIDS (Disease)—United States. I. Title.
HQ76.3.U5M38   1990b
306.76′6—dc20
                                            90-4987
                                               CIP

For Arnie Kantrowitz

In memory of my father,
Dr. Max Mass

To my friends with AIDS:
In memory of those deceased
In honor of those surviving

CONTENTS

Foreword   xi

Acknowledgements   xix

PSYCHIATRY VERSUS SEX RESEARCH

Perspective in Perspective   1
> *An Interview with William Masters*
> *and Virginia Johnson*

Homophobia on the Couch   7
> *A Conversation with Richard Pillard*

Homosexual Behavior   16
> *A Conversation with Judd Marmor*

The Birds, the Bees and John Money   29
> *A Conversation with Sexologist*
> *John Money*

Sex in the Therapeutic State   47
> *A Conversation with Thomas Szasz*

A Nation of Sexual Stutterers   65
> *A Conversation with Mary Calderone*

GAY FANTASIES, MALE REALITIES AND BONDING

The Church and Homosexuality   77
> *A Conversation with John McNeill*

Circumcision: Facts, Fallacies and Fantasies   87
> *A Conversation with George Stambolian*

Male Couples   99
> *A Conversation with Charles Silverstein*

Wrestling with Sexual Preference   105
        A Conversation with John Handley

FIVE INTERVIEWS FROM THE FIRST TWO YEARS
   OF THE AIDS EPIDEMIC (1981-1983)   113

Alvin Friedman-Kien   128

Donna Mildvan   133

Donald Krintzman   136

Dan William   143

David Sencer   156

GAY YOUTH, GAY HISTORY

Protecting Lesbian and Gay Youth   162
        A Conversation with Damien Martin
        and Emery Hetrick

The Swastika and the Pink Triangle: Nazis and Gay Men   189
        An Interview with Richard Plant

Nazis and Gay Men II   200
        An Exchange with Arnie Kantrowitz

"Sissyness" as Metaphor   213
        A Conversation with Richard Green

Keeping Time   223
        A Conversation with Martin Bauml
        Duberman

Index   241

ABOUT THE AUTHOR

Lawrence D. Mass, MD, is currently medical director of Greenwich House Alcoholism Treatment Program, Greenwich House Methadone Maintenance Treatment Program, and Greenwich House Counseling Center in New York City. He was the first physician to write for the gay press on a regular basis and became the first writer to cover the AIDS epidemic in any press. He is co-founder of Gay Men's Health Crisis, a co-founder and past vice-president of New York Physicians for Human Rights, and author of *Medical Answers About AIDS*, a publication of Gay Men's Health Crisis, which has been recommended by Jane Brody in the *New York Times*.

In recognition of his medical writing, Dr. Mass received the Gay Press Association Community Service Award for Outstanding Coverage of Health Concerns. He was also a recipient of the Gay Press Association Award for Outstanding Cultural Writing for *The Housemates Who Got Nailed,* the first published installment of *Synchronicities: Memoirs of Growing Up Gay, Jewish and Self-Hating In America.* Dr. Mass is a member of the editorial board for the *Journal of Homosexuality* and of the *Colloqium of CLAGS* (The Committee for Lesbian and Gay Studies) at the City University of New York. He has written for *The Advocate, The PWA Coalition Newsline, The Sentinel,* and the *SIECUS Report.*

Foreword

Dialogues of the Sexual Revolution

In my interview with her, Mary Calderone, a co-founder of The Sex Information and Education Council of the United States (SIECUS) and former medical director of Planned Parenthood, discusses her understanding of how we *learn* sexuality. Like most sex researchers of our time but without taking an unequivocal position on the eternal question of the etiology of sexual preference, Calderone states her belief that a lot of sexuality is learned the way we learn language. If everyone were taught language the way most of us, especially in America, were taught sexuality, she suggests, we would all stammer and stutter. In this analogy, then, we are a nation of sexual stammerers and stutterers. We are likewise sexual discourse stammerers and stutterers. And as readers of these dialogues are apt to appreciate, the language and discourse of sexuality — the constantly changing academic, medical and scientific vocabularies and phraseologies with which we keep trying to speak about sexuality — are probably less significant in broader perspective than the fact that we do keep trying to communicate about sexuality.

In 1979, when I did the first of these interviews, I had no conscious awareness of how motivated I was by the need to better understand myself. On the contrary, having recently completed seven years of conservative medical training, I must have regarded these initial efforts as physicianly models of neutrality and objectivity in which the self had little or no place. As such, I must have reasoned, they would prove to be potent weapons against the homophobic psychiatrists — textbook authors, media "experts" and other proponents of reclassifying homosexuality as a mental disorder, including my own medical school instructors and psychotherapists — they were so often trying to rebut. It just didn't occur to me, or faze me when it finally did, that the gay press was the last place these enemies or their allies in the mainstream press would care to look for perspective.

In those first years of my involvement in the gay liberation movement, I was occasionally asked about the long-range purpose of my writing, mostly by gay friends who were still in the closet. I had a sincere answer. With my precocious gay pride, I'd proclaim that I saw myself as a kind of watchdog for the gay community. As a physician, I had been trained to believe in medical models and scientific principles. Throughout my medical training, however, I had witnessed and been victimized by innumerable greater and lesser acts of homophobia and sexism, and felt we needed to pay a lot more attention to what was going on in medicine and the sciences, especially psychiatry, with regard to homosexuality and sexuality. In the late 1970s, in the face of overt lobbying by growing numbers of psychiatrists to repathologize homosexuality, this meant joining the sex research bandwagon. As I wrote in my first feature piece for *The Advocate*, which was an overview of the academic literature on sadomasochism ["Coming To Grips With Sadomasochism: Psychiatry versus Sex Research," 4/5/79], I believed this was a "cultural trend that has seen the credibility of opinion about human sexual behavior shift progressively from the temples of psychiatry to the laboratories of sex research." As a budding sexologist, I likewise believed that my "watchdogging" was as motivated by a desire to foster the larger confluence of struggles in our time that we called the sexual revolution as by concern for the gay community.

By the mid 1980s this perception had changed. In seeking the all-important objectivity and neutrality I believed would result from trying to consider every question about homosexuality in a larger context of sexuality and every question about gay liberation in terms of the sexual revolution, and from always trying to understand and define these phenomena in medical, scientific and academic languages, I had gone too far and not far enough. That is, I was moving too far away from the issues of gay identity and community that motivated me, as a gay man, more personally and fundamentally than any others. At the same time, I had barely touched on some of the largest issues of the sexual revolution and sexology (e.g., birth control). Hence the shift in the focus of these interviews: away from a preoccupation with the perspectives of medicine and science (in the exchanges with acclaimed sex researchers, sex educators and psychiatrists William Masters, Virginia Johnson, John Money, Mary Calderone, Richard Pillard, Judd Marmor, Richard Green and Thomas Szasz, all of whom were or became important allies in the protracted struggle to declassify homosexuality as a mental disorder and the subsequent struggle to maintain that declassification) toward a greater interest in those of gay politics, culture and history (beginning in the interview with Pillard, who was the first openly gay psychiatrist in the United States, and developing in the interviews with biblical scholar John McNeill, premiere gay wrestler and sports observer John Handley, gay *littérateur* George Stambolian, pathbreaking gay researchers and educators Charles Silverstein, Emery Hetrick and Damien Martin, veteran gay activist and writer Arnie Kantrowitz, and preeminent gay historians Richard Plant and Martin Duberman). This trend is especially apparent in *Homosexuality as Behavior and Identity*, the second volume of *Dialogues of The Sexual Revolution* (covering the years 1985-1989), none of whose interviewees is a psychiatrist, only one of whom speaks for the sciences (sexologist James Weinrich), and most of whom are artists, critics, historians and independent scholars (e.g., filmmakers Paul Schrader and Rosa von Praunheim, musicologist Philip Brett, opera critic George Heymont, composer Ned Rorem, psychologist and sex researcher John De Cecco in his role as critic of medicine and science, historians John D'Emilio, Estelle Freedman and John Boswell, and independent scholar Will Roscoe).

Eventually, I realized that the dialogues in which I was engaged often reflected my own as well as medically-oriented concerns and biases; that, however unintentionally, they sometimes reflected or abetted ethnocentric and androcentric biases; that they were open-ended, ongoing, in no way comprehensive or even balanced; and that they raised many questions they could never hope to answer. Having decided to continue this journey, however wandering, whatever the obstacles, I began to understand how personal it was, how deeply problems of sexual and community identity have pursued me all my life. Was my gay identity nothing more than an ephemeral byproduct of patriarchal homophobia and erotophobia? In the early 1980s I often believed that this was so, that there was nothing essential about being gay. In the mid- and late 1980s, coincidentally as homophobia and erotophobia reestablished their dominant influence on our culture, as I began to come to grips with a Jewish identity that had been even more repressed than my gay identity, and even as social constructionist historians demonstrated how gay identities have been shaped by social forces in the modern period, that belief became less secure.

In the early course of these explorations there was an unanticipated but predictable development, one that challenged me to integrate my perspectives as a physician, student of sexology, gay activist and writer. That development was the epidemic spread of a number of sexually transmitted diseases (STDs), including a newly reported one that became known, in the fall of 1982, as AIDS.

As the first writer to cover the AIDS epidemic in any press and as a gay activist highly critical of homophobia in medicine and increasingly skeptical that medicine and science had any real answers to questions of sexual identity and preference, I was now in the position of also having to be a physician, supportive of what I considered to be the best medical and scientific information and advice available. Did an epidemic, even one as serious as AIDS clearly was from the first reports, mean that the fundamental values of the gay liberation movement and what we were calling the sexual revolution had changed? As these dialogues demonstrate, especially the "Five Interviews From The First Two Years Of The AIDS Epidemic," I have consistently believed that the answer to that question is no; that the greater values of the sexual liberation movements of our time — equality of the sexes, civil liberties protections for sex-variant and minority persons, the cultural sanctioning of same-sex domestic partnerships, the accessibility of birth control, sex information and education, the fostering of sex-affirmative images and attitudes, the expansion and improvement of research and treatment of STDs — must coexist with the risks and responsibilities of STDs. It was with this viewpoint, that these values and realities were not in genuine conflict, that I conducted the first published interviews with early AIDS researchers and observers Alvin Friedman-Kien, Donna Mildvan and Dan William, with former New

York City Health Commissioner David Sencer, and with a person with AIDS—Donald Krintzman. And it was with this viewpoint that I continued my explorations of sexual preference and group identity.

The idea that these pieces might be collected didn't germinate until 1987, when I first noticed that the conversation with Martin Duberman I had recently completed seemed to resolve a question that is in the forefront of most of the early interviews—the question of the role of science in our struggles for sexual identity and liberation. When I conducted the first of these exchanges in 1979-80 with Masters and Johnson, Money, and Marmor, I really believed that the new science of sex research would guide the progress of what we were calling the sexual revolution and the gay liberation movement it contained. By 1987, however, I had to concede more fully what Duberman had maintained with such prescience in his critique of Masters and Johnson in 1979 for *The New Republic* and what Thomas Szasz argued with such passion when I interviewed him in 1980: that much of the new science of sexuality was turning out to be as pseudoscientific and subject to abuse as that which preceded it. Hence the principal cultural trend these dialogues document (a trend that is diametrically opposite to that with which they began): the slow, nonlinear but progressive shift in credibility of opinion away from a naive trust in a future that will be shaped by the insights and munificence of science toward a sober acceptance that the future is far more likely to be determined by the outcome of the learned versus the unlearned lessons of history. In other words, pursuing a science of homosexuality that could establish our "normality," even if there were such a thing, isn't nearly as likely to help lesbian and gay people come to terms with ourselves and guide us in the personal and political decisions that will determine our future as appreciating our history and, as Michel Foucault suggests, living and exploring our potential for all kinds of relationships, for *"becoming* truly gay." Science, in fact, is no more likely to foster the understanding, integration and well-being of lesbian and gay people in the future than it has helped women, blacks, Jews and others who have suffered discrimination in the past.

Conversely, however, these dialogues would appear to underscore the importance of one of those lessons of history, especially the later dialogues in *Homosexuality as Behavior and Identity*: with the experience of yesterday's science to guide us, we must be wary of entrusting any single perspective or discipline, even the currently ascendant history of homosexuality and sexuality that has exposed so many of the errors and biases of that science, to provide absolute definitions or explanations of human sexual preferences and behaviors.

As their focus changes from science to history, another important cultural and subcultural trend is discernible: the shift in credibility of opinion about gay life from nongay experts and allies outside our community (e.g., Masters and Johnson, Marmor, Money, Calderone, Green and even Szasz) to the observations, experiences and research findings of gay people ourselves (e.g., Pillard, McNeill, Handley, Stambolian, Silverstein, Hetrick and Martin, Plant, Kantrowitz, Duberman). This trend gathers momentum in *Homosexuality as Behavior and Identity*, wherein ten of the eleven interviewees are openly gay or lesbian.

From their engagement of the reactionary backlash in psychiatry that spasmodically still threatens to reclassify homosexuality as a mental disorder, to their discussions of sexual identity and political responsibility, to their immersion, in *Homosexuality as Behavior and Indentity*, in the essentialist/social constructionist debates about sexual identity, these dialogues bear witness to some of the controversies that have shaped thinking about sexuality and homosexuality in the 1980s. Because they are contemporaneous with many of the controversies they explore, the intersecting interviews and conversations of these collections are documents of the gay liberation struggle, the AIDS epidemic and what we have called the sexual revolution, as well as of my own personal journey. Together, I believe, they become among the few books to place the unfolding of the AIDS epidemic in a context, rather than as the consequence, of the sexual liberation movements of our time.

[A few words about technique and form. Except for the bracketed editorial notes, and with the exception of the interview with Masters and Johnson, each interview text was approved by the interviewee(s). In part because I'm not at my best in spontaneous conversation, my preferred method is to interview others as I myself would want to be interviewed: with a greater concern for considered, fact-checked and self-edited opinion than for less but also important values of spontaneity and style. What I've found is that when interviewees are assured that they will be able to edit their responses and share editorial approval, they tend to be more open, more willing to take chances, generally if not universally, than under more restrictive conditions.

The bracketed editorial notes that often introduce and otherwise give context to these interviews contain new or additional information compiled for this volume. Any introductory or bracketed information that is not designated as an editorial note ([Ed. note: . . .]) is from the original text or is being used to clarify, but not to update, that text.]

Acknowledgements

In regard to the preparation of *Homosexuality and Sexuality: Dialogues of The Sexual Revolution* Volume I, I wish to acknowledge the following persons for their assistance, information, friendship, support, insights or example: Peter Adair, Barry Adkins, Dennis Altman, Virginia Apuzzo, Bernadette Aquavella, Brett Averill, Dan Bailey, Ronald Bayer, Arthur Bell, Dixie Beckham, Mark Blasius, Chris Bram, Arthur Bressan, Len Brown, Jack Bulmash, Victor Bumbalo, Larry Bush, Joe Cady, Pat Califia, Michael Callen, Robert and Julio Caserio, John Cavendish, George Chauncey, Jr., Robert Chesley, Bill Cohen, Ed Cohen, Ron Christopher, Douglas Crimp, Melinda Cuthbert, Howard Cruse, Peter G. Davis, Martin Delaney, Michael Denneny, James D'Eramo, Richard Dyer, George De Stefano, Nick Deutsch, Tom Duane, Lucile Duberman, Lisa Duggan, Richard Dulong, Bruce Eves, Lillian Faderman, Nathan Fain, Anita Feldman, Robert Ferro, Ann Fettner, Frances Fitzgerald, Robin Foerster, Michel Foucault, Terry Fonville, Jim Fouratt, Dave Frechette, Sandy Friedman, Nanette Gartrell, Barry Gingell, Frances Goldin, Richard Goldstein, Alex Gotfryd, Stephen Greco, David Groff, Ron Grossman, Howard Grossman, Richard Hall, Sue Kiefer Hammersmith, John Hammond, Brent Harris, James Harrison, Michael Hirsch, William M. Hoffman, Andrew Holleran, Amber Hollibaugh, Richard Howard, Andy Humm, Joyce Hunter, Nan Hunter, Robert Isaacs, Doug Ireland, Alan Isaksen, Kris Jakobsen, Chester Jakala, Karla Jay, Mitchell Karp, Barney Karpfinger, Simon Karlinsky, Jonathan Ned Katz, David Kessler, James Kinsella, David Kirby, Don Knutson, Gregory Kolovakos, Hal Kooden, Phil Lanzratta, Linda Laubenstein, John Lauritsen, Martin Levine, Norman J. Levy, Winston Leyland, Sal Licata, Alex Lockwood, Diego Lopez, Peter Lowy, John Lunning, Michael Lutin, Daniel Margalioth, Harvey Marks, Ellen Mass, Steve Mass, Jed Mattes, Andrew Mattison, Boyd Mc-

Donald, Rodger McFarlane, Frank McGurk, Robert McQueen, David McWhirter, Patrick Merla, Tom Miller, Helen Mitsios, Richard Mohr, Paul Monette, Jon-David Nalley, Esther Newton, Stuart Nichols, David Nimmons, Frank O'Dowd, Jim Oleson, Charles Ortleb, Jim Owles, Marcia Pally, Pam Parker, Paul Paroski, Scott Parris, Cindy Patton, Felice Picano, Nathaniel Pier, Paul Popham, John Preston, Michael Pye, Nick Rango, Campion Read, Lou Rispoli, Darryl Yates Rist, Marty Robinson, Paul Robinson, Eric Rofes, Herb Rosenberg, Jane Rosett, Gabriel Rotello, Gayle Rubin, Frank Rundle, Ron Sable, Douglas Sadownik, Harvey Sakofsky, Terry Sandholzer, Gregory Sandow, Bert Schaffner, Michael Schnur, Robert Schwartz, Jay Scott, Laura Segal, Michael Shernoff, Randy Shilts, Ed Sedarbaum, Ed Sikov, Ira Siff, Michelangelo Signorile, Ira Silverberg, Ingrid Sischy, Maynard Solomon, Joseph Sonnabend, Susan Sontag, Barbara Starrett, James Steakley, David Stein, Terry Stein, Frank Sulloway, David Summers, Dee Sushi, Mark Thompson, James Tierney, Jaime Titievski, Gladys Topkis, Orlando Torres, Ron Vachon, Carole S. Vance, Judith Walkowitz, Joyce Wallace, Simon Watney, Steven Watson, Jeffrey Weeks, Edmund White, Walter Williams, Liz Wood, Ralph Wynn, Ellen Zaltzberg, Phil Zwickler, and my Greenwich House, ACT UP, GMHC, PWA Coalition and CLAGS friends and colleagues.

Very special thanks to Martin Duberman, Thomas E. Steele, John De Cecco, Jeffrey Escoffier, Norman Laurila, Arnie Kantrowitz, James Saslow, Vito Russo, Larry Kramer, Ida Walker, James Ice, Ann Schwartz, Eli Zal, Bill and Mignon Thorpe, Bruce-Michael Gelbert, Brandon Judell, David Alexander, Craig Rowland, Seymour Kleinberg and the friends from the meetings.

It is gratefully acknowledged that the interviews and conversations listed below were first published elsewhere, as indicated. Thanks to Thomas Szasz for his permission to use "Sex In The Therapeutic State," for which he retains copyright.

William Masters and Virginia Johnson, *The Advocate*, 5/31/79, pp. 19, 22-23, 42.
Richard Pillard, *The Advocate*, 10/4/79, pp. 18-19, 50.
Judd Marmor, *The Advocate*, 4/17/80, pp. 22-23, 26, 31.

John Money, *Christopher Street*, 9/80, pp. 24-30.
Thomas Szasz, *Christopher Street*, 3/4/81, pp. 32-39.
Mary Calderone, *Christopher Street*, 9-10/81, pp. 31-35.
John McNeill, *The New York Native*, 4/20/81, pp. 16, 21, 32.
George Stambolian, *Christopher Street*, issue 64 (1982), pp. 21-25.
Charles Silverstein, *The Alternate*, 4/81, pp. 30-31.
John Handley, *The New York Native*, 2/1/82, pp. 16-18.
Alvin Friedman-Kien, *The New York Native*, 1/27/81, pp. 21, 30.
Donna Mildvan, *The New York Native*, 1/27/81, p. 30.
Donald Krintzman, *The New York Native*, 8/24/81, p. 13.
Dan William, *The New York Native*, 8/16/82, pp. 31-32.
David Sencer, *The New York Native*, 1/31/83, pp. 23, 56.
Damien Martin and Emery Hetrick, *The New York Native*, 7/1/85,
    pp. 38-42.
Richard Plant, *Christopher Street*, issue 107 (1987), pp. 46-50.
Richard Green, *Christopher Street*, issue 110 (1987), pp. 18-22.
Martin Bauml Duberman, *The New York Native*, 12/22/86,
    pp. 25-31.

PSYCHIATRY VERSUS SEX RESEARCH

Perspective in Perspective

An Interview
with William Masters and Virginia Johnson

[Ed. note: When I asked to interview Masters and Johnson, I was told by press representatives of Little, Brown & Co, the publishers of *Homosexuality in Perspective*, that *The Advocate*, like all other such small-circulation publications, could not be granted a private interview. Instead, I was permitted to attend a general press conference with the authors and approximately twenty other journalists, one of whom was wearing a T-shirt that read "Virginia is for Lovers." At the time, I was persuaded that the decision not to give a private interview to *The Advocate* was egalitarian, a reasonable consequence of the overwhelming media response to the book, which included leading weekly magazine cover stories, a front page feature in the *New York Times*, a *Playboy* interview and television appearances on Phil Donahue and *Meet The Press*.

In retrospect, this subtle distancing of the authors from the gay and lesbian community should have seemed more disturbing than it did in 1979. In those earliest days of my involvement in the gay community and as a published writer (this was my first interview and one of my first pieces for the gay press), however, such discrepancies seemed a tiny price to pay for so many benefits. With perfect timing, in the midst of a growing trend within medicine and psychiatry to have homosexuality reclassified as a mental disorder and amidst the mass hysteria fomented by Anita Bryant, here was a study of unprecedented authority (public esteem for Masters and

1

Johnson was at its apex and vastly outweighed respect for any other sex researchers) and with unprecedented media exposure which said very clearly that homosexuality wasn't any kind of abnormality, and which explicitly denounced homophobia in the health care professions and endorsed civil rights protections for lesbian and gay persons. In fact, I felt so certain about the progressive impact *Homosexuality in Perspective* would and did in fact have on on the still ultraconservative, extremely homophobic worlds of medicine and psychiatry and on the public at large that I was apparently willing, not so unlike the authors themselves, to justify the means, to ignore some of the smaller details, with what I presumed would be the ends of greater political gain.

In perspective today, that political gain, though real, was relatively short-lived and mitigated by the authors' pseudoscientific work (ongoing today) with "homosexual dissatisfaction" and "homosexual conversion." However inadvertently, this aspect of their study fanned inquisitorial notions, psychiatric as well as religious, of changing sexual preferences by "voluntary" acts of will. Also in retrospect, on the other hand, it's difficult not to notice that this work is based on Masters and Johnson's stated belief that homosexuality, like heterosexuality and bisexuality, is a *learned preference*, a viewpoint that is shared by many of today's social constructionists.

As extracted from this general press conference, what follows the introductory comments by the authors is a transcription of only those questions I asked, and which were answered by Masters, Johnson and Kolodny. In *The Advocate*, the published interview contained an editorial introduction (not by me) and was accompanied by my review of the book. The review is mostly descriptive and unremarkable, except for the following statement, which betrays an unwittingly conservative, medical-model bias: "Yet again, whether permanent reversals of sex-partner preference or sexual orientation are effected, or whether the convert is simply facilitated in a temporary ability to perform heterosexually is left unanswered. This question remains the most important to be asked about 'homosexual dissatisfaction.' Inextricably bound up with the controversies of etiology, it is also the most important question that remains to be asked about homosexuality."

As I came to realize in the course of the ensuing interviews and conversations, I could not have been more wrong.]

In their suite at the Ritz-Carlton Hotel in Boston, Dr. and Mrs. Masters answered questions about their new book, *Homosexuality in Perspective*. They were joined by Dr. Robert Kolodny, a research endocrinologist and their Associate Director of Sex Research, and Dr. Raymond Waggoner, past president of the American Psychiatric Association and a senior member of the Board of Trustees at the Masters and Johnson Institute. The session began with introductory comments.

MASTERS: This is the first of what will be a series of new reports to the health care professions and the general population, based on data that has been collected over a 14-year period. What we have tried to do in *Homosexuality in Perspective* is to call upon the resources we developed to treat heterosexual dysfunction and apply them to homosexuals, something that really has not been done before. We can now state with real security that there simply is no difference between the facility (capacity or efficiency) of heterosexuals and homosexuals to respond to sexual stimulation. Nor is there any difference between males and females, homosexual or heterosexual, for such capacity.

KOLODNY: There has been an inferential treatment of homosexuality in the theme that has run through a great deal of the medical literature — particularly if we go back to the '40s, '50s and '60s — that homosexuality is a dysfunctional state and is less adequate than heterosexuality. For the first time, there is now laboratory evidence to suggest that this is not so.

JOHNSON: We are not by implication or intent making value judgments. Rather, we are talking to the issues of what happens. People who are making moral or value judgments should at least do so with the facts at hand.

MASS: The etiology of homosexuality is clearly and refreshingly *not* the focus of your study, as it is of nearly all the psychiatric and other studies. But you do comment on it. You summarize the endocrinological and genetic data which you believe to be inconclusive and of limited potential for research. Actually, you do state your belief that homosexuality is "a learned preference." In this perspective, what's to keep psychoanalysts from continuing to assert that this "learned preference" is always a maladaptive response to early sexual conflicts?

MASTERS: There is a basic fallacy inherent in your question . . .

KOLODNY: Learning is a very different thing from pure experience. Social learning theory posits that the entire sum of our experience in living — all post-natal events, not pure exposure to x, y or z sexual stimulus — results in adult learned roles. Learning is very different from just experiencing.

JOHNSON: Learning may take place by omission as well as commission.

KOLODNY: It would probably be a mistake to assume that homosexuality, or heterosexuality for that matter, are unitary phenomena; that under one rubric one can describe all the individuals that fall into a particular class and ascribe to them identical causative elements, styles of living, taste, etc.

MASS: But if it's a learned preference, it would seem by implication that there might be some way of treating or preventing it if one, or one's culture, preferred to view it as an undesirable variant of sexual expression, however otherwise functional and satisfactory it might appear to be.

KOLODNY: Of course, there are psychiatrists who view cross-gender activities in children as early signs of orientation disturbances. They feel that early intervention with such children is warranted. We don't subscribe to this view because this is not an area of our research. We cannot offer an opinion about etiology for a large portion of the homosexual population at the present time.

MASTERS: We happen to think that heterosexuality is also a learned behavior. We do not believe that we are born homosexual or heterosexual, but male and female sexual entities.

MASS: So what you are saying is different from, but does not directly contradict, the opinion of an orthodox psychoanalyst like Charles Socarides, that homosexuality is universally a maladaptive response to early sexual conflicts.

MASTERS: You'd be putting words in my mouth. We have no concept of homosexuality as maladaptive.

JOHNSON: That is a value judgment we do not make or feel, or find present in our work.

KOLODNY: In the same line, the maladaptive responses or behaviors of homosexuals with problems who seek help for these problems are entirely commensurate with the maladaptive responses or behaviors of heterosexuals who seek help for their problems. To that extent, how many of these maladaptive responses are learned, goes to a philosophical point of theory.

MASS: In your chapter on "Fantasy Patterns," you state that the homosexual males' fantasies frequently contained "more violence" than those of heterosexual controls. Is this simply a matter of degree? What if any social or psychological significance do you attach to this finding?

MASTERS: None. We have no evidence for that. It is simply a matter of degree in terms of reporting. We did not make any attempt to interpret it.

MASS: Would you care to do so now?

MASTERS: No, not until we've got a lot more data and a lot more time to study it. In a couple of years we will be publishing a much more detailed discussion of the fantasy material. At the present time, we would not dream of suggesting that our reported material purely represented a cross-section of the greater homosexual population.

MASS: The Kinsey II [*Homosexualities* by Bell and Weinberg] statistics suggest a far greater frequency of rectal intercourse than you do. This is important because you imply that homosexuals may sometimes be comparatively disadvantaged by not being able to enjoy and communicate sexual pleasure simultaneously as easily during homosexual rectal intercourse as during heterosexual vaginal intercourse. Do you dispute the Bell and Weinberg statistics?

MASTERS: All we can say is that for the group we worked with, the incidence was less. Our study did not necessarily represent a cross-section of the homosexual population. So we took no stand. We do not dispute the [Bell and Weinberg] statistics in any way.

[In their study, the authors describe a new classification of individuals as "ambisexual." Ambisexuals are said to be distinguished from bisexuals by an inability to establish relationships of any depth or duration with anyone, regardless of sex or sexual orientation. The authors qualify that although their data will not permit much speculation, "the ambisexual" might be more responsive to emotional involvement as he or she ages. The authors also characterize "the ambisexual" as uniquely devoid of sexual prejudice, and consistently comfortable and successful in sexual performance, regardless of the partner's sex, sexual orientation or activity preference.]

MASS: Given an ambisexual, is there any psychosexual or other reason why this person should have difficulty establishing an emotional commitment?

MASTERS: I don't know whether they have trouble establishing relationships or simply lack the interest to do so.

JOHNSON: Ambisexuality may be just a stage in the evolution of eroticism in the individual. We can't say as yet whether it is a more or less mature stage.

KOLODNY: There is nothing to suggest that these individuals are sociopathic. If anything, they are probably less so.

MASS: At the Masters and Johnson Institute, you treat both homosexual and heterosexual couples for sexual "dysfunction," but only the former (at the present time) for sexual orientation "dissatisfaction." Do you think that an undetermined number of your homosexually "dysfunctional" patients might under other circumstances also be interpreted as "dissatisfied"?

MASTERS: No. We interviewed for this and did not find this to be the case. We found that the dysfunctional subjects were interested in functioning effectively as homosexuals, *not* as heterosexuals.

MASS: For the sexually distressed single individual, wary of homophobia in psychiatry and the health care professions, what options for services such as yours are there?

MASTERS: There are now many types of gay health centers in most cities. This would seem to be a logical starting point. And, of course, the Masters and Johnson Institute accepts referrals and direct applications from individuals with partners.

Homophobia on the Couch

A Conversation with Richard Pillard,
the first publicly gay psychiatrist
in the United States

[Ed. note: Dr. Richard C. Pillard is associate professor of psychiatry at Boston University School of Medicine, is a founding member of The Association of Lesbian and Gay Psychiatrists, and has served as medical advisor of the Homophile Community Health Service in Boston. Dr. Pillard is the co-author of a book, *The Wild Boy of Burundi*, and has published a number of articles on psychotropic drugs and on the development of sexual orientation.

Dr. Pillard was also the first publicly gay psychiatrist in the United States. When I saw him identified as gay on a television panel discussion about homosexuality in 1976, during a time when any discussion of homosexuality on television was still a milestone event, I had an almost mystical experience of gay pride, one of the first such experiences of my life. Knowing very little about gay history or gay politics at that time (a fact I'm afraid these early interviews all too resoundingly confirm), I had never seen or even heard of another such physician or psychiatrist—one who was accepted and respected as openly gay. That's exactly what I dreamed of being.

The minute the television program was over, I called Dr. Pillard and made an appointment to see him. The next day, with Dr. Pillard's gentle support, I telephoned the homophobic Harvard shrink I had been in psychoanalytically oriented therapy with during the preceding year and explained that, henceforth, I'd be seeing Dr. Pillard.

Between 1976 and 1979 Dr. Pillard became my psychiatrist and mentor. Recognizing my budding gay activism and interest in the subject of homosexuality and psychiatry, he introduced me to Emery Hetrick, Damien Martin, Frank Rundle, Nanette Gartrell, Stuart Nichols, Jim Krajeski, Jean Munzer, Bert Schaffner, Jim Paulsen and other pioneering members of the fledgling organization of gay psychiatrists he had been working with. I already knew David Kessler, who later became president of the group. With their support, Pillard invited me to take over his position as its newsletter editor. Damien Martin, who was an authority on prejudice and who had done landmark work in defining the lesbian and gay community as a minority, was the only other nonpsychiatrist in the group.

At that time, in 1979, this insecure but very brave group was trying to call itself The Gay Caucus of the American Psychiatric Association, a name the nervous and still moderately homophobic APA hierarchy immediately asked us to change to Gay Caucus of Members of the American Psychiatric Association. Following several more name changes, including The Caucus of Gay, Lesbian and Bisexual Members of the APA, it is now known as The Association of Lesbian and Gay Psychiatrists.

A lot of the wrangling over the name of the organization had to do with the fact that the APA hierarchy, even those members who supported the declassification of homosexuality as a mental disorder six years earlier, were not convinced that lesbians and gay men represented a legitimate minority. So this became one of the earliest and most important goals of the organization: to secure minority recognition. At first, this goal was hindered as much by the unwillingness of many members to be openly identified as lesbian or gay as by the recalcitrance of the APA. Eventually, minority recognition was achieved in association with a partner organization called CHIP (Caucus of Homosexual-Identified Psychiatrists) of the APA.]

In the crowded exhibitions hall of the American Psychiatric Association convention in Chicago in March 1979, I looked vainly for the display booth of the [Gay Caucus]. At a coffee station, the Marcus Welby-ish attendant glanced about nervously in response to my question. "Gay *what?*" he asked. Eventually I was directed to the far end of the hall, where, behind a large pillar between the Latin American and Women's Committee booths, I could barely make out Frank Rundle, president of the caucus. "The location [behind the pillar] was assigned," explained Rundle with a straight face.

Though the assignment was in fact indicative of official psychiatry's attitude toward gay people within its own ranks, other signs were more favorable. By the end of the convention, membership in the caucus had swelled to more than 130, as participants attended panel discussions, symposia, lectures, films and consciousness-raising sessions. A child psychiatrist from Southern California confided that he had been moved to tears by the experience; he had come out first professionally, then emotionally without even realizing it. A specialist in family counseling from Atlanta, who had earlier been skeptical of a "gay caucus" appeared at every event.

The days seem past when—as once happened to me—you can hear an analyst say to her ostensibly straight colleague, "I don't care vut anyvun says. Ze ahnoos vus not meant to accommodate ze peenoos!" In the following interview, Dr. Richard Pillard, who was instrumental in the 1973-74 declassification of homosexuality as a "mental disorder," talks about the new Masters and Johnson study, anti-gay psychoanalysts and the changing perspectives of official psychiatry on gay issues.

MASS: After the American Psychiatric Association dropped its diagnostic category of homosexuality as a mental disorder, there was a petition to reinstate the classification. Where does this challenge now stand?
PILLARD: There has been a movement afoot to reinstate it as *ego-dystonic homosexuality*, which designates people who are unhappy about their homosexual impulses. I am personally opposed to including "ego-dystonic homosexuality" in the [Diagnostic and] Statistical Manual of Mental Disorders [DSM]. The reason people are ego-dystonic about homosexuality is *not* because they're suffering from a mental disorder, but because the social order makes it so painful to be gay.

I'd liken it to a kid who's masturbating and feeling guilty about it. Now, are you going to diagnose him as having a mental disorder? No. He's anxious over a particular situation which, in time, will resolve itself. There are many situations over which people become anxious, but I don't think we would give each of them a diagnosis. And I don't think this should have one.

MASS: As behaviorists, Masters and Johnson hypothesize that people are not born homosexual or heterosexual, but simply sexual; that homosexuality, like heterosexuality, is "a learned preference." Do you agree?

PILLARD: I would want to take a neutral position here for the time being. One option is that you learn homosexuality as you learn language. The second, analytic position is that you're sort of traumatized into it. That is, you've had such an unhappy experience trying to be heterosexual that you regress to homosexuality. What the relative validity of these two positions is we don't yet know. But there's no reason whatever to preclude a biologic or genetic component to homosexuality.

MASS: Does this sociobiological postulation have any scientific data to support it?

PILLARD: Unfortunately, not a shred at this point; but it is by no means a discounted theory. If a genetic component were to be identified, it would take nothing away from being gay. It wouldn't make it an illness at all so much as another treasured variant of human behavior.

MASS: . . . Until the technology is developed to decode and manipulate genetic structure. Then what?

PILLARD: Gay people will continue to be at risk that people will use whatever methods they can to oppose or prevent homosexuality. But then, people who are left-handed, brunette, short-statured or what have you could be similarly at risk.

MASS: Do you then question the Masters and Johnson hypothesis that there are gay people with deep-seated, unrealized heterosexual desires who are prevented from satisfaction because of homosexual patterning?

PILLARD: This hinges on a question that is very interesting to me: How do we define homosexuality? For Masters and Johnson, it is defined by behavior. [What they're saying is that] if you're fucking with a person of the same sex, you are homosexual—regardless of fantasy, history or anything else. The other position is that there's some underlying constitutional factor that determines whether or not you're homosexual. So that even though I might be having sex with females — if we could read this inner imprint — I might really be homosexual. Now if that's the case, *then* it would make sense to try to change my sexual behavior so that it's in accord with my basic sexual nature. Masters and Johnson don't make this latter distinction. What they're saying is that if your sexual experiences are homosexual, you *are* homosexual.

MASS: Some people have suggested that the Masters and Johnson study represents a mortal blow to traditional psychoanalytic theories of "normal" psychosexual development. What do you think?

PILLARD: All sciences have to deal with the problem of new evidence which contradicts established views. One might say that it's the test of a *science* whether it can absorb new ideas. If not, the discipline is more like a religion or a cult than a science. That is the dilemma, I think, which analysis faces.

MASS: In media coverage of homosexual issues psychiatric opinion is nearly always represented by orthodox analysts like Charles Socarides, Irving Bieber and Lawrence Hatterer. Where are the non-gay, progay psychiatrists?

PILLARD: I think part of this is the unfortunate tendency of the media to try to get views on opposite ends of a continuum. They'll get someone like Socarides who takes an extremely orthodox, gay-is-always-sick position, even though his view represents a miniscule number of people. But he'll get quoted because he's articulate, aggressive and way over on that side. I think there are equally prominent psychiatrists who completely disagree, but get lost in the shuffle because they are in a more middle ground. Richard Green, Judd Marmor, and John Spiegel are examples.

MASS: [Conservative] psychoanalysts seem to be more convinced than ever that homosexuality is, universally, a character pathology. What kind of influence are these analysts exerting on [the field] of psychoanalysis today, and on public opinion?

PILLARD: I'm not an analyst and am not wholly current with their thinking. One problem for the researcher is that the analysts tend not to get beyond their own jargon. They don't fertilize much with other disciplines. While their theories are impressive and command some respect, their data are appalling. Psychoanalytic theorists have been wrong so much that I think it's led to an almost tragic collapse of psychoanalysis as a credible intellectual discipline. I say "tragic" because I really think that psychoanalytic therapy has a lot to offer, and a lot to offer gay people. If only the theorists could get out of the persecutory bag they're in, the need to classify and label us. And by the way, many leading analysts are gay — or were, before they were weeded out of the profession.

MASS: What precautions should be taken by a gay person who wants to undergo analytic therapy?

PILLARD: Before agreeing to undergo analysis, he or she should inquire how the analyst views these matters. The central question is, "Can my analysis be considered successfully completed if I decide to continue being homosexual?" I would hope that there are analysts who would say "Yes," what is important is the quality, not the gender divisions, of the relationship.

By the way, recently discovered statements by Freud confirm his opinion that gay people could not only be successfully analyzed, but could be successful analysts as well! He endorsed that — it's only the neoFreudians who have taken this extremely hardnosed position.

MASS: In an interview in *Gay Community News*, you indicated that you plan to issue a statement about behavior modification intervention with homosexuals.

PILLARD: That will be in a chapter I'm writing for *Psychological Studies of Social Issues* called "Psychotherapeutic Treatment of the Invisible Minority" that should be out for the New Year. It will address analytic therapy. The analysts like to say, "We cure such and such percent." This is consumer fraud. Their studies are uncontrolled. My contention is that [these] analysts have no idea what the odds of change really are. Also, many people decide during psychoanalysis that they want to be gay! Why haven't those results been published?

MASS: In your GCN review of *Homosexuality in Perspective*, you questioned the ethicality of orientation "conversion" beyond the issue of its empirical validity. What, specifically, are these ethical objections?

PILLARD: Let me comment for a moment on the efficacy of this therapy. The number of people [Masters and Johnson claim to have] successfully treated for "conversion" was only six in ten years! So this is by no means a large-scale processing of gay people. The ethical objections are basically this: doctors are creating a paradox by saying on the one hand that being gay is not a sickness, then on the other, that there's a treatment for change "if you want it." If "treatment" is available, then sickness is implied.

MASS: [Psychiatrists] Richard Green and Robert Stoller have [worked] with [gay] youngsters, trying to make their behavior more appropriate to their physical gender. Is this ethical?

PILLARD: That's a hard question. Basically, they are treating effeminate boys whose behavior gets them into a lot of trouble. What it amounts to is that they're trying to butch these kids up. They do things like videotape them walking, show the children the tapes, and admonish them to "keep those hips in line." Clearly, their motivation is to prevent unnecessary suffering. But the problem, as I see it, is the parents, the school, the society—those who don't accept "swishy" boys. People don't object to a tomboy girl. If she wants to play baseball, she draws attention and admiration from her friends. If a little boy wants to cook and sew, why shouldn't that draw admiration too? Why try to homogenize these boys? I think it's a big social mistake. They [Green and Stoller] ought to be spending this time and money teaching the parents, the principal and the students how to accept and help such kids make use of their particular gifts. I think this aspect of their work just stinks.

Another consideration is this: What if it doesn't work?—as I suspect it won't. Will the child come out of the experience thinking, "Gee, I've got this terrible problem that they weren't able to change. I must really be awful."

MASS: Some phenomena have arisen in the gay community [*sic*] that have received little psychiatric comment—sadomasochism, bondage, fist-fucking, leather fetishism, tit-piercing. Do you have any general thoughts [about these phenomena]?

PILLARD: I think it would be very interesting to compare the gay subculture with other groups, like black men—people who have themselves been socially isolated and demeaned. There must be a lot of rage in gay men over the deprivation of their masculinity by straight culture. Perhaps some S/M phenomena are a kind of retribution for that, one way for a gay man to handle his anger. But as far as I know, you don't see this with black men.

MASS: In *The Pleasure Bond* (1975), Masters and Johnson maintain that exclusive commitment is where it's at. Their recent study reaffirms the same thing for gay people. Should we be encouraged to maintain exclusive relationships?

PILLARD: I'm not sure that encouragement would make any difference. Most people go through a period at some time in their lives when they need to do a lot of fucking around. I think it would be unfortunate if one never experienced a completely committed relationship as well. So committed, longterm relationships are wonderful, and fucking around is wonderful too.

MASS: Homophobia is a term liberally used by many people to describe the irrational and intense fear of homosexuals and homosexuality. Is homophobia a true phobia?

PILLARD: Homosexuality is feared but also coveted. It's that conflict that tends to convert it into a matter of phobic avoidance. Many people secretly envy homosexuality as a something within themselves they are prevented from expressing. It's almost a law of nature that the person who is most vociferously against homosexuality will, on examination, be found to have a lot of homosexual desires. So I think that homophobia is indeed a classifiable illness on some basis such as that.

[Ed. note: The Fifth Edition of the *Psychiatric Dictionary*, prepared by Dr. Robert J. Campbell and published in 1981 by Oxford University Press, includes the word "gamophobia," which it defines as "fear of marriage." It does not, however, include the word "homophobia." Dr. Campbell is a past vice-president of the American Psychiatric Association who unsuccessfully ran for President and a bachelor who lives openly with a male companion. Having witnessed his ferocious face-to-face debating skills against such homophobes as Arno Karlen and Charles Socarides at a conference on homosexuality at Long Island Jewish Hospital, I was disappointed to discover this serious and ostensibly incongruous omission when the dictionary was published in '81. When I asked Dr. Campbell to explain the omission in an interview in his office at Gracie Square Hospital in 1981, he could not.]

MASS: What kinds of research on homosexuality would you like to see carried out within psychiatry?

PILLARD: There's much that could be done. Kids growing up in lesbian families, for example, the whole issue of gay parents and gay kids. Another area of research would be homophobia. A study could also be done on the cognitive abilities of gay people; there's good reason to speculate that gay people have unusual cognitive and creative gifts. Likewise, it has been suggested that gay people have higher IQs. No one has tested even a simple proposition like this.

Homosexual Behavior

A Conversation with Judd Marmor

[Ed. note: As newsletter editor of the Gay Caucus of Members of the American Psychiatric Association, I was deeply committed to fighting the conservative backlash among American psychiatrists that was threatening to repeal the APA's 1973-74 declassification of homosexuality as a mental disorder. Just how serious this threat became is documented in Ronald Bayer's book, *Homosexuality and American Psychiatry: The Politics of Diagnosis* (Basic Books, 1981). My review of that book for *The Advocate* (6/11/81) concluded as follows: "When the dignified narrative voice gently confirms that 'as America enters a period of social conservatism,' it is likely that 'the psychiatric and scientific justification for once again declaring homosexuality an illness will be found,' you feel protective."

The threat was real and the fight valid by any but the most reactionary standards. But there were other, more personal motivations for my involvement. In addition to having undergone traditional, psychoanalytically-oriented psychotherapy with a Harvard-affiliated psychiatrist who was casually homophobic ("I've heard all fourteen homosexual jokes," he once sneered), I endured all but physically assaultive homophobia several years later, when I casually came out during interviews for a residency in psychiatry at Northwestern, the University of Chicago and the University of Illinois. These experiences are documented in my first essay for the gay press ("Trial By Ordeal," which was retitled "Psychiatry on Trial," *Gay Community News*, August 11, 1979).

I was angry about the behavior of mainstream American psychiatry, about its conservatism on social issues in general and as I had witnessed and suffered from it personally. As GCMAPA newsletter editor, I perceived that I would have a unique opportunity to respond to psychiatric ignorance and injustice, and I seized it. I did not realize it at the time, at least not consciously, but in accepting this position, I had become actively involved, for the first time in my life, in a struggle that would engage me for the rest of my life.

I knew that our battle was a largely political fight and our early newsletter headlines and pieces reflected this awareness. With GCMAPA President Frank Rundle's full support (but to the great discomfort of the more accommodationist President-elect, David Kessler), the banner headline of our first issue of the newsletter (Volume V, Number 1, Summer 1979) ran as follows: "Psychoanalytic Statute Prevents Legal Entry of Gay Aliens." The story dealt with the Immigration and Naturalization Services' use of the psychoanalytic concept of homosexuality as a form of "psychopathic personality" to exlude "undesirables." In several publicized court cases (Karl Kinder, Carl Hill), Dr. Charles Socarides had invoked this neo-Freudian terminology, which was first used by the INS in 1952, during testimony for the prosecution. The newsletter report concluded: "Although the substance of this testimony blatantly contradicted the official APA position on homosexuality, Socarides has continued to give similar testimony in court, in the media, and in his book, *Homosexuality* ('78). And he does so without official censure or other APA response." That policy, incidentally, is still on the books.

Although our struggle was clearly political, my conservative training as a physician continued to suggest to me that "science" ("truth") would prove to be our most powerful weapon. That is, I believed that if vicious homophobes like Charles Socarides and Irving Bieber, and less vicious homophobes like Lawrence Hatterer and Helen Singer Kaplan, could be more aggressively confronted with the more recent and credible findings of respectable scientists like Masters and Johnson, the Kinsey researchers Bell and Weinberg and, especially, their distinguished psychiatric colleagues (and former APA presidents) Judd Marmor, John Spiegel and Jules Masserman, they would eventually admit that they had been wrong and curb their homophobia, or be completely discredited. And this is mostly what happened. Socarides, Bieber and their ilk never admitted they were wrong, but were increasingly outvoiced by a consensus of psychiatric and public opinion. In the cases of Hatterer and

Kaplan, whose mentors were Masters and Johnson, however, this assumption proved to be very naive.

In this vein of believing in science as our most powerful weapon, subsequent GCMAPA newsletter headlines gave prominence to the "more scientific" work of persons who were seen to be allies such as Marmor, Spiegel and Masserman (e.g., "New Psychiatric Text by Marmor to be Published") and Masters and Johnson (e.g., "Masters and Johnson Answer Critics"), while encouraging political activism (e.g., "Spiegel, Masserman Speak Out for Civil Rights," "Does the APA Oppose ERA?"). Most of these "allies," like Judd Marmor and Masters and Johnson, continued to support the medieval concept of "voluntary" sexual orientation "conversion," and in the case of Masters and Johnson, their data turned out to be as biased as anything in the annals of pseudoscience. But in marked contrast to the still ultraconservative mainstream of American psychiatry, they explicitly endorsed the position that homosexuality *per se* is not a mental illness, they explicitly acknowledged the seriousness of homophobia, and they explicitly and publicly affirmed the legitimacy of and need for civil liberties protections for lesbian and gay persons. I think it is accurate to say that, however incompletely, they endorsed and facilitated the gay liberation struggle and were, in their time and place, true allies.

The interviews I conducted from 1979 through 1981 with Masters and Johnson, Richard Pillard, Judd Marmor, John Money, Charles Silverstein, Thomas Szasz and Mary Calderone were all conceived by me as weapons in this battle: the personal, academic and social struggle I had so optimistically if naively characterized in that 1979 overview essay on sadomasochism for *The Advocate* as a great cultural trend — the shift in credibility of opinion about human sexual behavior "from the temples of psychiatry to the laboratories of sex research." Unfortunately, as the conversation with Thomas Szasz makes very clear, too many of these "laboratories of sex research" have turned out to be no less biased, no more genuinely scientific in their methodologies and conclusions than the psychiatric orthodoxies they were supplanting.

The following interview was conducted in Dr. Marmor's office at the UCLA School of Medicine. When *The Advocate* declined to pay

my expenses to go to L.A. to conduct the interview, I proceeded at
my own expense.]

Dr. Judd Marmor, who is currently Franz Alexander Professor of
Psychiatry at the University of Southern California, is one of the
great heroes of the gay liberation struggle. Like another of its heroes, Dr. John Spiegel, he is a former president of the American
Psychiatric Association (APA). In 1964, when the word "homosexuality" had yet to make its first appearance in the *New York
Times*, when the APA declassification of "homosexuality" as a
mental disorder was still a decade away, Dr. Marmor was editing
the most sophisticated, scientifically objective thinking in his profession about "the multiple roots of homosexuality."

His new book, *Homosexual Behavior: A Modern Reappraisal*
(Basic Books, 1980) rests on the premise of his earlier volume,
Sexual Inversion (Basic Books, 1965). The same premise underlies
the findings of Bell and Weinberg in the Kinsey study, *Homosexualities* (Simon and Shuster, 1978) and of Masters and Johnson in
Homosexuality in Perspective (Little, Brown & Co., 1979): there is
no discrete clinical entity, "homosexuality," and no unitary explanation for homosexual behavior.

In *Homosexual Behavior*, ancient psychiatric shibboleths like homosexual "latency," "narcissism" and other stigmata of "mental
illness" are demystified. Drawing on an unprecedented number of
authorities from an unprecedented array of scientific disciplines and
socio-culutural perspectives, Marmor has edited and coauthored a
complicated, sometimes controversial, ultimately definitive outline
of American psychiatry's contemporary *positions* on "homosexuality."

At the beginning of the last decade, gay people with bags over
their heads made their first, timorous efforts at direct communication with official psychiatry. At the start of this new decade, Marmor was delighted to participate in an exclusive interview with *The
Advocate*.

MASS: In the otherwise remarkable chapter, "Homosexuality and
Stigma," Carol Warren concludes that if gay people are "too vocif-
erous" in their demands for civil rights, they will invite a backlash.

Should gay people not demonstrate, not protest, when they are fired, blackmailed, excommunicated, imprisoned, raped, mutilated and murdered? Should gay people just sit passively through all of this, verifying the worst psychoanalytic prejudices about homosexual passivity and masochism, prejudices that your book is clearly at such pains to dispel?

MARMOR: I don't happen to agree with Carol Warren's statement. As editor, I didn't censor everything that my contributing authors wrote. I wanted to allow as free an expression of their points of view as I could. When you rebel against inequity, that often creates a backlash. But backlash shouldn't be a reason for not rebelling. If we look at protests by gay people in a historical sense, we see that by and large they have achieved constructive results. Bruce Voeller's chapter in my book clearly emphasizes this. There will be backlashes from time to time, but that's part of the ebb and flow of any revolutionary struggle for civil rights.

MASS: In the concluding chapter, "Homosexuality and the Issue of Mental Illness," you forcefully condemn the psychoanalytic contention that "all homosexuals are deeply narcissistic." You counter that "such a formulation obviously does not explain why most individuals diagnosed as narcissistic personalities are nevertheless heterosexual in orientation." But nothing in this observation precludes the ongoing theoretical psychoanalytic contention that *all* homosexuals are afflicted with varying degrees of "pathological narcissism." What about female homosexuality [*sic*]?

MARMOR: My basic argument throughout the book is an argument against the stereotyping of homosexuals. The fact that narcissistic people are not necessarily homosexual means that there's no necessary etiological or causal tie between narcissism and homosexuality. There are homosexuals who are narcissistic and heterosexuals who are. How can these analysts generalize? Even if all the gay patients they see were "narcissistic," they can't extrapolate to the non-patient population at large. It's precisely this tendency to draw sweeping generalizations from a limited number of people that I object to.

Martha Kirkpatrick's chapter, "Psychodynamic Psychotherapy of Female Homosexuality" implies that some females fall into this group, and I take issue with her tendency to draw a causal connection between narcissism and homosexuality. However, we also have to recognize that female homosexuality may be a different kind of condition [*sic*] from male homosexuality. The mere fact that both involve same-sex relationships does not necessarily mean that they both derive from identical causes.

MASS: Your new book verifies that "many contemporary psycho-analysts continue to regard homosexuality, *per se*, as a form of psychopathology." You forcefully denounce this prejudice as sci-entifically untenable, socially counter-productive and morally rep-rehensible. You even specifically denounce Charles Socarides. Now that the APA has made it official, are the "cure"-determined psychoanalytic pathologists of homosexuality not committing a kind of *malpractice*? Should they not be held accountable, like ex-orcists or purveyors of Laetrile, for scientifically unsupportable claims?

MARMOR: In order to justify such an approach, one would have to prove first of all that the gay people who come to them are *not* seeking change. If they *are* seeking change, if they're troubled peo-ple, then it's perfectly legitimate to treat them psychiatrically. My objection to the "cure-oriented" people in this field is their implicit assumption that *anyone* who is homosexual ought to be treated in order to remove that sexual preference. That, I think, is wrong! But there's a protective mechanism here in that no one who doesn't *want* to change his homosexuality is going to come into treatment for that sort of thing, or stay in treatment if he really doesn't want to change.

I do differ from many of my gay friends on one issue. Many of them feel that no gay person should ever be helped to "convert" to partial or total heterosexuality. I don't agree with that. It depends on what the motivations of the individual are. If he is motivated to change only because of society's opprobrium, then one should en-courage him to recognize that the problem is society's and not his. On the other hand, if he wants to change because he feels a need to belong to the mainstream of society—to have children, to have a family—I think he's entitled to help, assuming there's a reasonable chance of success.

Some gay people *can* be enabled to function heterosexually. I think the feeling of gay people that one-never-changes-one's-gayness has some validity in the sense that one probably never loses the capacity to respond to one's own sex if one has developed that capacity. But that's really not a fundamental issue. If someone wants to be able to function as a heterosexual and can be enabled to do so, fine. *Only a small minority of gay people want that*. So under these circumstances, I wouldn't consider the effort to help such people as a form of malpractice.

I think there might be malpractice if a gay person went to a psychiatrist and was severely traumatized by the psychiatrist's prejudice — where a gay person went for help, not necessarily for conversion, and encountered antipathy, hostility and pseudoscientific interpretations that damaged that gay person. Then *that* individual could try to sue his analyst for damage to himself and might be able to buttress his case with the fact that this analyst acted unscientifically. But I can't see any sweeping legislative remedies to this problem.

MASS: Given a so-called "ego-dystonic" homosexual — someone whose negative feelings about his homosexual impulses are so profound that he feels he must convert to heterosexuality — how can you tell whether such an individual is truly or appropriately homosexual. In your view, as well as that of Masters and Johnson and psychiatric sex therapist Helen Singer Kaplan, the answer appears to be "depth and sincerity of conviction to convert," rather than fantasy content or past experience. Aren't "depth and sincerity of conviction to convert" what was being sought by Catholic magistrates during inquisitions? Stripped of their good intentions, are the positions of Judd Marmor, Helen Singer Kaplan and Masters and Johnson really any different from that of Charles Socarides, who also concludes that the critical factor in the conversion of "the homosexual" is his determination?

MARMOR: First of all, there's one major difference. My contention is that where conversion is not successful it is the duty and the obligation of the psychiatrist to help the ego-dystonic homosexual accept his homosexuality and recognize that it's possible nevertheless to lead a worthwhile, honorable and satisfying life. So I do differ from the inquisition in the sense that I don't think they should be burned at the stake if they can't convert.

I've been critical of some of Masters and Johnson's work in this

area. Ninety percent of the converts they discussed were really bisexual (Kinsey 2s, 3s and 4s). It's a great mistake to assume, as
Bieber and others do, that obligatory homosexuality rests on performance anxiety in the heterosexual sphere. This may be true of some
individuals, but with most gay people there's simply no sense of
heterosexual arousal. That is a deeper problem and can't be dealt
with simply by a two-week rapid treatment of the Masters and Johnson type.

The other criticism I have is the point you're making about "fantasy content." I don't agree. I don't think one necessarily changes
the fantasy life of gay people — men or women — with psychotherapy. But that depends. Human beings are not static, and even sexual preferences are not necessarily static, though they tend to be
rather deeply fixed. The capacity to respond homosexually, once it
is developed and facilitated by experience, is a powerful thing and
does not change easily. What probably happens with most gay men
and women who convert is that their ability to enjoy heterosexual
experience is facilitated. To the extent that they enjoy heterosexual
experience more, they may or may not, depending on the individual, indulge in homosexual experiences less frequently. If they so
change, it may be that even their fantasy life may be modified. But I
would think that for a long time at the very least — and maybe even
forever — they would continue to have homosexual fantasies. So
what? I don't think that's such a major issue if they are leading the
kinds of lives they want to.

I don't have a religious attitude toward whether one should be
straight or gay. I believe in letting people live the kinds of lives they
want to live. You can tell whether an individual *really* wants to
convert, whether the reasons given are valid or whether he simply
wants to avoid the criticism of society.

MASS: Can you?

MARMOR: I believe you can most of the time. But even if you can't
be positive (and nothing in psychiatry is absolutely certain), I'm
willing to give that person a chance to do it, with the difference that
I put it up front at the very beginning (and I think Masters and
Johnson and Helen Singer Kaplan would do the same thing) and
say, "Look, I'm willing to try with you, but I want you to understand that it is not essential that we succeed and if we don't succeed

you can still live a good life. It doesn't mean you're a sick person. If this is something you want to try to achieve, I'm willing to help you try to achieve it.''

MASS: Must we conclude from what you're saying that if our culture were to have stronger sanctions against homosexuality, many more homosexuals might be more "sincerely" motivated to seek conversion therapy?

MARMOR: I don't think so. Maybe to some degree, but not in a massive sense. Such sanctions would simply drive homosexuality underground again. You can't willingly change yourself that easily.

MASS: Is there evidence that sociocultural suppression of homosexuality would make it any less prevalent?

MARMOR: Absolutely none. I don't think that social disapproval of homosexuality would lead to more people entering or successfully completing treatment.

MASS: In your book's chapter, "Patterns of Sexual Identity in Childhood," Dr. Richard Green, an expert on gender identity problems in children, readily admits that there is much less emphasis on treating "tomboyism" in young girls than on treating "effeminacy" in young boys. Isn't Dr. Green advocating a kind of therapy that could psychologically traumatize these boys, perhaps severely and permanently?

MARMOR: I don't think so. I would support Dr. Green's stand here. First of all, there are different kinds of behavior modification therapy in the treatment of children. Ivan Lovaas used cattle prods; of course, that's inhuman and completely unacceptable! Green and his group have the father spend more time with the little boy, reinforcing so-called masculine behavior and ignoring so-called effeminate behavior. The rationale behind this is that we have no evidence that *all* effeminate boys are going to become homosexual, but we do know that a larger proportion of them will. The very fact that they are being subjected to ridicule and aggression from their peers means that they're being traumatized. Their sense of self-worth is being damaged. On a purely preventive, mental-health basis, it's legitimate to try to help them. We can't modify the behavior of their peers who are simply reflecting the dominant attitudes of society. If we ever get to the kind of society that doesn't have these spurious values, then maybe being an effeminate boy will be no worse than being a tomboyish girl. But we don't live in that kind of society yet.

MASS: Then why not direct your efforts towards educating the public? Why haven't psychiatrists like yourself and Richard Green been doing what Masters and Johnson have been doing for years — appearing on talk shows like Phil Donahue's or Dick Cavett's, being interviewed or writing articles for mass publications like *Playboy* and *Hustler*?

MARMOR: One has to be invited to do these things. I assume that Judd Marmor and Richard Green are not the kind of public names that Masters and Johnson are. If I were invited, I would be glad to appear on a talk show like Donahue's. So, I suspect, would Dr. Green. But we haven't been asked . . . as yet.

MASS: Would you (together with fellow egalitarians Masters and Johnson, and Helen Singer Kaplan) applaud the concept of teaching interested or dissatisfied *heterosexuals* to expand their sexual functioning to include *homosexual* relations?

MARMOR: If a heterosexual were to come to me with this kind of request — "I am attracted to another fellow with whom I would like to learn to function sexually" — I'd be glad to work with him. One doesn't get that kind of request . . . but I don't think any of the people you've mentioned has any built-in prejudices against helping an individual to achieve such an expressly desired goal.

MASS: Do you believe, like Masters and Johnson, that the monogamous pair bond is the most "mature" kind of sexual relationship that individuals of either persuasion can have?

MARMOR: I personally know of a number of valid and meaningful relationships that don't involve that kind of exclusive fidelity within the relationship. So I personally wouldn't impose that kind of a generalization.

MASS: Do you believe that bisexuality can be consistent with full psychosexual maturity?

MARMOR: In a very basic sense, bisexuality is the natural state, at least for mammals. You can't separate mental health from the cultural matrix in which it exists. One could have been bisexual in ancient Greece and have been optimally healthy. It's a little more difficult to be openly bisexual in our society and not be subjected to stresses that might impair one's health.

MASS: Why should sex play among children, or for that matter, between youngsters and adults, be so ferociously and categorically proscribed?

MARMOR: I feel very strongly that masturbation and sex between children are healthy manifestations of developing sexuality and should not be proscribed. The fact that they are treated as dirty or sinful is simply a carryover of our Judeo-Christian heritage.

In ancient Greece, in Sparta, you had a social context for healthy, constructive relationships between adult men and young boys. Here, the man transferred some of his nobility, his masculinity, to the youngster through a sexual bond. But we have to go a long way in our society before that kind of thing can be made an official aspect of contemporary human sexuality. I don't deny the possibility that such experiences could be healthy ones. But where do you draw the line? It's even possible that an older man might have a relationship with a preadolescent boy and make of it a very beautiful and tender experience. But I think that the danger of victimization in the kind of society we live in now, where feelings of individual responsibility are so corroded, is too great not to have laws prohibiting such behavior.

MASS: Arno Karlen's *Sexuality and Homosexuality* (Norton, 1971) has been widely criticized for its homophobic slurs and slants. In his chapter, "Homosexuality in History," in your book, Karlen sarcastically concludes: "Everyone knows that the ancient Greeks accepted and even promoted homosexuality — everyone who has not consulted the documents." "Everyone" here ostensibly includes Sir Kenneth Dover, President of Corpus Christi College, Oxford, whose prestigious and universally acclaimed study, *Greek Homosexuality* (Harvard University Press, 1978), is not even mentioned by Karlen. Why was homophobic, academically undistinguished Arno Karlen asked to write this chapter? Why not Vern Bullough? Or Martin Duberman? Or Jonathan Katz? Or John Boswell?

MARMOR: I have to plead ignorance on that. I didn't know the literature on the history of homosexuality sufficiently to make the best informed choice. I knew Arno Karlen's work and hoped he would restrict himself to historical fact and not indulge in editorial comments. If I had known the work of these other men, I might have made another choice.

MASS: Do you agree with psychoanalyst Robert Stoller's observation ([in his book] *Sexual Excitement*, 1979) that, in our culture, "sadomasochism is a central feature of most sexual excitement"?

MARMOR: I'm not sure that it's as widespread as he says. It may be relatively widespread and I think there's a good reason for that. As long as we are brought up to think of sex as dirty and sinful, then when we do have sex, no matter how much we love our partners, we must express that love with aggression.

MASS: Do you believe there are any significant differences between gay and straight S/M?

MARMOR: There are many complex motives in S/M, but I don't think it's fundamentally any different among gays than in a straight context.

MASS: Do you believe that sadomasochistic ritualizations between consenting adults can in some instances be healthy and constructive?

MARMOR: My own feeling is that whenever sexuality *must* be combined with the inflicting of pain on one's partner, there's something beyond sexuality that's involved — power, defiance of authority, the need for control, overcoming resistance. The mere fact that sexual excitement takes place is not necessarily an indication of a healthy process.

MASS: But where such acts are mutually consensual, how and where does one draw the line?

MARMOR: Where these acts are mutually consensual between adults and no one is seriously injured, it's nobody's business, neither the law's nor psychiatry's. It's not our job to be guardians of the morals of society at large.

MASS: Is any important research on homosexuality being carried on outside the U.S.A.?

MARMOR: The only such biological research that I'm aware of is that of Dorner in West Germany, as described in my new book. There probably is a certain group of homosexuals, particularly effeminate men, in whom there may be a genetic or constitutional factor. For some homosexuals, the implications of this work are obviously quite important. It may mean that there's a basic, constitutional difference between men who have felt effeminate and attracted to the same sex since they were children and those who become gay later in life. It may be something that also explains transsexualism. I think it does so better than Stoller's [psychoanalytic] hypothesis, of which I've never been convinced.

MASS: What is likely to be the future course of classical psychoanalysis?

MARMOR: Classical psychoanalysis as a form of therapy is on the decline. During the '50s and '60s, it dominated American psychiatry. It no longer does. Analytic doctrine is *slowly* becoming more flexible. The classical analysts will remain a strong, tightly knit, but shrinking group of people who cling to their outworn theories. The influence of classical analytic theory is declining because it has been superseded by other developments in behavioral science — ego psychology, communication and information theory.

MASS: Do you think that this "strong, tightly knit group" of classical analysts will attempt to cash in on the conservative backlash during the 1980 political campaign, and again confront the American public with their views? And if so, how should they be dealt with by gay people, by the APA?

MARMOR: There are some analysts who, in my opinion, suffer from serious homophobia and who might very well participate in such a movement. There's one psychoanalyst from the Menninger Clinic who is very much involved in the antigay movement. And Socarides, willingly or unwillingly, has been used by the antigay movement. Wherever they appear, they must be disputed by scientific fact. They are presuming to act as experts and there is a wealth, a predominance of scientific evidence against their point of view. We must counter these prejudices wherever possible.

MASS: For at least 20 years, you have been widely respected as the preeminent psychiatric authority on homosexual behavior. Yet some people, both gay and straight, are more familiar with names like Charles Socarides and Irving Bieber. Why should this be so?

MARMOR: There may be a valid psychological reason for this. It's more important to recognize your enemies than your friends.

The Birds, the Bees and John Money

A Conversation with Sexologist John Money

If limerence—the state of being love-smitten—is the newest frontier in the study of human sexuality, what about homo-limerence? And bilimerence? Is limerence genetic? What is the relationship between limerence and sexual attraction? Is religious faith a form of limerence? Can limerence be addictive?

As the science of love broadens the field of sex research, these and other questions are of tremendous importance to gay people. Psychologist Dorothy Tennov's *Love and Limerence* (Stein and Day, 1980) and sexologist John Money's *Love and Love Sickness* (Johns Hopkins University Press, 1980) further our understanding of love, its relationship to sexuality, its infinite variety, its "pathologies." Based on over a decade of clinical research, *Love and Limerence* examines the psychophysiological state of being in love through a correlation of thousands of subjective impressions from more than a thousand study subjects.

Dr. John Money, Professor of Medical Psychology, Director of the Psychohormonal Research Unit at Johns Hopkins, Visiting Professor of Pediatrics, Obstetrics and Gynecology, Instructor of Psychiatry, Doctor of Philosophy (Harvard), leading sex therapist, author of fifteen books on sex, gender identity, and pair-bonding, is probably the most respected figure in sexology.

Of *Love and Love Sickness* (only 256 pages in length), Dr. Mary Calderone, President of the Sex Information and Education Council of the United States (SIECUS), observed: "*Love and Love Sickness* provides a panoramic view of the entire field of human sexuality. The amount of information contained in the book is staggering, but it is information that must be mastered by anyone practicing in the relatively new field of sexology."

On his recent sojourn to New York "to see [the] Picasso [exhibition]," Dr. Money talked about his new book, Tennov's concept of limerence, the new sex therapists, recent developments in genetic and hormonal research, incest, transsexualism, sadomasochism, "cruising" and the relationship between sex and religion.

MASS: In *Love and Limerence*, Tennov concludes that it is *limerence*, the experience of being in love, that defines people as straight or gay. As one of her male homosexual subjects put it, "I fall in love with men, not women. Period. That's what makes me gay." How valid is [this] concept of *homolimerence*?

MONEY: Quite valid, I think. In my opinion, the most secure definition of heterosexual vs. homosexual or bisexual has less to do with sexual behavior or experience than with the sex(es) of the individual(s) with whom one is capable of falling in love. It would thus make more sense to classify people on the basis of their erotic imagery, their fantasies, than on the basis of visible behavior.

It's an irreparable defect of their entire study that Masters and Johnson did exactly that—classified people solely on the basis of current genital activity without regard to fantasy content. Young people who are trying to establish a long-term, pair-bonded (limerent) relationship gain a huge amount of predictability about one another if they exchange an understanding of each other's fantasies and fantasy expectations. It follows that researchers and therapists will gain predictability and understanding when they ascertain their subjects' fantasies.

MASS: But a major point of the Masters and Johnson study seems to be that fantasy patterns are far more variable and flexible than had previously been thought. According to them, even some Kinsey 0s—the most exclusively heterosexual of their subjects in*experience*—had some homosexual fantasies.

MONEY: One should more correctly say "Kinsey 0s" rated according to *their* criteria, but not Kinsey's. If they had been accurate, they would have classified these people with heterosexual experience and homosexual fantasy as bisexual right from the start. As one reviewer recently pointed out, there's an instance where they actually classify one man rated as Kinsey 1 in their heterosexual study group and another, also Kinsey 1, in their homosexual study group.

A point about fantasy. I'm very meticulous about the fact that a genuine masturbation or coital fantasy has the autonomy of a dream. You don't decide to do it voluntarily. I think Masters and Johnson have added to the general confusion by implying that fantasy can be changed by an act of will, as in sex therapy with the use of the technique of guided fantasy, so-called. What happens here is that the guided fantasy inevitably — often quickly — merges into the unguided fantasy that one is attempting to change.

MASS: In their "Fantasy Patterns" chapter, Masters and Johnson state that "as cultural mores change, so may fantasy patterns." In *Love and Love Sickness*, you hypothesize that "in the absence of rehearsing ordinary male-female sexual interaction, and the imagery of it in mental representation, children establish instead various improvisations and substitutes that become the basis of full-blown *paraphilias* (formerly called *perversions*) in later life. The bonding of exclusive homosexuality may also be facilitated in this way."

Does this imply that the whole business of fantasy is merely an artifact of culture? In other words, if we had been reared in optimum sexual freedom and health, would we be less likely to have *any* fantasies? Or would they just be different?

MONEY: Do you think Neanderthal man had fantasies of silk hose? More up to date, the rubber fetishism we saw earlier in this century is now giving way to plastics fantasies because of the change in diaper covers from rubber to plastic. It's fairly well established that masochism in this century as an upper-class "British and German disorder," correlates with the exaggerated attention paid to corporal punishment in the boarding schools of England and Germany. There's no question in my mind that the visual content of an erotic fantasy is surely not present at birth. The exact vocabulary and syntax of the visual imagery that becomes your fantasy is very much dependent on what we now have to say are the vagaries of development because we don't try to monitor erotic imagery in our children. That's why I've placed such emphasis in my book on the "sex rehearsal play" of children. We have a great research task before us to find out a lot more about the function of this play in primates and in the laying down of erotic imagery in children. If there were a socially shared program of child-rearing that included a proper perspective and toleration of these normal developmental sexual play activities, there would be a fairly solid guarantee that the content of the observed play would be built into the content of the children's subsequent erotic imagery. It would become one's "native eroto-sexualism," the counterpart of one's native language.

MASS: So there would be some kind of imagery, fantasy, regardless of developmental circumstances.

MONEY: With the rarest of exceptions, it is to be expected that members of the human race will have erotic imagery. But the vocabulary and syntax of it will never be demonstrable at the time of birth. The actual program of one's erotic imagery will not be written prenatally, by genes or hormones, but postnatally using the external receptors—specifically the eyes, ears, nose and skin—by light waves, sound waves, and tactual stimuli. This postnatal programming has the special characteristic of being simultaneously social and physiologic.

In my book, I stress that I think we've fallen into a hideous trap of thinking that if something is *learned*, it's ethereal, that it somehow doesn't involve the brain, that somehow we can assume that there's no biology of learning or memory. This, of course, is manifestly absurd. Our ignorance is not sufficient reason to pretend that something doesn't exist. This point about the biology of learning is important. It's going to be devilish for some time to come because we're going to continue to argue archaic "nature versus nurture" concepts. We're going to keep insisting on the differences between "the biological and the nonbiological." But what *is* the nonbiological? We never specify that. It's always the social, the learned, the spiritual, the astral. It becomes possible not to become entangled in this fruitless mind/body split by discarding the principle of motivation, and teleological thinking in general.

MASS: Masters and Johnson and their psychiatric disciple, Helen Singer Kaplan, have promoted the idea of "conversion" sex therapy for practicing adult homosexuals who *wish* to function as heterosexuals. Yet neither Masters and Johnson nor Kaplan appear to have any concept of limerence. Provided a person so wishes, is there any solid scientific evidence to suggest that an established pair-bonding (limerence) pattern can be truly or permanently "converted," whether by psychoanalysis, drugs, behavior modification, or aversion therapy?

MONEY: The monkey in the woodpile there, of course, is *"wishes* to be converted.'' I think that anyone who uses this concept ought to be severely chastised. We don't expect in any other branch of medicine that people will change or get better or do whatever it is that we expect them to do because they *wish* it. That's indefensibly passing the buck of responsibility from the physician or clinician back onto the patient. It's a cheap and sleazological trick of psychiatry and clinical psychology to blame the failure of this approach on the "resistance" of the patient. I simply won't use that motivational and teleological construct of wishing or desiring or wanting to change. Instead, I can now say that people who come to me, or to anyone, with the problem of wanting to have sex with or be limerent with a member of the sex he or she is not currently doing it with is really saying: "I'm a person who is somewhere on the bisexual continuum, and where I am right now isn't suiting me." I can't conceptualize attempting to convert an exclusive heterosexual to homosexuality or vice versa, no matter what his "motivation." The people that Masters and Johnson talk about are people with a degree of bisexuality that never got resolved into either dicrotic extreme; that is, either exclusive homosexuality or exclusive heterosexuality. As far as I know, that's also true of the cases Kaplan writes about. The people who come to us requesting change are partly bisexual. That's why we're there, for those people who aren't secure about where they actually are along the bisexual continuum.

MASS: Judd Marmor, Masters, Johnson and Kaplan seem to agree that some adults who have been *behaviorally* homosexual and who *wish* to function heterosexually can be enabled to do so by being taught to incorporate their homosexual fantasies into their heterosexual relations. Again, the critical factor here is this business of "depth and sincerity of determination to convert." If, hypothetically, a young man learns to repetitively function with his homosexual fantasies rather than to directly interact with his female partner, wouldn't he then be, technically speaking, a paraphiliac (or "pervert" in the old terminology)? In other words, aren't the new sex therapists actually running some risk of encouraging "perverse" sexuality, however "normal" it might appear to society?

MONEY: I share your genuine concern. I might be somewhat less critical if this kind of therapy were accurately presented for exactly what it is: a compromise that is nothing near the state of perfection being sought by the patient. But I would remain very concerned about the ethics of it. It's not very ethical as far as the partner is concerned, is it? To be fucking a fantasy? It creates a psychic distance. "You want me only for my body," the partner protests, and is not totally in error.

MASS: I think Marmor, Masters, Johnson and Kaplan would counter that over a period of time, their therapy will ideally facilitate the kind of greater communication of fantasy content and expectations between patient and partner that you mentioned earlier as being so essential to successful pair-bonding. In turn, this greater communication will, hypothetically, lead to more direct, fantasy-independent communications between patient and partner.

MONEY: But certainly this contention is sufficiently critical that it must be substantiated by long-term, follow-up studies. At present, we simply don't have this information.

MASS: Apparently not. Kaplan admits to having no such statistics and the Masters and Johnson study doesn't seem very satisfactory in this regard.

MONEY: The Masters and Johnson study certainly doesn't qualify as an adequate longitudinal study by my criteria.

MASS: Psychiatrist Marcel Saghir, author of *Male and Female Homosexuality* (Williams and Wilkins, 1973), recently said: "I do not believe that there is solid scientific evidence as to the presence of emotional and psychological bisexuality. Development of both homosexual and heterosexual orientations usually occurs early in life and despite overlapping experiences, there is usually a dominant preference." Likewise, Tennov doesn't rule out the possibility of *bilimerence*, but it was a phenomenon she did not observe.

MONEY: In her sample. And how often is "usually"? In my book, I emphasize that bisexuality should not be interpreted as sitting on a fulcrum of 50:50. The clinical task is to make some estimate of proportion — 60:40, 90:10, etc. I haven't actually encountered *simultaneous* bilimerence in my clinical experience. Limerence is usually experienced for one individual at a time. But I've known of a number of individuals who are close to being 50:50 in their capacity to experience limerence for either sex, but serially, not contemporaneously.

MASS: *Ambisexuality* is a term that has entered the recent literature.

Masters and Johnson have devoted an entire chapter to what they defined as their "Ambisexual Study Group." Denniston's chapter, "Ambisexuality in Animals," actually opens Marmor's [revised] *Homosexual Behavior* (Basic Books, 1980). [This term] is not once mentioned in your book. Why?

MONEY: In their study, Masters and Johnson credit their adoption of this term to Mark Schwartz, who had completed post-doctoral training with me at Johns Hopkins. There, in the early Fifties, I may have been the first or among the first to use the term, applying it to individuals with sex-organ anomalies such as hermaphroditism. Masters and Johnson use it in a new context to mean something about behavior. I didn't use the word in *Love and Love Sickness* because it wasn't relevant in my vocabulary. Therein, what is its virtue? What does *ambi*sexual say that *bi*sexual does not? Maybe "disexual or" "duosexual" will appear next.

MASS: According to Masters and Johnson, "an ambisexual is a man or woman who unreservedly enjoys, solicits, or responds to overt sexual opportunity with equal ease and interest regardless of the sex of the partners and who, as a sexually mature individual, has never evidenced interest in a continuing relationship." In terms of fantasy-independent sexual functioning, Masters and Johnson give the impression that ambisexuals are extraordinarily healthy.

MONEY: They sound more like Don Juans to me. I don't think I'd call that exactly healthy—not morbid, but not a paragon of health either. Don Juans would fall under what I classified in my books as *hyperphilia* ("supranormal in sexual or genital responsiveness or frequency"). The classical terminology for this has been *nymphomania* and *satyriasis*. There is a type of individual who finds himself on a merry-go-round of partnerships, who never settles down and who is able to have sex with both men and women. There is also the individual who must habitually repeat the initial courtship phase (*proception*) of a bonding relationship. Following sex and orgasm, such a hyperphiliac is incapable of reacting positively to the partner, except on an emotionally detached, social basis. Incidentally, this has a great deal to do with a particular type of *cruising*. In fact, I've coined a special term, *polyiterophilia*, to describe this particular syndrome. The polyiterophiliac is a person whose sexual responsiveness is built up toward orgasm by repeating the same activity many times with many partners. I coined this term also because it allows one to become much more logically precise in discussing such issues as the so-called promiscuity of homosexuals. It's a very particular criticism of homosexuals that they never have any "commitment," which means they're incapable of durable pair-bondedness. This simply isn't true. A subset of the total gay population has this particular phenomenon — the polyiterophilia — in *their* cruising. But one can't generalize that this applies to the entire homosexual population, or even to all "cruising."

MASS: Throughout your book, you stress that patterns of sexual behavior are programmed in early childhood. Psychoanalysts have consistently generalized that "cruising" is unique to homosexuals and always represents a compulsive flight from anxiety that is achieved by a kind of regressive, infantile "acting-out" of sexual conflicts with a fantasied parent figure. Beyond the issue of generalization, is this in any way congruent with what you're saying?

MONEY: Some homosexual individuals might do something *like* that. But I don't universalize! I quite specifically tried to bring more logic into the field by separately designating specific behaviors such as *hypophilia*, *hyperphilia*, *polyiterophilia*, and *paraphilia*. To illustrate, an individual whose sexual activities are exclusively masturbatory and who masturbates only with the aid of a *fetish* — say, the feces of a fantasy type — such an individual is polyiterative. That is, he must repetitively recycle this ritual of fantasy in order to achieve sexual gratification. He also has a *paraphilia*, the term I used (and persuaded the American Psychiatric Association to use in their *Diagnostic and Statistical Manual of Mental Disorders*) to replace the more pejorative and less specific *perversion*. The paraphilia in this instance is *coprophilia*: the condition of being dependent on the taste or smell of feces for erotic arousal and the facilitation or achievement of orgasm. I think it's valuable to be able to separate these various aspects of that individual's problem. It helps to avoid such oversimplification as "compulsive flight from anxiety," and "regressive, infantile acting-out with a parent figure," and to avoid attributing such maneuvers to homosexuals only. It's more logical and it's more fair-minded.

MASS: Tennov gives the impression that *nonlimerence*, the inability to become love-smitten, is widespread and may even be constitutional or genetic. What evidence is there to support this contention?

MONEY: There are some individuals with brain injuries or disorders who may be incapable of limerence – people who have defective pituitary functioning, for example. But to say that it is genetically determined is not justified. I was aware as I read through Tennov's case examples that the mightiest displays of limerence, as described by her informants, indicated a relative lopsidedness in the degree of limerence of one partner for the other. It was not very common to find people who had a totally reciprocated limerent affair. I would be inclined to say that Tennov was writing more about partially unrequited limerence than that which is perfectly reciprocal. We don't hear too much about the latter because it works so well. I would even speculate that for many people in our society, limerence has a sort of built-in booby trap because they're victims of the split between romantic love above the belt and carnal love below. They ride a pendulum of anguish when they become limerent because culture has prevented them from assimilating their "carnal knowledge" into their cultural picture of the ideal "romantic" love affair. We do in our society make it very difficult for young people to take off their belts, don't we?

MASS: Indeed. That seems to be the major point of your book. Tennov believes that the relationship between limerence and sexual attraction is far from clear. Is limerence simply one pattern of pair-bonding? Or is it rather, as you seem to imply, an optimum degree of a singular bonding phenomenon? Can it exist apart from sexual attraction in the same individual?

MONEY: Limerence cannot exist apart from sexual attraction in my opinion. Sexual attraction is a very essential ingredient of what the bonding (limerence) phenomenon is. But there's a related question. Can sexual and erotic communication between two people take place in the absence of limerence? The answer to that, of course, is yes. If you carry the question one step further, conception doesn't necessarily involve limerence either. The test case for that is artifical insemination.

In history, nearly all cultures have defined the basis of breeding partnerships economically, on the basis of family relationships, in order to match fortunes and power. Ever since the twelfth century,

Western civilization has undergone a great change in at least defining individual limerence, the romantic love affair, as the basis of marriage. But so great is the experience of limerence, of personally being affected by the feelings of being love-smitten, that it will inevitably express itself in any culture. Even a society that matches individuals regardless of limerent preferences must find some way of institutionalizing the feelings and experience of limerence.

MASS: You were on the subcommittee that prepared and approved the gender-identity section of the new, third edition of the American Psychiatric Association's *Diagnostic and Statistical Manual of Mental Disorders* (DSM-III). As we've noted, you were also responsible for the change in terminology from *perversion* to *paraphilia*. You were said to be against the new classification of *ego-dystonic homosexuality* (describing as mentally disordered only those who are unhappy with or wish to change their homosexual impulses or behavior). What were your arguments?

MONEY: I think it's a political cop-out. My big argument was, if you're going to have ego-dystonic homosexuality, then you should also have ego-dystonic masturbation, ego-dystonic heterosexuality, etc.

MASS: But the response to your argument, a response that is actually printed in DSM-III, is that ego-dystonic heterosexuality, at least in our culture, is not something one sees.

MONEY: Oh? . . . Oh? . . . Oh! That's not my experience! The inclusion of this category must be faced for what it is—a political maneuver to appease the opposition. It's also a way of guaranteeing insurance payments for those who decree treatment for homosexuals. Intellectually, as a matter of the logic of classification, it cannot be defended.

MASS: If there were optimum sexual health and freedom in our culture, there might be less so-called ego-dystonic homosexuality and correspondingly more ego-syntonic bisexuality. Would there, on the other hand, be less exclusive homosexuality?

MONEY: The way in which children develop gender identity is to an important degree programmed by the cultural environment in which they are raised. If there's a cultural program in which everyone is to be heterosexual, then heterosexual rehearsal play cannot be inhibited in children. Otherwise, you have a culture that won't function. If our culture openly espouses heterosexuality or even bi-sexuality as the end product of adolescence, then it must openly and explicitly program children from their earliest development to achieve that end, which frequently it does not do. That's why there isn't a higher prevalence of uncomplicated heterosexuality than ex-ists at present. Instead, we've allowed erotosexual development to take place willy-nilly, in a milieu of secrecy, threat and punish-ment. Your question is problematic in suggesting that there's a kind of pre-ordained pattern of development, a pristine destiny of nature that will express itself regardless of cultural programming. Genes always unfold themselves in an environment. And when it comes to erotosexual development, our social traditions dictate that environ-ment. There are some ethnic societies in which the social traditions of erotosexual development encourage an absence of exclusive adult homosexuality.

MASS: In your chapter, "Genetic and Chromosal Aspects of Homo-sexuality" in Marmor's new book [*Homosexual Behavior*], you as-sert almost simultaneously that although the currently available evi-dence suggests that "the sex chromosomes do not directly determine psychosexual status . . . it remains to be seen whether an as yet undetected genetic origin" for these variations will be found. I get the impression that you believe a genetic basis for at least some homosexuality will be further substantiated in the future. If this is so, would you hazard a guess as to what percent of exclusively homosexual adults this might apply to?

MONEY: Not yet. But I will guess that genetic determinants will probably turn out to be on some kind of a curve, along a spectrum of distribution. There's a newer piece of information that is not in *Love and Love Sickness*. It pertains to transsexuals. Dr. Wolf Ei-cher in Munich presented evidence that in female-to-male transsex-uals, the male determining H-Y antigen is incongruously present. Likewise, in male-to-female transsexuals, it is incongruously miss-ing. Since this factor, H-Y antigen, is carried on the Y sperm and is normally found in every Y-bearing cell of the male body, it has been thought to be present only in genetic males and absent in ge-netic females. The new finding throws all the prior security of theo-retical thinking about sex determination into chaos. Here, transsex-uals are disobeying what was thought to be a universal rule. Who knows where this will lead in terms of understanding the genetic and other prenatal programming of neurohormones or neurotransmitters that pertain eventually to pair-bonding? This might help to explain a predisposition to, but never the exact programming of, the homosexual and bilimerence patterns mentioned earlier, and it may possibly have shed light on the percentage of exclusive homosexuals in a population.

MASS: You emphasize the logical appropriateness of "Minimizing Sex Differences," the title of Chapter 7 in *Love and Love Sickness*. Yet a criticism of your work with transsexuals, as expressed at some length by Janice Raymond in *The Transsexual Empire* (Beacon Press, 1979), is that it supports a patriarchal commitment to *maintaining* sex differences. Is there some conflict in your positions?

MONEY: The President of the Canadian Medical Association, Dr. Lawrence Wilson, recently questioned the availability of national health insurance for transsexual surgery and was quoted as saying that transsexuals "volunteer for their diseases; they bear the self-inflicted wounds of peacetime." Ms. Raymond is basically saying the same thing. She's also saying that it is a condition that is "volunteered" by the doctors who treat it rather than by the patients who have it. But it's the transsexuals themselves who have insisted on extreme sex stereotypes of being a woman or being a man.

MASS: Ms. Raymond states that "transsexual surgery turns into an antisocial activity that promotes the worst aspects of a patriarchal society by encouraging adaptation to its sex roles." Prophetically, she perceives gender-identity clinics as "future centers of sex-role control." Such gender-identity clinics are already flourishing. And they are treating effeminate boys with much greater emphasis and in much greater numbers than masculinate girls. This is parallel to the treatment of transsexuals, among whom a sex change is requested with at least a fourfold greater frequency by males than by females. Are we building a transsexual empire?

MONEY: If we had a society that was less obsessed with maximizing sex differences, we'd be living in a society without the unbelievably pervasive, traumatizing sexual taboo that affects us all our lives. If we were living in a society where sex differences were minimized to the extent that they are currently maximized, we would probably be able to get rid of virtually all the paraphilias, transsexualism, the hyperphilias, the hypophilias — premature ejaculation, impotence, anorgasmia — and other erotosexual handicaps. At the very least, we could expect a drastic reduction in the prevalence of most erotosexual disorders. We create most of the psychosexual disorders in our society, transsexualism included, with our excessive addiction to the sexual taboo from infancy onward. But I wouldn't call that the building of a "transsexual empire."

MASS: Psychoanalysis has introduced the fear that young children cannot distinguish their sexual from their aggressive drives. Is there any scientific evidence to support the contention that aggression is innate in the sexuality of children?

MONEY: Now you see why I got rid of the concept of "motivation"! In the constructs of psychoanalysis, the aggressive and sexual "drives" are like little machines that are going to force themselves out . . . like demons. Looking at the whole matter historically, psychoanalytic theory is very closely related to the theories of human behavior that preceded it. In fact, psychoanalytic theory can be found principle by principle in the Old Testament. It's simply a rewording of concepts of sin, free will and salvation by grace.

MASS: If the sexuality of children were to be less taboo-ridden, if society were to be more concerned with nurturing "erotic/vocational synchrony," as you put it in your book, wouldn't this result in some degree of sociosexual chaos?

MONEY: No. The cross-cultural evidence is very clear that sex-rehearsal play in children is not at all obtrusive, even when completely uninhibited. Nor does it occupy a major portion of the childrens' attention or activity. But deprivation and punishment of this play has dire developmental consequences.

MASS: What about the problem of adolescent and teenage pregnancies?

MONEY: Why must this be considered a problem? Why not a solution? The very possibility of reversing this question in *Love and Love Sickness* is related to the fact that we now live in the age of birth control. There can be little doubt that our sexual taboo is historically very much related to society's struggles to deal with the issues of child care. In the ultimate analysis, it was pregnancy and its relationship to property and wealth that was being regulated by the taboo. We are now confronted with new options. We could develop a society in which all people would be supplied with birth control up to a certain age. Another option is for society to recognize that it might be healthier for people to complete their breeding at an earlier age — by 18 or 20, for example. Instead of bemoaning "the problem" of teenage pregnancies, we'd take an entirely new view: what an ideal time for breeding! All you'd need to change is the economic support system for young parents. That would be imperative.

MASS: That's a big "all."

MONEY: It is, because it would threaten the patriarchy.

MASS: What would be the effect of making healthy, explicitly erotic pair-bonding images available to young children?

MONEY: Probably 80 to 90 percent of the world's children know what copulation is because they sleep in the same room with their parents, brothers, sisters, and other relatives or friends. So we're really asking a lot of questions that reflect our own obsessions with our own taboo against sex, don't you think? The business of the traumatic dangers of the "primal scene" is so middle class that I find it difficult to believe that people can still take it seriously.

MASS: In your book, you explain that the prototype for adolescent and later adult pair-bonding is the bond that is established between infant and parent. Does the existence, then, of an hysterically extreme incest taboo have an inhibitory effect on the erotic component of adult bonding? In other words, is the incest taboo of patriarchy actually the "original sin" of sexual disorder?

MONEY: Yes, but it is only one manifestation of the overall sex taboo. The mechanism of this negative effect is that it requires guilt for any degree of erotic feelings that the child may experience for the parent, almost always the mother, and vice versa. We've confronted people with terrible problems about incest, even if it should occur in a dream or fantasy that is not subject to voluntary control. We then tell people that such dreams and fantasies are products of immaturity, sin, evil, immorality, degeneracy. In effect, we impose the agony of forced secrecy and deceit. No guidance, no reassurance, no sexual health. This is the mechanism by which the incest taboo has its most traumatic effects on growing children. And, of course, if incestuous behavior is later practiced, as it may be when brothers and sisters play in childhood, the taboo of earlier infancy will continue to work just as traumatically.

MASS: Is religious faith a form of limerence, or pair-bonding? Is a child taught to love an imaginary deity in much the same way, and with the same intensity and permanence, that he is taught to love his or her parents? In other words, have the scientific principles of pair-bonding been applied to the study of religious behavior?

MONEY: To my knowledge, they have not been so applied. But it would be worthwhile. To me, it's obvious that the phenomenon of limerence, personally experienced, is the one on which the entire structure of religion has evolved. "God is love," the Bible proclaims. Many thousands of years ago, perhaps in the neolithic age, certain elite priest-rulers were probably experimenting with ideas, using their elite IQs of 150 to 200. Religion didn't just evolve from a bunch of monkeys in a tree. It evolved from human thinking in the category known as "revelation." Every major religion begins with its myth of creation, its Adam and Eve story, based not only on sexual mating but also on love. Change sexual love into affectional love and profane or earthly love into sacred love, and you have love of God.

MASS: Throughout your book, you stress the role of religious ignorance and proscription in the genesis of crippled sexuality. At one point, you actually imply, as did Larry Flynt in a recent issue of *Hustler*, that individual ministers and their institutions might someday be sued or otherwise held directly responsible for the sexual disorders of individuals. How far are we from such confrontations?

MONEY: Very far; I'm not too optimistic. One proviso, however! Sometimes, there are sudden, earthquake shifts in the course of social history. Quite unexpected, completely unscheduled changes can appear. Who would have predicted OPEC, for example?

MASS: You describe the paraphilias, like "sexual sadism" or "sexual masochism" as "erotic/sexual addictions" where "role reciprocity" and "role collusion" appear to be common. But you qualify that "in the present state of knowledge, the extent to which the accommodation of the partner to a paraphiliac's addiction begins as a mutual attraction is not known." In Massachusetts, a sadomasochistic relationship recently came before the courts (Appleby). The sadist was judged responsible, guilty, and given a stiff prison sentence for minor, allegedly unsolicited injuries sustained by the plaintiff ("the masochist," according to the defendant). Do you think this will establish a trend wherein the sadist in such a partnership will usually be held responsible, even where "role collusion" is beyond question? Are there other implications?

MONEY: Isn't prior role collusion already the basis of many divorces? Just how this terminology will be manipulated by the courts is a big question. For now, I would simply observe that whenever sex is approached with a negative criticism, it receives far more attention than when it is positively endorsed. Thus, there is reason to expect that the courts will, as they always do, apply the adversary rule, identify a victim (the masochist) and an oppressor (the sadist), and accuse and punish the sadist.

MASS: You mention the endorphins, the body's recently discovered, internally produced, morphine-like narcotics, and hint that they may be involved in bonding pathways and sexual pleasure. Does this, then, complement the hypothesis that pair-bonding (love), both healthy and sick, can be an addictive phenomenon?

MONEY: Can be? I think I said it *always* is. Limerence is the prototype of all addictions — getting "fixed" onto an external stimulus.

MASS: If this is so, does it mean that physical and psychological sadomasochism, the suffering or inflicting of pain, can be part of a process of addiction to pleasure?

MONEY: Yes, but the addiction is *to* something — one's partner, ritual, fetish, etc. The transvestite, for example, is addicted to the fetish of women's clothing. As with any addiction, his fetish-demand to cross dress will eventually prove overwhelming, no matter how much he may *wish* or struggle to resist.

MASS: If love is an addiction, does its termination precipitate withdrawal phenomena similar to what is experienced during withdrawal from narcotics?

MONEY: Inevitably, there's a period of agonizing bereavement. In humans, it lasts about two years, on the average.

MASS: There has been some study by New York psychiatrist Paul Sacerdote, attempting to link the release of endorphins to hypnotic phenomena — prayer, meditation, group/mob leader interactions (leaders like Hitler or Rasputin are often characterized as "hypnotic"), and group bonding. If endorphins are involved in various forms of group and auto hypnosis, does this mean that opiate-mediated sensations are the indistinguishable results of both religious and sexual "self-transcendant" experiences? If so, does this imply that sexual abstinence would facilitate the pursuit of endorphin pleasures through alternate pathways, principally religious behavior (i.e., religious "faith")? Finally, is there evidence that endorphins are released during aggression, or in the preterminal stages of death?

MONEY: These are not unreasonable hypotheses, but there's no solid evidence about endorphins on much of anything yet. It's worth knowing, however, that this is the newest frontier of knowledge in sex research.

MASS: You are a scientist. Your statements are made in the name of science, not politics. Nevertheless, how does it feel to be in the vanguard of the greatest cultural revolution since the dawn of "civilization"?

MONEY: The discovery of effective birth control planning has had as great an impact on us, I think, as anything since the harnessing of fire, because it influences our lives continuously. I identify the onset of the Birth Control Age with the Philadelphia Exposition in 1876, where the first rubber condom was displayed to the world. But the Birth Control Age didn't really take hold until the latex-rubber process put the modern condom on the market around 1927. It could have started earlier, but male gynecologists wouldn't fit women with rubber diaphragms. Instead, it required something that men could buy from vending machines in men's rooms in gas stations. Birth control is the one basic cultural factor of change that has allowed everything else that we call the sexual revolution to proceed.

Of course, there have been other factors: the control of venereal disease; the need not to overpopulate the earth; the change in life expectancy of adults from age 35 at the time of the American revolution to 75-plus today, and the unexpected lowering in the age of puberty from 17 to 13 or lower in less than one hundred fifty years; and the discovery of labor-saving devices that have given women the capacity to do everything that men had done formerly only by virtue of their brute strength—and likewise, the development of baby foods and formulae that allow men to take on all the responsibilities of childrearing that were once the exclusive province of women (except for breast feeding, which I think is terribly important; here's a basic difference between the sexes that we haven't been able to change . . . yet).

All of these factors, these developments, became part of the making of the sexual revolution. So I see what I'm doing as being merely a commentator in the midst of a process that's loose in society. I'm in what I've called a great tide of history.

Sex in the Therapeutic State

A Conversation with Thomas Szasz

Dr. Thomas Szasz, a psychoanalyst and member of the American Psychoanalytic Association, is professor of Psychiatry at the State University of New York, Upstate Medical Center, in Syracuse. In the course of writing seventeen books, countless essays, and making many public appearances, Dr. Szasz has probably done more to expose and clarify the ethical dilemmas and failures of American psychiatry than any individual in history. Prominent among those dilemmas and failures, of course, has been his profession's historical pathologization of "homosexuality."

MASS: In *Law, Liberty and Psychiatry* (1963), you wrote: "Upon those willing to heed peaceful persuasion, the values of the state will be imposed by force: in political fascism by therapists, especially psychiatrists. I think that we are rapidly heading toward the therapeutic state."

In 1984, this warning will be 21 years old. Generally speaking, how has your prediction of "the therapeutic state" come of age?

SZASZ: The accuracy of that prediction has been borne out by subsequent events. Indeed, the phrase "therapeutic state" has become part of our language. Since I wrote *Law, Liberty and Psychiatry*, I wrote several papers and books on what are, in effect, the expanding frontiers of the therapeutic state — drug controls, the medicalization of sex, the whole business of the so-called "psychiatric diversion" in the criminal justice system. For example, every crook from congressman down who gets caught in a criminal act now claims that his actions were caused by alcoholism. Then he cops a plea by accepting court-ordered counseling. It's becoming hard to tell which is the bigger fraud — the crime or the punishment.

MASS: The direction of your thought, somewhat like Jung's, has been to urge that much of what we call psychiatry, especially psychotherapy, be demedicalized and [more appropriately appreciated] as moral-religious enterprises. But hasn't the "progress" of the mental health movement actually been in the opposite direction?

SZASZ: Of course it has. The mental health movement has become like a hurricane. One may be able to predict its course or describe the havoc it wreaks. But one cannot stop it. With all the leaders of society supporting "mental health" — from the President's Commission on Mental Health to Dear Abby — what do you expect?

MASS: The new third edition of the American Psychiatric Association's *Diagnostic and Statistical Manual of Mental Disorders* (DSM-III), which was in preparation for nearly a decade, was published in May 1980. It is the manual that will be used to medically and sometimes medicolegally classify "mental illness" in 1984. Generally speaking, how will the so-called mental patient benefit or suffer from the greatly expanded terminology of DSM-III?

SZASZ: As a practical matter, I don't think the DSM-III will make that much difference. It's a symbolic act. It's another attempt by organized psychiatry to prove to the world how medical and scientific psychiatry is. Smoking and gambling are now mental diseases! I don't see how anyone can take this outpouring of psychiatric nonsense seriously. But it will expand the medical and legal frontiers of psychiatric casuistry. And it will expand the numbers of suckers who are dazzled and deceived by its rhetoric.

MASS: According to a leading figure in the preparation of DSM-III [Dr. Robert Spitzer], "exactly how DSM-III will be used in the courts is not yet known, but is not the responsibility of psychiatry." Do you agree?

SZASZ: Sure! The psychiatric Eichmanns only run the railroads. That claim is too contemptible to deserve a reasoned rebuttal. The whole history of psychiatry cries out in protest against it.

MASS: Do you think there is anyone, anywhere, who would not qualify as being afflicted with the *narcissistic, borderline* or *antisocial* "personality disorders," as defined in DSM-III, or combinations thereof?

SZASZ: I am unable to take such psychiatric and psychoanalytic diagnoses seriously, to give them "scientific" credence. But why do you worry about these recent diagnostic obscenities? They are just the latest delicts in a very long list — a list that includes such gems as Freud's diagnoses of Adler and Jung as psychotic-after they broke with him, of course. I am trying to take a Mark-Twainian attitude toward the madness-mongering of the psychiatric inquisition. The narcissistic, borderline and anti-social personality disorders are simply the latest fashions in psychiatric semantics, invented to justify a psychiatric industry imbued with an insatiable ambition. There's no clear definition of "narcissism," for example. But I can give you one. That's the mental illness that afflicts patients who love themselves too much . . . and their analysts too little.

MASS: *Law, Liberty and Psychiatry* emphasizes the need for "mental patients" to organize if they expect, as human beings, to "achieve" their fundamental legal rights. You characterize the plight of these individuals, in being afraid to stand up for those rights, as similar to that of the Jews in Nazi Germany or blacks in the pre-civil rights South. In the words with which you conclude *Law, Liberty and Psychiatry*:

> This [their passivity], more than anything else, may have made them and may continue to make them convenient scapegoats. Instead of protecting their own integrity, they have, as the psychoanalyts put it, identified with the aggressor. Perhaps the most effective method of securing the mental patient's liberty — not to become mentally well but, if need be, to remain as he is and yet enjoy the rights of an American — lies in *legal action against his oppressors*.

In the case of "the homosexual," whom you characterized as "the model psychiatric scapegoat" in *The Manufacture of Madness* (1970) and in your recent expose of psychiatric complicity in the Dan White verdict (*Inquiry*, 8/79), exactly what kinds of legal action were you referring to?

SZASZ: I was referring to suits for false imprisonment, when the diagnosis serves as a basis for commitment. To suits for malpractice, where there is coercion, where consent is inadequately informed, where "less restrictive" alternatives are inadequately explored. I also had in mind efforts to repeal laws that discriminate against mental patients or homosexuals, such as the immigration laws.

MASS: In *Sex By Prescription*, you join the growing list of critics who accuse Masters and Johnson of maintaining an anti-gay bias. Yet a problem with this criticism is that it invariably ignores their pioneering designation of "homosexual dysfunction." In this category, homosexual men and women were treated for problems of sexual functioning (like heterosexuals), but with no attempts at orientation conversion. Unlike Cornell psychiatric sex therapist Helen Singer Kaplan, who does not treat homosexual dysfunction, Masters and Johnson thus unequivocally recognize and respect homosexual preference. What seems to upset the critics is that Masters and Johnson were willing to convert some individuals who appeared to be inappropriate candidates. What the critics didn't take into account is that these individuals *volunteered* for their so-called conversions. In siding with these critics, is Thomas Szasz, the great champion of individual liberties, suggesting that Masters and Johnson should interpret for their subjects what these individuals *should* want?

SZASZ: Certainly not. Because X criticizes Masters and Johnson and because I also criticize them does not meant that I agree with X. That's a simple logical fallacy. Let me just offer two brief comments about your rather complex question. First, my contention that Masters and Johnson are anti-homosexual is amply documented in *Sex By Prescription* (Doubleday, 1980), and I would like to refer the interested readers to that documentation—which you have not questioned or challenged. Secondly, I interpret Masters and Johnson's invention of the diagnosis of "homosexual dysfunction" differently than you do. You say it signifies respect for their subjects and for homosexuals in general. I say it signifies their "illness-*uber-Alles*" philosophy. You think they want to expand homosexual rights or opportunities. I believe they want to extend the physician's rights and opportunities by creating new "diseases" and new "treatments." You speak of Masters and Johnson's pioneering designation of "homosexual dysfunction." How about their pioneering designation of "masturbatory orgasmic dysfunction?" Does that signify their special respect for the rights of masturbators?

MASS: It may seem silly to many that Masters and Johnson try to give scientific credibility to such concepts. But as you yourself have so amply documented in your many books, the history of psychiatry is all but founded on the principle that masturbation causes insanity. Perhaps the rights of masturbators, like those of homosexuals, transvestites, etc., still need to be specifically, "scientifically" [defended].

SZASZ: That is precisely the positivistic, scientific approach to ethics and politics to which I object. People do not have rights qua homosexuals or masturbators, qua Jews or Christians, qua males or females. They have rights qua persons, human beings. I believe the differences between science and ethics, between sexual behavior and political rights, should be clarified, not obscured. Masters and Johnson are guilty of engaging in a naive inversion of the logic of "scientific materialism" or National Socialism. Those vicious political creeds invoke science for taking rights away from certain individuals and groups of people. Masters and Johnson invoke science to "give" rights to certain people. I maintain that it's wrong, it's evil, to biologize morals—whether you do it to select scapegoats or to "unselect" them. If masturbators and homosexuals have been persecuted by psychiatrists, as obviously they have been, why not say *that*? Why say that they are biologically similar or the same as heterosexuals?

MASS: You stated that I had not challenged your documentation of Masters and Johnson's anti-homosexual bias. I'd like to do so now. In *Sex By Prescription*, you accuse Masters and Johnson of fraudulently claiming that no patients are accepted at their institute unless referred by a medical "authority." As you point out, they broke their own rule when they independently recruited homosexuals for their study. But they did so in the absence of alternatives, because psychiatrists had no concept of homosexual dysfunction. A homosexual who did not wish to convert was simply rejected, not referred to sex therapists!

You likewise criticize them for not engaging a "homosexual therapy team" to treat their homosexual couples. This, you allege, is inconsistent with their policy of having heterosexual therapy teams treat heterosexual couples. But at that time, there *were* no specifically designated, trained homosexual therapists! I could go on. Do you *really* think Masters and Johnson were in favor of the Briggs initiative?

SZASZ: Let me answer those questions, one at a time. In the first place, it's not true that homosexuals who did not wish to be converted were invariably rejected by psychiatrists. I know, from my own long experience as a practicing psychotherapist, that many homosexuals have been "treated" by psychotherapists and have been helped to lead better lives, as homosexuals. If Masters and Johnson had made as much noise about their homosexual study as they did about their heterosexual study, psychiatrists and psychotherapists might have sent them homosexual patients.

Your second defense of Masters and Johnson's inconsistency is even less persuasive. If there were no homosexual treatment teams to begin with, Masters and Johnson could have trained some — *before* undertaking the "work." But, so far as I can recall, they don't ever mention the need for such a team. So your claim that they felt such a need but could not accommodate it is without foundation.

Finally, you ask me what I think about Masters and Johnson's *real* feelings about the Briggs initiative. That's not cricket. A reporter asked *them* what they thought of it, and they refused to tell him. Such a refusal, I submit, says a lot. But there is other evidence as well, which I haven't mentioned in my book, that casts serious doubt on Masters and Johnson's claims to being sexual egalitarians.

MASS: What is this other evidence?

SZASZ: I have in mind a UPI news release. It was filed from Miami, was dated October 31, 1980, and was a report of a seminar on "Sexual Problems in Medicine," at which Masters and Johnson were the featured participants. Instead of telling you what struck my attention in this story, let me just quote the relevant sentence from the news release: "Women attending the seminar Wednesday night were disappointed when the seminar chairman, Dr. Ronald Schoer, announced that only men would be allowed to see a showing of hard-core movies depicting sexual encounters of various kinds." If Masters and Johnson objected to this policy, the story failed to mention it. We do know, however, that they participated in a seminar where *that* was the policy.

[Ed. note: Privately, when I asked Dr. Szasz why he maintained his membership in the ultraconservative, homophobic American Psychoanalytic Association, he asserted that he believed he could be a more effective proponent of change from within that organization than from without. It seemed to me that Masters and Johnson were doing something analagous by agreeing to participate in a conference whose sexist policy their work tacitly contradicted and exposed.]

MASS: So we're to disregard the entirety of their published work and accept, on the basis of these two newspaper-clipping anecdotes, that Masters and Johnson are really closet sexists? Come on! Earlier, you almost implied that nonconverting homosexuals were rarely rejected by psychiatrists. Yet a major observation of *Homosexuality in Perspective*, Masters and Johnson's tome, that has yet to be credited by its critics (including yourself, of course) has to do with exactly this "Prior Rejection By Health Care Professionals" of such individuals. Masters and Johnson are apparently the first researchers to *document* this prejudice with statistics.

SZASZ: You are much too concerned about the so-called scientific method, even when its use is trivial or patently absurd. You don't have to "measure" some things in order to be certain of their existence. Did one need "clinical studies" or statistics in Germany in the Thirties to prove that the Nazis didn't like the Jews? You take Masters and Johnson seriously as scientists. I don't. Masters may be a competent gynecologist. But his so-called sex research is pure deception. Measuring, or claiming to measure, the obvious, and describing what one has done in pretentious, pseudo-medical terminology is not my idea of what a serious scientist does.

MASS: Obviously, then, you are not impressed by their documentation of the comparative similarity of homosexual and heterosexual functioning?

SZASZ: That's an example of precisely what I'm talking about. It's an example I discuss in *Sex By Prescription*. But perhaps Laud Humphreys has done it better because he did it with humor. In his review of *Homosexuality in Perspective* in *Society* (October/November 1980), Humphreys writes: "The preclinical study's principal finding is that, in regard to sexual behavior and response, there are 'no significant physiological variations that can be attributed to sexual orientation alone.' That means that homosexuals don't ejaculate out of their ears or have orgasmic contractions of the sinus cavities but climax like everyone else." That's a perfect summary of Masters and Johnson's expertise concerning homosexuality.

MASS: Is it? If it's so obvious that the sexual behaviors and responses of homosexuals are identical to those of heterosexuals, why has virtually every psychoanalytic study of homosexuality (and the vast majority of psychiatric studies of homosexuality have been psychoanalytic) characterized homosexuals as dominated by distinctive patterns of fantasy, behavior and compulsion bizarrely different from those of heterosexual "normality"? Why hasn't a single psychiatric study ever taken the simple Masters-and-Johnson step of observationally comparing overt homosexual with overt heterosexual behavior and fantasy patterning? *Homosexuality in Perspective* may be primitive and flawed in its methods, naive and biased in some of its conclusions, but in comparison with any existing psychiatric study (or, frankly, all of them lumped together), it strikes me as an empirical milestone, a masterpiece of objectivity. The response of the psychiatric community to this work, it seems to me, has been unmistakable in its taste — that of sour grapes.

SZASZ: Well, let's just agree to disagree about that "masterpiece."

MASS: When recently interviewed together with Irving Bieber for the *National Enquirer* [1/22/80], psychiatric sex therapist Helen Singer Kaplan stated that gender-identity disturbances could be easily "cured" if they are "caught" early enough. Even if informed consent becomes fully established in psychiatric practice, how will it apply to children? Will parents have the right to insist on "gender-reinforcement" therapy for children who are subjectively judged to be "effeminate" or "homosexual?" What *are* the sexual rights of children?

SZASZ: That's a very difficult question to answer in an interview, because the rights of children are a very complicated affair. How can one speak of the sexual rights of children when male children don't even have protection against their penises being mutilated by circumcision? I can only offer a few general remarks apropos of your question.

My first comment is that we cannot deal intelligently with the sexual rights of children in isolation, as it were. We must also grapple with some of their other, perhaps more obvious rights — for example, their right not to go to schools where their health and physical safety are endangered. And before we can do that, we have to grapple with the rights of adults to self-determination or self-ownership — that is, their rights to consensual sexual acts, drugs, "mental illness," suicide. In other words, just as one cannot do calculus until one has mastered algebra, one cannot discuss the rights of children until one has come to grips with the rights — and duties! — of adults. It is precisely this endeavor that psychiatrists and psychoanalysts have consistently undermined.

MASS: Your chapter "Legal and Moral Aspects of Homosexuality" was by far the most liberal and, it's now clear, prophetic voice in Marmor's *Sexual Inversion* (Basic Books, 1965). This voice, in fact, sets the narrative tone of Marmor's new book, *Homosexual Behavior: A Modern Reappraisal* (Basic Books, 1980). Yet Thomas Szasz is not among its contributors. Nor are you mentioned. Were you "expurgated" from *Homosexual Behavior*, and, if so, why?

SZASZ: The term "expurgated" refers to motives, and I don't know what Marmor's were or are. I only know what people do. Actions speak louder than words. But there's another proverb that may be more to the point — that imitation is the highest form of flattery.

MASS: In *Sex By Prescription*, you state that "the unremitting hostility of psychiatrists and psychoanalysts to homosexuals is, in my opinion, now greatly underestimated, especially by homosexual organizations and their leaders." But aren't Marmor's book and the APA's de-listing of homosexuality as a mental disorder proof that there has actually been a lessening of this hostility?

SZASZ: I regard the APA's "delisting" of homosexuality from the DSM-III and books such as Marmor's revised edition on homosexuality as acts of intellectual and political opportunism. As you know, the APA still categorizes "ego-dystonic homosexuality" as a disease, but it does not so classify ego-dystonic heterosexuality. The proposition that it is the gay person's dissatisfaction with his sexual orientation that makes his so-called condition a *disease* is, to my mind, a dead giveaway. The APA has confused and conflated two different concepts—namely, having a disease and being in the patient role. I don't want to get too far afield but, obviously, one can have a disease without being a patient, and vice versa. Is having an unwanted penis, or vagina, or eyes that can see also a disease? Remember Oedipus? That way, to paraphrase Shakespeare, lies madness.

MASS: Actually, whether or not Marmor approves of the new classification, "ego-dystonic homosexuality," is not clear. I don't think it's mentioned in his new book.

SZASZ: Marmor pretends that there is something scientific in his present assertion that homosexuality is not a disease. But look at the evidence. In 1965 Marmor was not a young, naive psychiatrist. He was 55 years old. He was an influential training analyst. He then wrote, and this is a quote from his 1965 volume (*Sexual Inversion*): "My basic orientation in assembling the papers that follow has been that causality in this area—no less than in any other area of *psychopathology* (my emphasis) . . . is multifactorial." That's not all. Under the heading, "Is Homosexuality an Illness?" Marmor then wrote, "Most of the psychoanalysts in this volume (except Szasz) are of the opinion that homosexuality is definitely an illness." Actually, it wasn't "most" of the psychoanalysts—including Marmor himself—who maintained that homosexuality is a mental illness. Every one of them did—except me.

MASS: But even you, Dr. Szasz, somewhat qualified your history-making defense of homosexual preference in *Sexual Inversion*.

[Ed. note: In *Sexual Inversion* (Basic Books, 1965), Chapter 7, "Legal and Moral Aspects of Homosexuality" by Thomas Szasz, opens as follows:

Ever since the Freudian revolution, and especially since the Second World War, it has become intellectually fashionable to hold that homosexuality is neither a sin nor a crime but a disease. This claim means either that homosexuality is a condition somewhat similar to ordinary genetic maladies, perhaps caused by some genetic error or endocrine imbalance, or that it is an expression of psychosexual immaturity, probably caused by certain kinds of personal and social circumstance in early life.

I believe that it is very likely that homosexuality is, indeed, a disease in the second sense and perhaps sometimes even in the stricter sense. Nevertheless, if we believe that, by categorizing homosexuality as a disease, we have succeeded in removing it from the realm of moral judgment, we are in error.]

What were your impressions of the new *Homosexual Behavior*?

SZASZ: My overriding impression is that Marmor has "converted" — from homophobia to anti-homophobia. I would say that Marmor is dishonest and hypocritical. He pretends that his present views are based on scientific evidence about homosexuality, just as he pretended his previous views were. In his preface to *Homosexual Behavior*, Marmor explains that since 1965, when the previous volume was published, "there have been considerable advances in our understanding of the phenomenon of homosexual experience . . . so that the previous volume . . . must now be considered to be in large part outdated."

MASS: And you object because you believe there hasn't been any such accumulation of important new research?

SZASZ: Right. But that's only part of it. Marmor's claim really packs two lies into one. First, it is simply not true that we now know significantly more about homosexuality — "biologically, sociologically, and clinically" — than we did in 1965. Marmor loves that word "clinically"! But how can you know *clinically* about X unless X is a disease? Can you know *clinically* about Jews or anti-Semites? About liberals or conservatives? So my first point is that it's an intellectual con-job for Marmor to claim that he gave up his previous homophobic attitude under the influence of new scientific knowledge.

My second point has to do with Marmor's admission that diagnosing homosexuals as sick is a manifestation of *prejudice*. That's crucial, because prejudice is not a matter of facts or logic. So, typically, it is not something that can be dispelled by enlightening the prejudiced person with "scientific evidence." Let's take a crass example again. In 1940, there was widespread prejudice against Jews in Germany. In 1980, there isn't. Is this because new scientific evidence has been submitted to the Germans about "religious inversion" which made them revise their ideas about the nature of "Jewish behavior"?

MASS: So you would consider the term "homophobia" to be just as unscientific and morally inflated as the prejudice it is attempting to redress?

SZASZ: That's right. In his introduction, Marmor has a whole section entitled "Homophobia and Its Derivations." Homophobia, he says, "represents a pathological fear of homosexuality." He attributes his newly discovered "phobia," among other things, to "a strong religious indoctrination." Is this science? Or is it pitting one prejudice against another? Why does Marmor use a Greco-Latin term implying a disease to "diagnose" the anti-homosexuals? Why not simply say that they are bad people? That they are evil, ugly?

MASS: You seem to believe that Marmor's objection to classifying homosexuality as a disease does not necessarily mean that he is sympathetic to the gay rights cause. On what do you base this interpretation?

SZASZ: One interpretation might be that Marmor objects to classifying homosexuality as a mental disease because he no longer believes it is. That would mean that Marmor now sincerely believes that people who smoke or gamble or are sexually "masochistic" or "sadistic" are mentally ill, but homosexuals are not. I don't find that persuasive. Another interpretation is that Marmor wants to protect homosexuals from the psychiatric persecution entailed in being diagnosed mentally ill. But he hasn't shown the least interest in protecting other, psychiatrically stigmatized groups from persecution. In fact, throughout his professional life Marmor has been in the forefront of the psychiatric persecutors — apologizing for and defending involuntary psychiatric interventions of all kinds. Did Marmor protest Ezra Pound's psychiatric imprisonment? Marilyn Monroe's? Ernest Hemingway's? The psychiatrists who locked up these "psychotics" were Marmor's buddies. How do you think Marmor became president of the American Psychiatric Association?

There's a more plausible interpretation. Marmor knows that the traditional anti-homosexual posture of organized psychiatry is now making psychiatry look bad. So he is urging psychiatry to take a "progressive" position on homosexuality to save psychiatry from itself—from looking ridiculous, from being even more discredited as a science, as a therapy, as a branch of medicine, than it already is. Marmor is like a good investor or portfolio manager: he is telling his client, psychiatry, to cut its losses, to divest itself of homosexuality as a disease. Obviously, today, there is no economic future in homosexuality—as a psychiatric disorder. There are other, more promising investments—like "masturbatory orgasmic inadequacy," and the dread "diseases of desire." The psychiatric "sex researchers" are making new mental diseases faster than the APA can absorb them—and you don't hear Marmor complaining that all these sexual behaviors are not diseases.

MASS: You seem to be suggesting that Marmor is less interested in the freedom and dignity of gays than in the power and prestige of the psychiatrists. Must these loyalties be mutually exclusive?

SZASZ: That's precisely what I'm suggesting. And I ask you and your readers to judge for yourself whether this interpretation isn't the one that is most consistent with the facts. I claim that Marmor loves psychiatry more than he loves the civil rights of gays. He was, and still is, a labeler and defamer—only the objects of his psychiatric scorn have changed: from homosexuals to anti-homosexuals. I don't see anything admirable in this. The Anita Bryant type anti-gays are at least sincere. They are bigoted and they don't pretend to be scientific and liberal. But Marmor pretends to be "unprejudiced"—which is absurd. Doesn't he hate Nazis? Does that make him into a "Naziphobe?" Actually, Marmor is so steeped in the style of psychiatrically disparaging anyone who isn't like him or who doesn't share his values that his writing is often patronizing and downputting toward homosexuals. What he says still often implies a disease-concept of homosexuality.

MASS: Can you give a specific example of this?

SZASZ: Okay. Here is an example from your interview with him in *The Advocate* (4/17/80). Marmor says: "There's no necessary etiological or causal tie between narcissism and homosexuality." Saying that there is "no necessary etiological tie" between A and B implies that there *may* be such a tie. It is like saying that there is no necessary or etiological tie between smoking and lung cancer. Some, but not all, smokers get lung cancer and some non-smokers get it too. Thus, Marmor's statement about the connection between narcissism and homosexuality makes homosexuals, implicitly, into patients. The statement I cited is not isolated. It's the way Marmor speaks. It's the way most psychiatrists speak. And they are proud of it. In your interview with him, Marmor exudes this paternalistic-psychiatric attitude. For example, he says that "female homosexuality may be a different kind of *condition* [*sic*] from male homosexuality." You see, Marmor hasn't changed all that much. He used to maintain that homosexuality was a *disease*. Now he regards it as a *condition*. But it's not a condition either. In another twenty years, if he lives that long, Marmor will no doubt claim that that is his opinion too — and he'll produce "scientific" evidence to back it up. And there is something else — namely, that Marmor's seeming defense of the rights of homosexuals is contradicted by his whole career as a psychoanalyst.

MASS: What do you mean?

SZASZ: Do you know of any analyst accredited by the American Psychoanalytic Association who is an avowed homosexual? Is there a gay caucus of the American Psychoanalytic Association? In the late Forties and early Fifties, when I was in psychoanalytic training and on the staff of the Chicago Institute for Psychoanalysis, the exclusion of homosexuals was firm policy. As far as I know, it still is. You have asked Marmor some probing questions, but they weren't probing enough. You should have asked him why he hasn't protested these exclusionary policies of the most prestigious psychoanalytic training institutes.

MASS: I've heard Marmor protest these policies, however indirectly. He often quotes Freud's assertion that homosexuals could be fully competent analysts.

SZASZ: Come on! You have *heard* him protest such policies. Has he protested them in writing?

MASS: I believe he does so in the new book.

SZASZ: The quote from Freud you mention is news to me. I don't believe he ever said such a thing in print — or in person, for that matter. The evidence is overwhelming that Freud was anti-homosexual, and homosexuals — and their born-again psychiatric defenders — are kidding themselves by quoting a scrap here and there from Freud to support their position. Let's get Freud straight, if I may use a pun, once and for all. He considered homosexuals to be *perverts* — and, indeed, not just homosexuals! In 1916–17, in his classic *Introductory Lectures on Psycho-Analysis*, Freud wrote: "On the other hand, the abandonment of the reproductive function is the common feature of all perversions. We actually describe a sexual activity as perverse if it has given up the aim of reproduction and pursues the attainment of pleasure as an aim independent of it." I think we should not forget this opinion of Freud's, and should not forgive him for it. And I think we should hold it against all the psychoanalysts who have failed to repudiate it.

MASS: You are one of the rare critics to overtly discuss what you call the "Jewishness" of the psychoanalytic movement. In your previous work, *The Myth of Psychotherapy* (Doubleday, 1978), you characterize Freud, whose grandfather and great-grandfather were both orthodox rabbis, as "The Jewish Avenger." In your perspective, Freud's psychoanalytic movement has been and remains political. Could you be more specific?

SZASZ: I hardly know where to begin, it's so obvious to me. The psychoanalytic movement — note the word "movement" — is, in its recruitment policies, in its lobbying activities, in the regulation of its members, and so forth, just like any other special interest group, such as a labor union, or a monopolistic business, or a religion. Here is a specific example: The American Psychoanalytic Association is now engaged in lobbying to secure official governmental acceptance for psychoanalysis as a medical treatment, so that it will be covered by National Health Insurance, should such a scheme be enacted into law. What was good about psychoanalysis is that it was a way of "curing souls." Now that that's been totally repudiated, what's left is too stupid and sordid to deserve much attention, much less any respect.

MASS: In *Sex By Prescription*, you discuss the primitive, tribal origins of circumcision, a procedure that has subsequently been promoted by medicine as a "natural" precaution for optimum health and hygiene. You conclude that circumcision not only "lacks any medical justification," but is hazardous. Several hundred needless infant deaths result annually from bleeding, infections, and other complications of the procedure. But you don't specifically mention the allegedly higher incidence of cancer of the penis in uncircumcised men and of cancer of the cervix and of herpes infections in women whose male partner(s) have been uncircumcised. Are these also rationalizations?

SZASZ: I do not know how reliable those statistics are. But even if we assume that such a correlation exists, it would hardly justify the routine circumcision of male infants. It would only prove that poor genital hygiene in males may be hazardous for the females with whom they have sexual intercourse. After all, although circumcision may be magical from a religious point of view, there is nothing medically magical about it. There are ways of keeping the penis clean without cutting off the foreskin.

MASS: Should a parent have the right to have his or her child circumcised?

SZASZ: I don't believe so. But I am not an Orthodox Jew or Mohammedan. Prohibiting the practice would obviously be interpreted as a violation of the First Amendment's guarantee of separation of church and state. This is another example of the sort of basic problem that we would have to confront if we really wanted to develop a "modern" sexual ethic based not on religious tradition but on respect for the integrity of the body and for the intelligence of the individual.

MASS: In *Sex By Prescription*, you criticize the "transsexors," as you call them, for offering sex-change surgery as a "life-saving" procedure for individuals who threaten to commit suicide. You point out that by resorting to such reasoning, virtually anything displeasing to a person could be defined as a disease and its "medical" alteration as treatment. At the same time, however, you seem to be most supportive of the individual's right to make his or her own decisions. You seem to be saying, on the one hand, that transsexual surgery shouldn't even be offered. On the other, you would support a self-identified transsexual's right to pursue surgical transformation. Is that correct?

SZASZ: That's correct. It is consistent with the ethic of respect for persons. I explain to the reader that, on the one hand, I don't like the idea of "transsexing" persons and that I, personally, would neither want to perform such an operation nor submit myself to it.

At the same time, I make it clear that anyone who wants to provide such an operation, or to receive one, should not be prohibited by law from doing so. This principle has many applications. For example, I wouldn't want to give or get electric shock treatment or LSD — but if other people do, let them give it or get it, *provided they have been properly informed* about the nature and the consequences of the act in question.

MASS: Dr. John Money is criticized in *Sex By Prescription* as a leading "transsexor." As co-editor of a new book, *Traumatic Abuse of the Child at Home* [The Johns Hopkins University Press, 1980], he is apparently the first sexpert to imply that we should henceforth conceptualize the overt prevention, deprivation and punishment of normal childhood erotic play as acts of child abuse and neglect. What do you think of Money's position?

SZASZ: What I think about Money's position is this. First of all, I don't like it and I don't agree with it. Second, he has a right to his ideas, just as I have to mine. Third, I think he is dishonest when he presents moral values and social policies as if they were scientific facts or were derived, or derivable, from such facts. Finally, I think that Money, like many other sexologists, is a sexual totalitarian who has actually convinced himself that he is a "sexual liberator" — in the classic Robespierrian style. He wants to take away the power to impose sexual values on others from those who now have it and wants to give it to himself and other "sex experts" who agree with him. If Money believed in sexual freedom, he would advocate getting the state out of the business of sex education, sex therapy, sex research and sex legislation. As you know, that's the last thing he wants. Money's position epitomizes the position of most contemporary American sexologists: they all want to replace the religious sex educators, the Anita Bryants. That's why they are so eager to get sex education into the public schools — to gain control over it as "science."

MASS: In *Sex By Prescription*, you express concern that sex education has assumed forms that are as subtly coercive in their insistence on what is "normal" or "moral" or "healthy" as the sexual ignorance they purport to transcend. In your view, adherents to true sexual freedom should oppose what currently passes for scientific objectivity in sex education. Instead, what they should support "is an economic, legal and political order that allows the individual a maximum amount of freedom to learn about and engage in sexual activities.'' You believe, then, that there can be no absolute definitions of sexual health?

SZASZ: Yes: there can be no absolute definitions of sexual health. But let me add, without going into details, that I believe qualifying "sex" with the adjective "healthy" is misleading. Why I think so is explained in [my book] *The Myth of Mental Illness* and some of my other writings. I maintain that there cannot be any such thing as "sexual health" or "sexual illness." Human beings have sexual desires and engage in sexual behavior. In what sense behavior may be said to be normal or abnormal, healthy or sick — these are matters about which I have said enough. "Sexual health," in my opinion, is part of the mirage of "mental health." So we are back to square one, to mental health — and the mental health movement. Anyone who believes that the advocates of "mental health" value and support individual liberty and responsibility — and advocate sexual liberty and responsibility — well, such a person, as Sam Goldwyn put it, "should have his head examined."

A Nation of Sexual Stutterers

A Conversation with Mary Calderone

As the daughter of pioneering photographic artist Edward Stei-
chen, Mary Calderone first knew fame as a child. Today, at 76, she
looks forward more boldly than ever from the perspective of her
internationally respected life's work as a pioneering champion of
responsible sexuality, and as a great-grandmother, secure in her
Quaker faith of the goodness and purpose of life.

Mary Calderone, M.D., M.P.H., is a co-founder, former Executive Director and current President of the Sex Information and Education Council of the United States (SIECUS). Her honors, appoint-
ments, memberships and publications are too numerous to list, but
include the medical directorship of Planned Parenthood, nine honorary doctorates and, most recently, *The Family Book About Sexuality* (Harper and Row, 1981), which she co-authored with sex edu-
cator Eric W. Johnson.

MASS: *The Family Book About Sexuality* seems to be written for
traditional family people. Yet it contains some very sex revolutionary concepts. The book's drawings, for example, are almost senti-
mentally sweet, but include such subjects as naked small boys and
girls cavorting together around a pool. Another shows a happy,
loving lesbian family. This is the kind of material that would still be
burned in some parts of the country. Thus far, has there been any
such response to your book?
CALDERONE: No, on the contrary, response and sales have been
excellent. I don't regard nudity among children as revolutionary,
and I didn't back in the Twenties when I raised my own first two
kids, or in the Forties when I had the last two. But I suppose others
do. It pains me to see little girls on the beach with bikini tops. Over
what? Over exactly the same anatomy that the little boy has. In any

case, the book was specifically designated to be as low-key and non-threatening as possible, hence the lovely drawings which everyone mentions liking. Except for Dr. [Thomas] Szasz, there have been no negative responses, specifically to the book, that I'm aware of. But it will probably be attacked by the people who have been attacking me all along. I'm in at least one of Jerry Falwell's letters. I'm also targeted in a fascistic 1977 book, *The SIECUS Circle*. Here, we're characterized as an octopus at the center of a web with tentacles extending to the American Medical Association and the National Association for Mental Health, among other organizations. The guilt-by-association chain is just unbelievable. For instance, I "must be a communist" because my daughter took a couple of night courses at the New School for Social Research! And look what it says on the cover here: "Sex, Drugs, Education, Evolution, Abortion, Euthanasia." By implication, we're not only *for* all those awful things, we're *causing* them. This book is not only dishonest, it's unchristian. In bearing false witness, it breaks the Ninth Commandment. And it does so deliberately.

MASS: In his recent critique of *The Family Book About Sexuality* (*Inquiry*, May 1981), Dr. Szasz observed that you've become a lot more liberal in recent years. He cites an article you wrote for the *Humanist* in 1973 in which you characterized rape together with "a childhood homosexual experience" as the kind of trauma that people can often "survive" very well. Similarly, Ian Young points out in his *Advocate* review (June 11, 1981) of Szasz's *Sex By Prescription* that "she did after all regard it as the obligation of every parent to read one of the most viciously anti-homosexual books ever, Peter and Barbara Wyden's *Growing Up Straight*."

CALDERONE: Oh, that awful book . . . Why don't they take the trouble to see what I'm saying *now*, eight years later?

MASS: Are there other skeletons in your closet?

CALDERONE: I have none anywhere. The truth is that when I made these statements the literature on homosexuality was scarce and printed opinion was still extremely conservative and distorted. Many of the important developments in the understanding of homosexuality had not yet taken place. On the other hand, when I began in this field in 1964, I certainly had to be a victim of some of the prejudices of my time and place. The interesting thing is that such prejudice is so pervasive that it tends to operate unconsciously. I had never actually thought of myself as homophobic. Well, I had a lot to learn. It wasn't until I became involved with SIECUS that I was able to update my understanding of sexual variance. In fact, I wrote to the *Journal of the American Medical Association* urging substitution of *variant* for *deviant*, because the latter was pejorative. A major influence in the evolution of my thinking was my first gay film. Here, a real-life couple was shown making *love*. From that time on, I had no more doubts that homosexuals are doing and feeling exactly the same things that heterosexuals — and I myself — enjoy.

To arrive at my present thinking and statements about homosexuality, I had to do a lot of growing, and that's exciting. Even at my great age of 76, I am continually learning, changing and my life is immeasurably enriched by the privilege of growth. As you know, my present position on homosexuality is not just supportive, it's outspokenly realistic. The reason is that I deeply believe it's the heterosexuals, those who are in power, who should be standing up for gay rights. Unfortunately, gay people are having to fight their battles practically alone, in much the same way that blacks, women, and too many other minorities in America have had to struggle for their fundamental human freedoms. Ha! In coming out so strongly for the rights of gay people, I suppose I run the "risk" of being labeled homosexual myself. I'm probably a Kinsey 0, but why not? I've been called *much* worse, even in the eyes of homophobes.

MASS: What else have you been called?

CALDERONE: "Moral degenerate," "pervert," "raper and seducer of children in the classroom," and (my favorite) "aging libertine."

MASS: At the broadest level, Szasz criticizes you for claiming to provide morally neutral descriptions of sexual behaviors. "Calderone and Johnson seem to be utterly oblivious to the fact that preferring a nonjudgmental term to a judgmental one is itself a judgment." Does he not have a point?

CALDERONE: It's ridiculous — you're damned if you do and damned if you don't. I think Szasz is so busy disliking *anything* anyone else does that he hasn't had time to open his mind in a fresh way to the emerging issues — the *facts* of sexual medicine. He won't grant what I insist we must begin with — the value-independent and central importance of the existence of sexuality of every baby and young child. It seems to me that Dr. Szasz, far from bringing clarity to this area, is actually just avoiding it. My prescription would be a good, basic, window-opening course of education for sexuality.

MASS: Implicit in Szasz's critique, I think, is a Cassandra-like concern that people like Mary Calderone, today's "friends" of sexual tolerance, health and happiness, are analogous to the people who seemed to be our friends in the psychiatric establishment.

CALDERONE: I'm not analogous to anyone but me.

MASS: It all looked and sounded good in those days but ended up moving in some extremely repressive directions. I think that Szasz might say that if Mary Calderone really believed what she preaches, she'd be lobbying to change the laws.

CALDERONE: Why should I use my energies for things I'm not qualified to do? I'm not a lawyer or a politician or a theologian. Nor am I a lobbyist. I'm a teacher, a conceptualizer, an opener of windows that enable people to see a fresh landscape. I'm devoting all my energies to work for change at a more fundamental and, I believe, more important level. What good are laws if society still thinks and acts in the old ways? How helpful, for example, have civil rights *laws* been in changing things? Minds and hearts have to change first; laws follow after. That's what I'm about.

MASS: There was some altercation between you and Dr. Szasz over *Sex By Prescription*.

CALDERONE: No there wasn't. We've never met or corresponded.

MASS: Then what did happen?

CALDERONE: Dr. Szasz's references to my writings in his book were second and third citations of very old publications. But what I objected to most was the demeaning and utterly untrue categorization of myself on the front fly leaf of the book's dust jacket. (Masters and Johnson were also.) It was not in the book. When this was brought to their attention, the publishers [Doubleday] were sufficiently appalled that they rejacketed all the books and issued a full public apology distributed to press, reviewers and the like.

MASS: "Is the School House The Proper Place To Teach Raw Sex?" This is the title of a [1968, seventh printing 1974] Christian

Crusade publication that actually opens like this: "Dr. Mary Calderone has a burning mission: to alert and convert the youth of America to a new sexuality. . . . Dr. Calderone's concern — after tossing God aside — is to teach American youth a new sexual morality independent of church and state." At the bottom of this concern, its seems to me, is a recurrent theme: that you are promoting the sex and sexual problems you are attempting to demystify.

CALDERONE: Do umbrellas promote rain? Actually, SIECUS has never published sex education materials per se. And, though we support the concept, we have never directly promoted sex education in the schools. From the beginning, for more than fifteen years, we have said that if a community wants to provide sex education, it should involve *itself* in devising the methods for doing so. What we now promote is education *for* sexuality to be conducted by parents at home.

MASS: What, then, is the primary objective of SIECUS?

CALDERONE: SIECUS was founded to help establish sexuality, like nutrition, as an aspect of the total health of every individual. I think this objective has now been achieved, at least in the eyes of peer health professionals. A recent example of this recognition was the 1980 Edward Browning award for Prevention of Disease, which I received as President of SIECUS from the American Public Health Association. With our preventive medicine approach, what we're really trying to prevent is the *dis*-ease regarding sex that the entire country exhibits. What I'm saying is that the vast majority of Americans are uneasy about sex. The proportion of people who are, at any age, warm, controlled, happy and comfortable in and with their sexuality is pitifully small.

[Ed. note: The following statements are excerpted from "The SIECUS/NYU Principles Basic to Education for Sexuality":

- The expression of sexual orientation is a fundamental human right.
- The majority of individuals have some elements of both homosexuality and heterosexuality in their makeup which may or may not be identified or expressed by the individual throughout his or her life.

- Social structures or attitudes which lead to repression of sexuality in general, and homosexuality and bisexuality specifically, may cause individual and interpersonal difficulties.
- The sexual orientation of any person, whether child, adolescent, or adult, cannot be changed solely by exposure to other orientations. Occasional experiences are not necessarily indicative of a person's sexual orientation.
- It is the right of every individual to live in an environment of freely available information, knowledge and wisdom about sexuality, so as to be enabled to realize his or her human potential.]

MASS: In its discussion of masturbation, your book asserts that "one of the main sources of failure to achieve sexual satisfaction in adult life is interference by parents early on with the child's discovery of its own body as a source of pleasure." How pervasive is this interference among the world's cultures?

CALDERONE: Not being a world anthropologist, I couldn't say. I'm quoting sex therapists in *this* country. But we are a particularly sexophobic nation. Much of this can be traced to our Puritan ancestry. We fear sex so terribly that we literally cripple if not destroy the natural, emerging sexuality of our children. Most people can't cope with the fact that *children are born sexual*. As John Money points out, little boys have as many as three erections every twenty-four hours. Likewise, little girls experience vaginal lubrication from infancy on.

MASS: Like John Money, you have used the analogy of language to conceptualize the learning of sexuality.

CALDERONE: Yes. I borrowed his analogy. It is especially appropriate because the most intensive period during which the child learns spoken language coincides with the most intensive phase of sexual learning—between the ages of one-and-a-half or two to five years. By the time the child is five, it has done the most intensive sexual learning of its entire life. By age five, in other words, the child's developing sexuality has either been nurtured or crippled, often prematurely. The analogy to language becomes dramatic if you imagine what the speech patterns of children would be like if they were slapped every time they mispronounced words, or every time it was feared that they might be learning "dirty" words. If we treated the learning of language by our children the way we treat their learning of sexuality, we would have a nation of stammerers and stutterers. By this analogy, then, we are a nation of *sexual* stammerers and stutterers.

MASS: But how, exactly, do you teach a toddler about sex?

CALDERONE: We don't have to teach it. It's there, inborn. We simply must recognize, accept and socialize it. There are three things parents need to do in order to validate their child's natural sexuality. First, they need to give proper names to all the genitalia. With the little girl, this means taking a mirror and a flashlight and showing her the clitoris, the urethra, the vaginal opening, and the anus. The little boy must have explained to him that, unlike the little girl, he has a single organ for pleasure, urination, and reproduction.

The second priority is to accept, to nurture the pleasure principle as valid in and of itself. "Sex is for pleasure and it is good. I'm glad you found that out." The socialization of sex play can be accomplished by teaching for privacy and appropriateness of place and person, the same way one teaches children to socialize their eating pleasure. Sex should be socialized without destroying or crippling it. Finally, the relationship between present sex and future *elective* reproduction should be reinforced. Johnny has a penis for pleasure, for urination and because someday, *if he wants to*, it will help him become a Daddy.

[Ed. note: Like the thinking of many sex researchers and most of my lesbian and gay friends, my understanding of sexual preference or orientation as something that is learned versus something that is "constitutional" shifted back and forth during this period (as it has ever since), especially with the publication of the second Kinsey Institute study of homosexuality in 1981. The first, which was published in 1978, was called *Homosexualities* and wasn't as involved in questions of etiology, except by implication, as in dismantling stereotypes of abnormality. In the new book, *Sexual Preference*, however, authors Bell, Weinberg and Hammersmith concluded that "homosexuality is as deeply ingrained as heterosexuality;" that sexual preference may well arise — "like left-handedness and aller-gies" — from "a biological precursor." As I concluded in my re-view of *Sexual Preference* for the *Native* (10/5/81), "It's true that the literature of sex research, including the studies of Masters and Johnson, John Money and the Kinsey authors, has raised more questions than it has answered." Translation: As Helen Singer Kaplan unwittingly observed in an interview for *Omni* (8/81), "Whenever you find a number of different explanations coming from the medical profession, then you know we don't know what we're talking about."]

MASS: But if children are merely told about sex, if they aren't al-lowed to actually see healthy, loving, explicit sex in the home, in the community, or in the media, how are they ever going to appro-priately *learn* it? Wouldn't their so-called sex rehearsal play be best guided by direct images?

CALDERONE: I don't agree with that at all, and certainly not in this century, in our culture. At the level of the family, which is where such change would have to begin, we really don't know how high a degree of relaxed openness is necessary for positive learning. Any child from such a family would certainly run the risk of severe censure and traumatization if it attempted to live those values in a sexophobic community. No, in our culture, with its pluralism, there must be a delicate balance of the forces that nurture our children with those that protect them. That's why we must maintain the strong emphasis on socialization, on privacy, on not moving too fast. Acceptance must be the first phase.

MASS: In your recent address at the American Psychiatric Associa-tion convention in New Orleans, you observed that the pediatricians and family practitioners, the physicians who should be most con-cerned with developmental sexuality, are actually "scared to death" of these issues. Why should this be so and what can we do about it?

CALDERONE: First, most physicians are afraid of sexuality be-cause, like most of us, they know so little about it and are them-selves "sexual stammerers and stutterers," just as often as are non-physicians. The medical course work in human sexuality, which was never much more than elective, has now been dropped by most medical institutions. So interns and residents receive no training—indeed, they resist it. Still, the obstetricians, gynecologists, and psychiatrists have managed to remain involved in many aspects of sexual medicine in a way that glaringly contrasts with the nonparticipation of pediatricians and family practitioners. The pediatricians, for example, aren't even doing routine (periodic) genital exams. The lecture I gave in New Orleans would reach its most important audience in the pediatricians. But so far, the American Academy of Pediatrics has kept its distance.

MASS: Did you have any reservations about crossing the ERA boycott of the APA convention in ERA-nonratified Louisiana?

CALDERONE: Being an ERA supporter, I thought about it very carefully. But I had to make a choice. I might not get another invitation to speak at the APA. What I had to say was, I felt, sufficiently fundamental to women's liberation that it justified my action.

MASS: I understand that you did not specifically discuss homosexuality in the APA address.

CALDERONE: That's because the speech was only thirty minutes long and very general. I didn't discuss sexual variance at all. I spoke broadly about what I see as the core issue: the sexuality of young children. Being in the fields of public health and preventive medicine, I've come to realize that we must get at the roots of sexual health if we wish to lead, as Margaret Mead would say, a whole generation of parents in new directions.

MASS: In your book's chapter, "Understanding Ourselves as Sexual Persons," you discuss the Pilaga Indians of Argentina. You point out that their remarkable openness about sexuality, coupled with their tolerance of sex play among children, appears to correspond with an equally remarkable absence of sexual problems among adults. Is homosexual play included within this tolerance?

CALDERONE: At a given age, six or seven, the boys in this tribe go to the all-male big hut to live, and they have exclusively homosexual relationships until they are eighteen or whatever the marriage age is, when *every* male marries. They no longer have homosexual relationships unless they are separated from their wives for extended periods, out in the jungle hunting, for example. This information is detailed in John Money's book, *Man & Woman, Boy & Girl*.

MASS: I suppose such patterns argue that at least some homosexuality may be situational or adaptive.

CALDERONE: Yes. If this example were truly representative, it would argue that much of what we've called permanent or fixed homosexuality doesn't really exist. That raises difficult questions for gay people. If an intelligent, well-poised group of male and female homosexuals were truly together and could play with this idea, if they were hypothetically allowed to decide what sexual orientation their children "should" have, I wonder what they'd say. If there were a button that could decide the sexual orientation of your child, which one would you press?

MASS: More important than the "orientation," I think, is the "sexual." I would want my child to be fully, lovingly, comfortably sexual.

CALDERONE: I'd like that for every child.

MASS: If I *had* to press a button designating what we rigidly call sexual orientation, I would press "bisexual." If bisexuality weren't among the options, I wouldn't press.

CALDERONE: That's fair, I think. You're saying you'd choose bisexuality over exclusive heterosexuality. But you're also saying you'd choose bisexuality over exclusive homosexuality.

MASS: I think that's fair.

[Ed. Note: Clearly, what is missing from this shameful exchange is the kind of political perspective Harvey Fierstein provided when asked the same question on a late-night talk show eight years later. His response: "Would you ask Jesse Jackson 'if you could press a button that could make you black or white' . . . Do you have any idea how offensive it is to be asked such a question?"]

The information about homosexuality among the Pilaga Indians also touches the subject of intergenerational sex. In our culture, can you conceptualize any circumstances in which sex play between a pubescent or even pre-pubescent youngster and an adult might be viewed as constructive rather than destructive?

CALDERONE: No, I can't. I'm not sure it wouldn't be damaging in most cultures, but certainly in ours. As a culture, we are nowhere near the level of sexual maturity, honesty and health that we can even begin to study sex itself with equanimity. In any case, much of the child molestation and pedophilia that we see is actually directed at three-and four-year-olds, and *these* would be considered pathological in any culture, for there simply is no possibility of "choice" by a frightened child. The main thing to emphasize now is how little we know about child/adult sexuality. The studies on these subjects are few and inconclusive. Did you know that 31 percent of traumatically (including sexually) abused children were prematurely delivered, as compared to 7 percent prematures in the general population? This is an example of the kind of new, complex and obscure data we'll have to assimilate if we're to reach a broader understanding of the whole issue.

MASS: What would prematurity have to do with childhood erotosexual development?

CALDERONE: One could guess that the bonding process between mother and father and infant, the basis for all later bonding, is disturbed by the otherwise life-sustaining procedures of incubation, necessitating separation of infants and parents. How delicate it all is. Did you know prematures bedded on soft sheepskins gain better weight than when they're on sheets? We are only at the beginning of our understanding of these phenomena. But as the data accumulate, we are more certain than ever that the earliest establishment of the infant-mother bond has a tremendous influence on adult patterns of sexual and interpersonal intimacy.

MASS: Does your perspective of childhood sexuality imply any dissatisfaction with the present age-of-consent laws?

CALDERONE: This touches complex legal questions I'm not really competent to discuss. Formerly, the legal marriage age was around 17. This roughly coincided with the age of puberty. Today, the great majority of young Americans are undergoing puberty three, four or five years earlier. So some changes may eventually have to be thought about.

MASS: Although you do not specifically characterize it as such, circumcision is viewed by some (including Thomas Szasz), as a prime example of the arbitrary, perhaps destructive interference by culture with natural erotosexual development. Is there any real defense for routine circumcision?

CALDERONE: I don't know much about this, except that the reason usually given is "cleanliness." But the child can easily be taught genital hygiene. Even when there's phimosis (constriction of the foreskin), there are less drastic alternatives to circumcision. The prepuce could simply be stretched or incised, not removed.

MASS: Shouldn't the affected individual have any say-so about whether or not to undergo such a procedure?

CALDERONE: I would think so. The truth is that one must be rather religiously oriented to want circumcision. What do you think?

MASS: As a Jew, I was circumcised during infancy. As an adult, I've come to resent this arbitrary, theological violation of my bodily integrity. With all due respect to the rights of parents and for religious freedom, I personally feel that the elective circumcision of infants, as it is currently practiced — without anesthesia, without the patient's informed consent, without the slightest medical or hygienic justification — belongs, like clitoridectomy, in the archives of natural history.

CALDERONE: As you know and as my co-author Eric Johnson and I point out in our book, there's no solid evidence to suggest any difference in penile sensitivity or sexual functioning between circumcised and uncircumcised males. But why not have things as natural as possible?

GAY FANTASIES, MALE REALITIES AND BONDING

The Church and Homosexuality

A Conversation with John McNeill

[Ed. note: To some extent the conversations with Money, Szasz and Calderone have a kind of subtext that is also discernible between the lines of the interviews which follow with John McNeill and George Stambolian. As a gay Jew, I was deeply upset by the homophobic statements and behaviors of what I perceived to be a distressingly large number of psychiatrists and intellectuals whom I knew to be Jewish. As members of an historically oppressed minority — a minority, like the gay and lesbian community, that has experienced the denial of its civil rights and much worse, how could they not be more sympathetic? Sometimes this incredulity was transformed into a much too generalized anger at the nonexistent monolithic group whose representatives I identified as people like *Commentary* editor Norman Podhoretz, writers Midge Decter, Joseph Epstein and Norman Mailer, *New York Times* editor Abe Rosenthal, psychiatrists Irving Bieber and Helen Singer Kaplan, and the state of Israel, which maintained laws against homosexuality and whose officials had even refused to allow a group of gay Jews to plant Holocaust memorial trees. (In 1988, the laws against homosexuality in Israel were abolished.) Like Gore Vidal, I went after "the Pod people," as Vidal referred to Podhoretz, Decter and their ilk, by hammering away at what were perceived to be areas of collective vulnerability. The vulnerability Vidal chose was that of American Jewish loyalty to the state of Israel. My choice, circumcision, was more subtle and less vulnerable to charges of anti-Semitism. In both cases, however, there *was* prejudice in the motivation, however preconscious, to retaliate against one group for insults perceived from individuals of that group against another. I do not regret one word of these contributions to the debate on circumcision, but I do now feel freer to reflect on the intensity of my involvement in them.

In the interview with Father McNeill, with whom I had been in psychotherapy during the preceding year (at a time when I was having a love affair with a Polish Catholic gay man whose Catholic identity was a lot stronger than his gay identity), I continued to probe the phenomenon of group bonding that seemed to be the central puzzle of my own life as well as that of the gay liberation movement and the sexual revolution. With what groups do I/we claim identity? Does one preclude the other? If there are multiple identities, which are more important and why and how? This preoccupation with issues of group identity and bonding—and eventually, "patriotism"—are at least subtextually apparent in all of the interviews in this collection, but the concerns and questions they engender become more explicit and complex over time, as in my interviews with Richard Plant and Paul Schrader (included in *Homosexuality as Behavior and Identity: Dialogues of the Sexual Revolution—Volume II*). Meanwhile, I can now see that I was exploring and subconsciously seeking acceptance from Christianity in much the same way I was still exploring and subconsciously seeking acceptance from heterosexuality.]

Like Hans Kung and Edward Schillebeeckx, two Catholic theologians who have been rebuked by Rome for their outspoken liberalism, Father John McNeill is among the most controversial figures in contemporary theological scholarship. When his book, *The Church and the Homosexual*, was first published in 1976, it created a furor. Despite Rome's subsequent withdrawal of the *imprimi potest*, its official permission to publish, the book has since been translated into five languages.

John J. McNeill is a Jesuit priest, a moral theologian and a founder of Dignity New York. He has taught at Fordham University, Le Moyne College, and Woodstock Seminary. In addition to his S.T.L. degree from Woodstock Seminary and his Ph.L. degree from Bellarmine College, McNeill received his Ph.D. in philosophy from the Institut Superieur de Philosophie, Louvain University in Belgium.

Lawrence Mass wishes to dedicate this interview to the memory of Vernon Kroening, founder and director of Music at St. Josephs (New York) and a member of Dignity New York. Kroening was one of two gay men who were shot and killed in a machine-gun attack on the Ramrod bar November 19, 1980.

[Ed. note: *The Church and the Homosexual* (Beacon Press) is now available in a revised third edition that includes two new chapters: (1) "Some Pastoral Reflections on AIDS" and (2) "A History of the Publication of This Book." In the latter, Father McNeill relates the events that led to his dismissal in early 1987 from the Jesuit order because of his public dissent from the Church's teaching on homosexuality.]

MASS: What were the circumstances surrounding the withdrawal of the *imprimi potest*, the official permission to publish, from your book, *The Church and the Homosexual*?
McNEILL: The *imprimi potest* was granted to allow me to present this subject and my point of view for scholastic debate, but only among my peers in academic theological circles. The problem arose when it became a media success. I appeared on many talk shows and lectured in thirty cities. Rome felt that the public nature of the ensuing debate was contrary to the understanding with which the *imprimi potest* had been granted. American bishops subsequently protested to Rome that some of my public statements were causing confusion about church doctrine and raising false hopes.
MASS: This explains why you were subsequently forbidden to speak publicly on the subject of homosexuality and ethics, a prohibition you continue to rigorously obey. But it does not explain the unconditional withdrawal of the *imprimi potest*.
McNEILL: I think the withdrawal was felt to be necessary as a means of emphasizing that the church's position on homosexuality had not, in fact, undergone any official change.
MASS: Certainly the Pope's statements about homosexuality while

in Chicago strongly reaffirmed the church's traditional position. Nevertheless, wasn't John Paul II the first Pope in history to publicly recognize the legitimate existence of a theologically-independent, constitutional "homosexual orientation" [i.e., wasn't he the first pope to ever publicly mention this phrase]?

McNEILL: Yes. In this sense, I think his statement did indeed represent a very definite advance. His explicit recognition of a psychic homosexual orientation is, in fact, unprecedented. Of course, he continues to maintain the traditional Church position that all non-procreative sexuality is sinful.

MASS: Gay people sometimes observe that some of the worst opposition to their social acceptance and integration comes from gay people themselves; that is, the powerful, successful, but closeted homosexuals who feel that their reputations would be jeopardized by any affirmative involvement with gay concerns. Some infer that this is especially true of the priesthood. Do you agree?

McNEILL: I think that in many instances the homophobia you are speaking about is irrational and unconscious, the result of repressed homosexuality. But you find this everywhere, including the church. I must say, however, that my sense of the priesthood's openness to gay concerns, to the gay community, is extremely positive. I'm very much in touch with the grassroots clergy, the priests and the nuns out in the parishes who are working with the poor, the needy, the sick, etc. I have been deeply and consistently impressed by their warmth and support and by their genuine understanding. The number of reactionaries, those who are phobic about homosexuality, is, I think, extremely minimal. Unfortunately, some of these individuals are in positions of power in the Church, as they are everywhere else. But again, I must emphasize the true power of the grassroots movement that has grown so strong during the last ten years and that is so clearly with the gay community in its struggle for dignity.

I also want to say that many of the greatest spiritual leaders I've known, tremendously productive individuals, were and are homosexually oriented. This has been generously acknowledged by other distinguished theologians, like Paul Moore. In his new book, *Christianity, Social Tolerance and Homosexuality*, John Boswell also points this out. It is interesting to speculate why this should be so. In my book, I quoted Jung's observation that the homosexual is often "endowed with a wealth of religious feelings, which help him to bring the *ecclesia spiritualis* into reality, and a spiritual receptivity which makes him responsive to revelation." Of course, Jung was generally much more open to questions of spirituality than his mentor, Freud. In fact, their differences proved to be irreconcilable.

MASS: You are a practicing psychotherapist as well as a Jesuit scholar. Are you also a Jungian?

McNEILL: My psychotherapeutic orientation, at least for now, is in the object relations school — more Sullivanian. But Jung had much to say. Each of the special qualities he attributes to the homosexual community is usually considered a striking characteristic of Christ himself, like the extraordinary ability to meet an individual's unique person free of stereotypes, or the refusal to accomplish goals by means of violence. The point I'm trying to make here is not, of course, that Christ was a homosexual any more than he was a heterosexual. His example clearly transcends our current homosexual-heterosexual dialectic. My point is that Christ was an extraordinarily free and fulfilled human being.

MASS: What about the many scholarly observations (including Boswell's) that Christ's most deeply intimate human relationship was with [Saint] John?

McNEILL: I think what we see in Jesus is the total freedom to love, to relate to *any* human being. Many priests have succeeded in incarnating these positive qualities of Christ. And, as we've said, many priests in many denominations are homosexually oriented. The gay community, if it were allowed to be itself, to develop its special qualities, has a major role to fulfill in helping to bring about the ideal that Christ represented.

To better understand how and why homosexuals have this special place in the human community, one must examine some critical differences between Old and New Testaments. It is important to remember that the new people of God are no longer bound by blood relationship; membership in the New Testament community is no longer a question of human descent. Consequently, marriage no longer occupies the central place it had in Israel. As T.C. Deleruijf stated in *The Bible on Sexuality*, "In the new covenant it is given to anyone to be fertile in the new people of God through a love which surpasses even marital love in value and therefore in fertility." This new understanding of love lies at the origin of other vocational choices besides marriage, such as a life of sexual abstinence, and other forms of human community.

Another important difference between the Old and New Testaments concerning human sexuality has to do with the belief in personal immortality. In the Old Testament, there was little stress on the afterlife. The New Testament emphasis on resurrection, however, carried with it the belief in personal immortality and, consequently, freed the individual from the *necessity* of marrying and bearing children. This change of emphasis is of particular interest *vis-à-vis* the homosexual, since, as many psychologists point out, one of the most profound roots of homophobia is the connection, unconscious for the most part, between homosexuality, barrenness and death.

MASS: We hear much about the Old Testament condemnations of homosexuality (based on the Sodom and Gomorrah story or on erroneous translations and interpretations of them). Are there any explicitly positive references to sexual variance in the New Testament? Is there anything that legitimizes the special role of homosexuals in the "New Testament community"?

McNEILL: Nowhere is the new attitude concerning human sexuality more evident than in the account of the baptism of the Ethiopian eunuch in the Acts of the Apostles (8:26-39). Here, the Lucan author stresses that people who were considered outcasts by Israel for various reasons were to be included in the new community. The first group is the Samaritans. The second group, symbolized by the eunuch, are those who for sexual reasons were excluded from the Old Testament community. In Isaiah 56:2-8 the prophecy is explicit: "For thus says the Lord: 'To the eunuchs who keep my sabbath, who choose the things that please me, and hold fast my covenant, I will give in my name better than sons and daughters . . . For my house shall be a house at prayer for all peoples.' Thus says the Lord God, who will gather the outcasts of Israel."

The word *eunuch*, it must be noted, did not have the circumscribed meaning that it has today. In Matthew 19:12, Jesus, discussing marriage and divorce, says to his apostles: "There are eunuchs who have been so from birth, and there are eunuchs who have been made so by men, and there are eunuchs who have made themselves

eunuchs for the sake of the Kingdom of heaven.'' The first category — those eunuchs who have been so from birth — is the closest
description we have in the Bible of what we understand today to be
a homosexual. It should come as no surprise, then, that the first
group of outcasts of Israel that the Holy Spirit includes within the
new covenant community is symbolized by the Ethiopian eunuch.
The Holy Spirit takes the initiative in leading the new Christian
community to include among its members those who were excluded
for sexual reasons from the Old Testament community.

MASS: In his review of Ronald Bayer's new book, *Homosexuality
and American Psychiatry: The Politics of Diagnosis*, for *The New
Republic* (3/21/81), historian Paul Robinson states his belief that the
''intellectual and moral forces predating the rise of psychiatry,
above all Christianity, have exercised immeasurably greater influence on the circumstances of homosexuals.'' I assume you would
agree that religious indoctrination accounts for a great deal of anti-
homosexual prejudice.

McNEILL: I would agree. But there's a paradox here. I believe that
the greatest ally of gay people in their quest for acceptance is the
Church. This is because the historical role of the Church has been to
take the side of the oppressed. On this issue of homosexuality, for
example, the Catholic bishops have individually and collectively
made statement after statement in support of civil rights for gay
people.

There has been a lot of appropriate and justifiable gay anger towards the Church. Through Dignity, the Catholic gay community
has been able to channel its anger to bring about constructive
changes. The prophets, of course, were all angry men. They were
angry about injustice. Anger was a loving motivation for them as it
is for the gay community. But it's important that these energies not
be destructive. The ''Sisters of Perpetual Indulgence,'' for example, tend to trivialize — if not ignore — the positive, selfless face of
Christian service. How indulgent were the assassinated nuns in El
Salvador, or Archbishop Romero?

MASS: Some of John Boswell's most important findings were credited to him and published by you in *The Church and the Homosexual*. Clearly, you enthusiastically respect his work. [But] are there

any major statements in [Boswell's book,] *Christianity, Social Tolerance and Homosexuality*, with which you would take issue?

McNEILL: I read it through immediately and now must give it more careful study. But I had a loose, puzzled sense that somehow John had missed the basic root of Christian homophobia. He's inclined to attribute it largely to the intellectual work of St. Thomas Aquinas at the University of Paris. I believe that of far greater significance was the general, traditional use of the homosexual as scapegoat.

MASS: But at the broader level, isn't Boswell saying precisely this? I think he not only gives credibility to your thinking, he extends it further. In what struck me as one of the most impressive syntheses I've ever read in a cultural-political work, Boswell concludes that not only have homosexuals historically been culturally scapegoated, they have been so in tandem with other minorities — the Jews, the gypsies, heretics, etc. When one minority was scapegoated, the others followed. As Boswell documents it, this pattern became unmistakable by the 12th century. Although it is not explicit, I get the sense that he believed this tandem pattern has probably recurred right up through the Nazi exterminations of the present day.

McNEILL: Yes, but I would have emphasized the historical trend to *specifically* scapegoat homosexuals — in order to win the war, stop the plague, end the natural disaster. In order for things to get better, you have to get rid of the homosexuals. This is stated very clearly and repeatedly in Justinian's codification of Roman law. Paraphrasing: God destroys cities because of the homosexuals. We learned that from Sodom and Gomorrah. I feel that Boswell tended to minimize the importance of the Justinian laws. They established the legal-psychological tradition of homophobia that has continued right through to Blackstone, who says that homosexuality should be a criminal offense to protect the state against God's vengeance. This thinking is repeated throughout American law. In fact, a court in Virginia recently upheld this example. Again, my point here is that this tradition was strong and quite independent of the theoretical-intellectual thinking of Saint Thomas Aquinas.

It's true, of course, that Jews have been similarly scapegoated. That's why I find it incredible that the Jewish community does not fully support the gay struggle.

MASS: As a Jew, I have been even more perplexed and, of course, deeply saddened by the phenomenon of Jewish homophobia — or "homosexophobia," as John Boswell prefers to call it. Like Christian homophobia, it can't all be attributed to the Old Testament.

McNEILL: I don't feel that the religious teachings of the Old Testament explain the Jewish prejudice toward homosexuals. To my knowledge, most Old Testament scholars are fully aware that there is no universal condemnation of homosexuality in these scriptures. There is, in fact, a large body of scholarship in the Jewish community that fully supports my interpretation. In any event, even the most recalcitrant theological traditions do not explain the current inability of the Jewish community to publicly acknowledge and condemn the Holocaust extermination, side by side with the Jews, of homosexuals.

MASS: When you speak of your disappointment with the Jewish response to the gay struggle, what else did you have in mind?

McNEILL: Here in New York, when the City Council tries to pass a gay rights ordinance, the opposition is strong at the level of Jewish community leaders.

MASS: In *The Church and the Homosexual*, you conclude that "the primary argument for the continued oppression of the homosexual is the continued belief, in reality unfounded, that the stability of the family and the moral health of society demand such an oppression." Once again, what are the fallacies in this argument?

McNEILL: Actually, as I say in my book, it is the oppression itself that undermines the family structure by limiting the heterosexual to narrow and dehumanizing stereotypes and also by forcing homosexuals into loveless marriages.

If children — whose sexual orientation everyone now agrees is involuntarily, unconsciously directed from the earliest development — could grow up with strong, loving, healthy heterosexual and homosexual role models, there would be much less fear and destructiveness in their sexuality. We would all be immeasurably freer to direct our sexuality in the loving service of God.

Look at the relationship of gays to their own families. Who is it that cares for a sick, elderly mother or father? It's usually the gay son or daughter. The great irony is that many of these gay persons lovingly care for parents or other relatives who refuse to discuss —

to say nothing of accept — their children's individuality. In this sense, gays are living the fullest expression of Christ's example. They are suffering on the cross.

MASS: One of the most exciting and highly original of your book's contributions to social thought deals with the future role of the gay community. How has your vision of gay humanity developed since the book was published?

McNEILL: In my travels throughout the country, I've been profoundly impressed by the enormous number of gay people who are engaged in and deeply dedicated to loving human services — priests, physicians, psychotherapists, nurses, teachers, gay people working with retarded children, the sick, the blind, the poor. Since most of these people do not have children of their own, they tend to direct a vast reservoir of unselfish love into the human community. So great is this reservoir that the world could not bear its loss. Despite their personal suffering because of social ostracism, their loving presence is the oil that keeps the entire machine going.

Circumcision:
Facts, Fallacies and Fantasies

A Conversation with George Stambolian

[Ed. note: Although this conversation was not published until early 1982, it was begun and largely completed, as were the interviews with Mary Calderone (which was published in September 1981) and John Handley (which was not published until February 1982), before I began my full-time coverage of the AIDS epidemic in June 1981. What follows is an uncut version of the interview that appeared in *Christopher Street*. The published version was entitled "The Unkindest Cut of All."]

George Stambolian is professor of French and Interdisciplinary Studies at Wellesley College. His most recent books are *Homosexualities and French Literature*, *Male Fantasies/Gay Realities*: *Interviews with Ten Men* and *Men on Men*, an anthology of gay fiction [volumes I, II and III].

STAMBOLIAN: I think many people do not know the facts about circumcision—for example, how many men are circumcised in this country, how this practice has evolved over the years, what justifications are given for it, and what kinds of consequences, both medical and personal, result from it.

MASS: The book you and I have been reading, *Circumcision*: *An American Health Fallacy* by Edward Wallerstein (Springer, 1980), documents the alarming growth of this practice in the United States over the last hundred years. In 1870, only about 10 percent of male infants were routinely circumcised. Today, 85 percent of them are. It has been suggested that circumcision may outrank abortion as the most frequently performed unnecessary surgery in America.

STAMBOLIAN: Are parents consulted on this matter beforehand, or is it just automatically done?

MASS: Legally, the parents must always be consulted. But in fact, the information is often presented to them in such a way that they are strongly urged to do what has become the norm rather than what is in the child's best interests.

STAMBOLIAN: Well, I understand that if parents do not wish their son to be circumcised, it takes some effort to prevent the operation.

MASS: I think that in a growing but still small number of quality medical centers, leading opinion *against* circumcision is now such that parents probably wouldn't encounter much difficulty. However, if parents aren't aware of at least some of the facts, their baby is far more likely to be circumcised.

STAMBOLIAN: What are the justifications offered by the medical profession for the operation?

MASS: For those who are informed, there are currently no medical or hygienic justifications of any kind. In the recent past, the most potent justification had to do with the suspected relationship between smegma (from the secretions of the foreskin) and cancer of the cervix in women, which is one of the most commonly diagnosed cancers in America. But this supposition has never been ascertained. On the basis of less impressively circumstantial evidence, cancers of the prostate and of the penis were also said to be risks for uncircumcised men.

STAMBOLIAN: I have read that when surveys were done regarding the connection between smegma and cervical cancer, many of the women who were interviewed didn't know whether their husbands were circumcised or not. There are even men who are not sure of the difference.

MASS: I think this is part of the erotophobia that has characterized our culture specifically and patriarchal cultures in general. Religious fundamentalist attitudes and beliefs continue to hide the most basic knowledge of sexual anatomy and functioning from our children. As Mary Calderone puts it, we are still "a nation of sexual stutterers." In fact, the reason circumcision persists probably has less to do with the cancer associations than with masturbation and other manifestations of pre-pubescent eroticism which violate the sexual taboo. I think there is a kind of tacit understanding between medicine and the public that circumcision will prevent "precocious sexuality."

STAMBOLIAN: So if the child doesn't have a foreskin, he is less likely to be touching himself or playing with himself than if he did?

MASS: Yes. The uncircumcised boy must be taught to periodically retract his foreskin in order to clean the penis. During infancy the mother must do this, which means actual "incestuous" contact. In our culture, the incest taboo is so hysterical that anything that would minimize even the potential for such contact would be seen as good. I personally believe that this factor beyond all others has made the practice of circumcision acceptable, even attractive to many individuals.

STAMBOLIAN: It is also believed that uncircumcised men are more likely to contract venereal disease, again because it is supposed that the foreskin will retain contagious organisms.

MASS: If an uncircumcised male never practices any hygiene, he may be more likely to develop certain infections, if he has been exposed to the organisms that cause them. By maintaining genital hygiene, however, he is at no more risk than someone who is circumcised.

STAMBOLIAN: There are many, especially within the gay community, who believe that the uncircumcised penis is more sensitive, and who are against circumcision for that reason. But there are also doctors who advocate circumcision because it supposedly prevents or reduces premature ejaculation.

MASS: This is part of the psychiatric thinking that is still so powerful in this country. It's basically a kind of medical updating of the Old Testament. Like the Bible, psychoanalytic psychiatry recognizes the existence of childhood sexuality, but ultimately judges it, like all nonconjugal sexuality, to be undifferentiated, uncivilized, dangerous, abnormal. What contemporary sexology characterizes as the normal, developmental sex-rehearsal play of primates is still regarded by the Freudians as "polymorphous perversity." What is really being said is that the uncircumcised penis is too *sexual*. With this logic, premature ejaculation is seen to be a problem of "hypersexuality." By similar reasoning, removing the foreskin will render the penis less "sensitive."

STAMBOLIAN: Earlier you mentioned the incest taboo in our culture. But in Europe, the vast majority of men are not circumcised, and their mothers have taught them penile hygiene without any apparent ill results.

MASS: I suspect that in many European countries constriction of the foreskin, the condition we call *phimosis*, is more common than it should be because these cultures are also anti-sexual. If a child is encouraged to regularly retract his foreskin, phimosis is far less likely to develop. European parents may be more successful in teaching genital hygiene to their children, but they probably don't apply that hygiene very rigorously.

STAMBOLIAN: If these European cultures are so anti-sexual, and if circumcision is also anti-sexual and allegedly so effective in preventing various medical conditions and diseases, why haven't these cultures promoted circumcision more than they have?

MASS: I think one answer is probably to be found in the historical European tendency to distinguish Christian from Jew. We know that although the church has been doctrinally anti-sexual, it has also been virulently anti-Semitic during many periods of history, especially in Europe.

STAMBOLIAN: When I discuss the issue of circumcision in America with European friends, many of them propose that this is largely because a more signficant and influential segment of the American medical establishment is Jewish.

MASS: The possibility that a significantly Jewish medical establishment of this country may have been consciously or unconsciously motivated to seek ''scientific'' justification for circumcision is awfully speculative at several levels. It would be impossible to prove and could be interpreted as anti-Semitic. Even so, it can't be entirely ruled out. On the other hand, one can't overlook the profit motive. Circumcision requires only a few minutes of the physician's busy day and is a substantial source of income. But once again, what is certain is that there has been a preoccupation in American medicine and psychiatry with the idea that circumcision will prevent or at least inhibit the evil ''self-pollution'' of masturbation.

STAMBOLIAN: Since the early nineteenth century Europeans have also been obsessed by masturbation, but somehow in this country the idea that circumcision was going to reduce masturbation took hold in a way that it didn't in Europe. Even then the reasoning is not clear. After all, circumcised boys masturbate all the time. As for the incest taboo, in my own life some of the most loving moments I ever shared with my mother were in the bathroom when she was bathing me as a child and teaching me to wash my penis.

MASS: Incidentally, most nonhuman primates periodically inspect, lick and play with the genitalia of their infants.

STAMBOLIAN: What can be traumatic in this country is when the child is not informed what it means to be uncircumcised. I remember there came a day when I looked around and saw I wasn't like everyone else, and this upset me very much. When I asked my parents why, they said, "The doctor asked us if we wanted it done, but we said no." My uncle explained how he had had his penis circumcised when he was in his twenties because of a problem, but added that the operation was very painful, and that if my penis didn't bother me, I should keep it the way it was.

MASS: Did those explanations dispel or strengthen your impression that the others were normal and maybe a little better than you?

STAMBOLIAN: I did feel "irregular" to a certain extent. The pressure toward conformity is an important factor. Parents usually want their son to be like everyone else, or in some cases to be like the father.

MASS: My experience was the inverse of yours. As a Jew, I was circumcised during infancy in Macon, Georgia [where I was born and raised]. You would think that there would be a lot of uncircumcised men in the South, and I suppose there were and are. But in fact, the majority of men and boys in my environment were also circumcised. Unlike you, I actually had a certain sense of being more normal and natural than my few uncircumcised friends. I didn't really develop a conscious sense of regret about circumcision until much later.

STAMBOLIAN: There are men in this country who are not circumcised, and who probably wish they were. The other day at my gym, where almost all the members are gay, I saw an attractive young man in the shower who made a point of carefully pulling back his foreskin so that it rested behind the glans and made it look as if he were circumcised. He seemed very self-conscious and probably thought that his foreskin would be a sexual turnoff to others, despite the fantasy material that has been published on uncut cocks.

MASS: I have a parallel story. A good friend with whom I went to medical school underwent circumcision several years ago because his lover preferred that he be circumcised. The irony is that the lover is himself uncircumcised. The lover came from a poor rural environment and had little education. For him circumcision apparently had powerful associations with many of the things he felt he wasn't but wanted to be.

STAMBOLIAN: One thing that reassured me when I was young was that none of the statues were circumcised. Even Michelangelo's David is uncircumcised. This is usually explained by saying that he represents more the ideal beauty of a Renaissance Florentine than a biblical Hebrew. But still, I was dismayed when I read the Old Testament story of David slaying the Philistines and gathering their foreskins. I imagined all those bodies on the battlefield being systematically mutilated and sacks of foreskins being carried back to Saul's palace.

The aesthetic question is important. I remember reading Herodotus, the great Greek historian, talking about the culture of Egypt and mentioning that he could not understand why the Egyptians circumcised their male children and so mutilated the male body. For Herodotus circumcision was a form of ugliness.

MASS: And the way circumcision was done in those days, I'm sure it frequently resulted in horrendous mutilations.

STAMBOLIAN: The question of erotic tastes and sensibilities is a complex one. I was recently in France and spoke to a friend who, unlike most of his compatriots, wishes he had been circumcised because, he says, it is "sexier, cleaner, nicer, better."

MASS: But you've pointed out to me the great infatuation that many French gay men are currently having with what they perceive to be gay culture in America. Since so many Americans are circumcised, it may be that for some Frenchmen circumcision has acquired affirmative cultural associations.

STAMBOLIAN: I don't know if that is so, but certainly a lot of one's erotic sensibilities are determined by one's culture. I recently looked at the personal ads in *The Advocate* and discovered that there were several men who were seeking men with uncut cocks. But I should also say that whether a penis is cut or uncut is mentioned far less often than penis size or even body musculature. So this is a significant but still relatively minor "fetish," as some would call it, in our culture. However, if you look at the personal ads in a French gay newspaper like *Gai Pied*, there is not a single mention of circumcision in any form whatsoever.

MASS: Yes, but I think that the largely West Coast gay culture that reads *The Advocate* is far more into discussing and exploring every aspect of sexuality than are the gay cultures of Europe. Also, it's simplistic to stereotype gay Americans as "fetishistic" just because some of them are expressing an interest in aspects of sexual anatomy. It would be no more appropriate than labeling as fetishists straight men who have an erotic preoccupation with female breasts.

STAMBOLIAN: I agree, but the erotic always works in strange ways. I knew a man in the Midwest who was obsessed by foreskin and was ecstatic whenever he found a sexual partner who was uncircumcised. His friends often said to him, "Why don't you go to Puerto Rico or to Europe?" And his answer was always, "I would go mad if I went there." But that wasn't what prevented him from going. He liked America precisely because he knew that the odds were *against* his finding uncircumcised men, and that made the hunt all the more exciting for him. I also met a man once who had a rather remarkable collection of pornographic photographs of uncircumcised men. Looking through these photos, I found that the men who turned me on the most were not the European-looking ones whom one would expect to be uncircumcised, but the American-looking men. In fact, the more clean-cut and typically American the model looked, the more erotically exciting it was for me. "Clean-cut" is itself an interesting expression because although it does not refer specifically to circumcision, it does describe a total erotic image of which circumcision is a part. In these photos the cock was the exception and played against the rest of the image. That tension was very arousing. When I go to Europe and suddenly find myself in the majority, the erotic value, for me at least, of uncircumcised cocks diminishes greatly. I also find far fewer men who are excited by that aspect of my own body, or who pay special erotic attention to it.

MASS: Fascinating. So you think that the status quo is a bigger erotic factor than many of us have realized.

STAMBOLIAN: To be uncircumcised in this country is to be different, and any difference can be eroticized. Of course, differences that are attractive to some people are often repellant to others depending, as always, on circumstances. There's no question that the foreskin is associated with those tastes and practices we call "dirty sex" as opposed to "clean sex." Smell is an important factor here.

MASS: Freud agreed with his young colleague, Wilhelm Fliess, that smells are important in the sexuality of many animals, including human infants. But he also believed that the achievement of "genital" ("mature," "civilized") sexuality in humans involved the transcendence of these "archaic" behaviors. In view of the recent discovery of human pheromones (hormones which, when smelled are sexually arousing [but which have yet to be demonstrated to be involved in human sexual pathways]), Freud's implicit denial of the importance of smells in "mature" sexuality seems manifestly erotophobic.

STAMBOLIAN: One can, of course, like uncut penises and not be attracted to smell. Also, most uncircumcised men bathe so regularly that there is no smell. But the erotic associations persist. I saw a graffito that said "Smell my uncut cock," and then added a phone number. In fact, one of the signs of contemporary sexual mores has been the rediscovery of the natural smells of the body that were once hidden or avoided because they were "dirty" or "not nice." In a way, it *is* a revolt against the over-civilizing of sex. We should add, however, that today it is primarily gay men who eroticize such things. And in this respect, one of the dangers inherent in our talking about circumcision, and particularly against it, is that some people will think the subject is interesting only to gay men.

MASS: Indeed, psychoanalysts have consistently identified the "disease" of homosexuality by the following "symptoms": "fetishism," "narcissism," "masochism" and "paranoia." Of great importance here is a recent report called "Prepuce Restoration Seekers" (from *The Archives of Sexual Behavior*, 8/81). It describes the experiences of several American surgeons who were approached by a number of homosexual males requesting plastic surgery to create foreskins. Each of the patients had been circumcised during infancy and claimed a lifelong preoccupation with his absent foreskin. They complained of feeling "incomplete" or "mutilated." What's most intriguing is how much of this report is devoted to the question of "psychopathology." It is suggested, for example, that many of the patients were "narcissistic" and suffering from "mothering deficits." By contrast, if a woman requests an augmentation mammoplasty [silicone implants], psychopathology is almost never a question because the predominantly male surgical, medical and psychiatric establishments respect the importance of big tits in women. In the *Archives* report, the authors mention the Uncircumcised Society of America (U.S.A.), many of whose members are gay. Did you say there are several such groups?

STAMBOLIAN: I don't know how many organizations there are, but I think USA is the largest. The members are supposedly 80 percent homosexual and 65 percent uncircumcised. I do know that at one time they held special nights at the Mineshaft where only men who were uncircumcised were allowed to enter first; then, later on, it was opened to the others. They had a newsletter in which they traded information concerning the medical, erotic and "fetishistic" aspects of circumcision.

MASS: I think that as the subject of circumcision becomes more public, gay men will be scapegoated. It will be said that being against circumcision is yet another example of gay fetishism, narcissism, masochism and paranoia.

STAMBOLIAN: But the fact is that everyone — straight or gay, man or woman — has a self-image and body-image to which reality, unfortunately, does not always conform. These men who sought to have their foreskins restored wanted to bring the reality of their body in line with the image of their body that they had nurtured in their minds, and when they succeeded they experienced great psychological satisfaction. They gave a variety of interesting reasons for seeking this operation. They said that the uncircumcised penis was more beautiful or more pleasing. Some even said that it was more masculine, and one man associated it with greater creativity.

Now that may be considered going too far, but the essential issue is still the right that each of us has to have a choice in this matter. There are many circumcised men who resent that their bodies were changed without their consent.

MASS: For me, that is by far the most objectionable aspect of routine circumcision—that it is done without the patient's informed consent. It's bad enough that the procedure is done without anesthesia. As you know, this business of the baby not being able to experience pain or psychological trauma is ridiculous. It's probably an exceedingly traumatic event for the baby. I am a qualified believer in religious freedoms and parental prerogatives. But in the case of a dangerous, physically and psychologically traumatic, medically unjustifiable religious ritual like circumcision, I believe that those freedoms and prerogatives need to be reevaluated and redefined.

STAMBOLIAN: I agree. But we should recognize that by saying this, we mean that a child will have to wait until he is older before making a decision, and how many young adults will then opt for circumcision, given the [postoperative] painfulness of the procedure?

MASS: If a young man, once he has reached legal adulthood, wants to undergo circumcision because of religious or other beliefs, that's his business. He should have that right.

STAMBOLIAN: I'm glad you mentioned the problem of mutilation because although circumcision is widely performed in this country, it is not always done with great expertise. Sometimes underlings or people who aren't very well-trained are assigned this task, and we know that there are a significant number of cases each year where the circumcision is badly performed leading to infection and pain. There have been instances where the circumcision has led to a major infection resulting in the loss of the penis, and there have been legal suits brought by parents against hospitals. I believe there are also a certain number of deaths each year.

MASS: The upper estimates are that two hundred deaths result annually from complications of circumcision. Complications necessitating repeated plastic surgeries for reconstruction of the urethra and other sequellae have also been reported. But we don't yet know what the real rates are. That's because unlike tonsillectomy, hysterectomy, abortion, etc., there has never been a major study of circumcision. However, in recent years a number of leading medical organizations, journals and spokespersons (many of them Jewish) have come out with strong statements against the routine practice of circumcision. These include the American Academy of Pediatrics and the American College of Obstetrics and Gynecology, which are among the most respected voices in neonatal medicine. On the other hand, there is almost no discussion of this subject in the psychiatric and psychoanalytic literatures. It seems mind-boggling that Freud, the great theorist of infantile sexuality and the conceptualizer of the Oedipus complex and of castration anxiety, never wrote a paper on circumcision! [By telephone from Boston, Frank Sulloway, author of *Freud: Bioloqist of the Mind*, confirmed that he knew of no such paper.] To my knowledge there is only one paper in the entire psychoanalytic literature that is devoted to "The Psychological Effects of Circumcision" (by Cansever, *British Journal of Medical Psychology*, 1965, 38, 321).

STAMBOLIAN: That paper is also interesting because it shows to what extent psychoanalysis enters an impasse when it discusses such questions. After studying a culture in which circumcision is performed during puberty rites, the author remains uncertain whether this involves a healthy separation from the mother and an indentification with the father leading to a heterosexual manhood, or whether the separation from the mother is so traumatic and the pain inflicted by the father so great that the circumcision in fact enforces homosexual tendencies in the child. There is the suggestion that circumcision expresses submission to the father, and that it was performed in the Jewish religion because it also meant submission to God. Christians supposedly rejected circumcision because Christianity is a religion of the son and therefore did not require submission to paternal authority. All that is fascinating, and one could even use such perceptions to support the idea of a homosexual revolt against patriarchal society. But these ideas don't change the fact that circumcision, like other sexual issues, is riddled with contradictions. What impressed me most in the Wallerstein book was a statement on circumcision by a Dr. Karen E. Paige, who said that when a custom persists after its original functions have died, it may be accorded the status of a ritual, particularly when it supports antithetical goals, such as repressing *and* liberating sexuality, making the penis more *or* less sensitive, etc. I think it is going to be much more difficult to get rid of something that has become ritualized to that extent. More is involved than ending a fallacious medical practice.

MASS: I couldn't agree more. But I believe it is a worthy struggle. I don't think we can retreat as physicians, as intellectuals, and as advocates of fundamental human rights who happen to be gay just because we may be more likely to become (once again) the scapegoats of those who endorse the perpetuation of such anti-sexual rituals.

Male Couples

A Conversation with Charles Silverstein

Charles Silverstein is a psychologist and psychotherapist in private practice in New York City. He is Founding Editor of the *Journal of Homosexuality*, the co-author with Edmund White of *The Joy of Gay Sex* (Simon and Schuster, 1977) and the author of *Man to Man: Gay Couples in America* (William Morrow, 1981). It was Dr. Silverstein who made the presentation on the declassification of homosexuality as a mental disorder in 1973 before the Nomenclature Committee of the American Psychiatric Association.

MASS: The title of your new book, *Man to Man: Gay Couples in America*, makes it implicit that "gay" means male homosexuals rather than the homosexuality of both genders. This was similarly true of your previous book, *The Joy of Gay Sex*, (co-authored with Edmund White). How did this distinction come about?

SILVERSTEIN: For some time, there has been a growing insistence on this distinction by growing numbers of lesbians. The more militant of these individuals seem not to want *any* generic word that represents everyone whose affectional preference is for the same sex. At the very least, they want to maximize the differences between gay men and lesbians.

Where appropriate, I emphasize these differences, but I still think of gay as referring to both male and female. That's why I used the word in my subtitle rather than the title. I wanted to make clear that in this particular book, but not necessarily otherwise, gay is referring to male homosexuals.

MASS: Like sociobiologist Donald Symons (*The Evolution of Human Sexuality*), you suggest that male homosexuality is predominantly a phenomenon of masculinity and that lesbianism is similarly a phenomenon of femininity. But doesn't this observation skirt the issue of the frequent, though by no means regular, cross-gender identifications and behaviors of many homosexuals?

SILVERSTEIN: I don't think so. What I'm saying is that there are certain *general*, perhaps fundamental similarities between gay and straight men. Statistically, androgyny can be appreciated as an overlapping of "masculinity" and "femininity." In this sense, I think gay and straight men are, by and large, similar. The same *general* similarity is, I think, likewise true of lesbians and straight women. Another way of saying the same thing is that the differences between male and female explain more than the differences between gay and straight.

MASS: *Generally* speaking, are you saying that gay men now identify more comfortably with straight men than with lesbians and straight women?

SILVERSTEIN: In order to answer that question, one first has to talk about geographical differences. In large urban centers, there's a much greater segregation of gay men from women. This segregation is particularly striking in bars. In the city, there are far too many gay men's bars where lesbians are prohibited, where the attitude is we-don't-want-any-women-here. I think that in the large, politicized urban centers, many gay men are frankly mysogynous. But the men-hating and self-imposed segregation of many big city lesbians is equally impressive.

In the rural midwest and southwest, by contrast, gay men and lesbians go to the same bars, dance together and mix comfortably. They seem to enjoy each other's company enormously. In the smaller communities, in fact, the question I was most often asked by both lesbians and gay men was why their brothers and sisters in San Francisco and New York were always fighting.

MASS: Do you think this trend towards segregation of lesbians from gay men will continue?

SILVERSTEIN: I can't predict the future. Certainly a tension exists today. What concerns me most is the antisexual tone of some recent lesbian feminist voices. There seems to have been a drastic shift from a liberal emphasis on civil rights to fascistic calls for censorship. In their overall attitude towards sexuality, the lesbians who would endorse censorship are much closer to the most conservative straight women (e.g., the lesbian-hating Phyllis Schlafley) than to the most conservatively feminist gay men.

Most lesbians I've spoken with in recent months say they're offended by what they see as the association of gay men with "pornography," "S&M," "promiscuity," "pederasty," etc. If they had their druthers, they would put a stop to it all. This is summed up in that infamous statement from N.O.W. The irony is that this attitude is as oppressive to many women as it is to men. They seem to be completely unaware that "S&M" is also enjoyed by some women, as in intergenerational sex, brief encounters, even "pornography."

The lesbians who claim that such deviations from their own ideal of femininity are merely the acting out of male oppressions are primarily ignorant and dangerously fascistic.

MASS: In *Man to Man*, you address the touchy subject of "man-boy love," which arouses such negative, fearful reactions from many gay men as well as lesbians, together with liberal and conservative straights. In her recent interview for the *New York Native*, for example, *Ms. Magazine* editor Letty Cottin Pogrebin retrospectively qualified the extremely liberal, pro-gay position of her new book, *Growing Up Free*: "The powerful relationship between the adult and the child automatically invalidates the sexual rights aspect." Is sweeping generalization the only way we can deal with this issue?

SILVERSTEIN: First, what's a child? I have relatives who think, like most religious leaders, of forty-year-olds as children. I can't argue for or against anything so generalized as "man-boy love," but I would argue for a sophisticated perception of the complexity of issues and variations involved.

As was the case with "homosexuality," people now want to stigmatize any intergenerational sex as "pederasty" or "pedophilia." This is not to say that terrible exploitation doesn't exist. But positive, nurturing, extremely loving relationships in which there is a genuine balance of power also exist. Unquestionably.

MASS: Commenting on the relationship of gay sons to their fathers, you suggest that one can conceptualize the gay son's sexual fantasies about his father (frequently, in your experience) as the mirror image of Freud's Oedipus complex. In this "Laius complex," as you call it, the boy's sexual attraction is originally for his father rather than his mother. Do we know that this attraction does not take place [for heterosexual sons]or is different from that of heterosexual sons for their fathers?

SILVERSTEIN: I have no idea and would not want to speculate at this time. It's an idea I would like to pursue in future research. But I do want to stress that I consider the Laius complex—characterizing the gay son's original, primary attraction for his father (as opposed to the mother of the Oedipus complex)—to be no more than a convenient metaphor; not a rigid, universal paradigm.

MASS: Does this imply that the gay son would resent his mother as a consequence of desiring his father?

SILVERSTEIN: One would then be hypothesizing that the Freudianly bisexual son experiences jealous hostility towards his mother because she gets to fuck with daddy. In this paradigm, the son *then* becomes homosexual by identifying with his mother, in order to vicariously satisfy his desire for his father. That's *not* what I had in mind! I do not want to build a new *theory* on top of an archaic, unproven one.

MASS: I've never read anything about the homosexuality of Sophocles's Laius (Oedipus's father) or about a Laius complex in the analytic literature. How do you think analysts would respond to your metaphor?

SILVERSTEIN: Some would dismiss it out of hand. Others would decorate old theories with it. I doubt that any good would come of psychoanalytic manipulations. I have a rather jaded view of analysts, having worked with them throughout my career and having trained in psychoanalysis. I find them extraordinarily impervious to new knowledge. I don't think any amount of research will ever change their minds.

MASS: How can fathers better relate to their gay sons? Are there analogies to be drawn between the sexual attraction of straight daughters and that of gay sons for their fathers?

SILVERSTEIN: The sexual attraction of little girls for their fathers is more widely acknowledged and to some degree tolerated, though overt sexuality (incest) remains, of course, taboo. The father might learn to better handle the gay son's eroticism towards him without indulging it. I think the important thing is not to disapprove of the son or his sexuality while appropriately, gently and lovingly reproving his incestuous behavior: "We don't do that in the family."

MASS: What if he asks, why?

SILVERSTEIN: Beyond custom, there is no completely satisfactory answer to this question . . . at the present time.

MASS: Are lesbian daughters known to be attracted to their mothers in a way that is comparable to the attraction of gay sons to their fathers?

SILVERSTEIN: I have no idea. Nor, I think, does anyone else.

MASS: In your chapter, "Cock Rings and Lovers," you suggest that "cult masculinity has replaced femininity as the social behavior of gay men." How do you account for the fact that there isn't a comparable phenomenon of cult femininity that has replaced masculinity as the social behavior of many lesbians?

SILVERSTEIN: I think there is such a phenomenon, one that exaggerates such traits as nesting. But it is only beginning to emerge. That's because the *history* of women has been so suppressed, so ignored, so distorted.

MASS: How do you distinguish cult masculinity from sadomasochism?

SILVERSTEIN: In cult masculinity, the symbols of masculine power become more important than sex itself. In true sadomasochism, symbols are only secondarily involved. Here, roles are assigned and are mutually acceptable and respected. What distinguishes true sadomasochism from cult masculinity is that in the former, sexual behavior is genuinely intimate, loving and not competitive. In the latter, it is exclusively competitive. In cult masculinity, two men are competing *against* one another in the arena of sex.

I think the growing trend towards cult masculinity in the largest urban centers is among our biggest problems. Invariably, masculine cultists, unlike true sadomasochists, have great difficulty sustaining, or even commencing intimate relationships. I would actually say that I see more "sadomasochistic" relationships among gay men than I do among sadomasochists.

MASS: Do you think that cult masculinity and the growing identification of gay men with their masculinity suggest that many gay men wish they were straight?

SILVERSTEIN: I don't think so. It's often assumed that gay men want to be more straight because they're homophobic; because they've internalized negative cultural images specifically of homosexuality. But this hasn't been my experience. I think the problem is more related to sexuality than to sexual orientation.

MASS: You say that many gay men have a phobia about closeness. Because of this, you suggest that it is "ironic that many gay male love affairs break up *because* of the closeness and intimacy that has developed, not because men can't become intimate." Is this phobia any different from that which prevents heterosexuals from achieving greater sustained intimacy in our anti-sexual culture?

SILVERSTEIN: I think it's exactly the same. In our anti-sexual culture most people — gay and straight, but male more than female — have serious difficulties initiating and sustaining intimacy?

MASS: Is intimacy more characteristic of "home builders" than "excitement seekers," as you distinguish them in your book?

SILVERSTEIN: No. Excitement seekers are just as capable of intimacy as home builders. But the former are often in conflict with the latter; they're unable to establish the intimacy that may be fully potential between them because they have different styles of expressing intimacy.

MASS: What was the reaction of the Phil Donahue audience to your appearance on that television program?

SILVERSTEIN: There was a gasp of disbelief when one of the three gay couples appearing with me stated that they had been together for twelve years. As you know and as I verify in my book, impressive longevity — 30, 40, 50 years — is not at all uncommon among gay couples. Yet the myth that gay men can't sustain intimate relationships is pervasive among straights and not infrequent among gays themselves.

MASS: Your book concludes on a strongly optimistic note. Have the political events of recent months dampened this optimism?

SILVERSTEIN: I fear the rise of fundamentalist bigotry. I don't think there's much gays can do to stop this craziness. Speaking realistically, I think the only thing that will stop them is the more traditional, established religions, when they realize that the Fundamentalists are against them as well. So our hope is that one religious power will put a stop to the other. I think this is beginning to happen and I expect it to continue.

Wrestling with Sexual Preference

A Conversation with John Handley

Should there be separate competitions for women athletes? If so, what about gay athletes? If we endorse separate competitions for women athletes and gay athletes, does this mean that it is OK for there to be separate competitions for black athletes and white athletes? Whatever the answers, can we say that the psychological mechanisms involved in physical combat sports like wrestling and boxing are fundamentally similar for all competitors regardless of their race, religion, gender or sexual preference?

John Handley, who heads the largely gay male New York Wrestling Club, believes that where differences are perceived, they invariably reflect the political loyalties and personal fantasies of spectators. Handley argues that competitive skills in the arena, like competitive skills in any other area of human endeavor, transcend political distinctions.

MASS: Why do you believe that gay men are becoming more involved in physical contact sports like wrestling and boxing?

HANDLEY: I don't think it's unusual that gay men are interested in fighting. Not all fighting is physical, of course. But physical aggression has always been of profound concern to most *men*, straight or gay. As General Patton said: "Men love to fight—they always have and they always will, or they are not real men." The fact is, gay men have only recently begun to throw off the shackling stereotypes imposed upon them by both the straight *and* gay worlds.

The gay man is breaking sociological rules with every breath he takes. Breaking rules in the ring is psychologically symbolic of further role-breaking—flaunting social conventions, getting back at the confinements, the frustrations of daily life. Why else do so many boxers come from underprivileged backgrounds? The equation is exactly the same for both straight and gay men: oppression + frustration = aggression.

MASS: Are there significant differences between gay and straight wrestlers?

HANDLEY: I don't think so. In fact, I think of myself not as a gay wrestler, but as a wrestler who happens to be gay. Those people who try to classify athletes on the basis of sexual preference are invariably noncompetitors who don't know much about athletics. These days, gay is too often in front of rather than behind sports endeavors.

MASS: Like "gay softball." But what about "The 1982 Gay Olympics?"

HANDLEY: I'd be more comfortable with a name like "The 1982 San Francisco Olympics." I think it's great that gay individuals and groups want to sponsor sports events and encourage community participation, but I don't think we should do so in a way that defeats our purpose. As I see it, we should be striving to integrate these endeavors, not to polarize them. I think genuine progress for gay people in athletics, as in other areas of achievement, will depend more than anything else on those individuals who are willing to come out amidst — rather than apart from — the greater society.

MASS: So you would stress the similarities between competitors who are gay, to use your phrasing, and those who are straight.

HANDLEY: Yes. There may be important differences off the field of competition. But I believe that whether the wrestler, baseball player or chess player is gay or straight, they have identical participator interests in their sport. Spectator interest, however, may differ — and may, where wrestling is concerned, relate to sexual preferences.

MASS: If it's no more appropriate to emphasize sexual preference than skin color in the appreciation of the art of athletic competition, is it similarly inappropriate to emphasize the gender of competitors?

HANDLEY: That depends on the sport. For diving, certain gymnastics, tennis, golf and many other sports, gender distinctions are beginning to fade. But female participation in wrestling has never been legitimized. The female wrestling you see in Las Vegas is showmanship. It's an exhibition, strictly for audience entertainment. It's not genuinely competitive. Female mud wrestling, as in the recent film, *All The Marbles*, is a kind of sex show for straight men. If the structures were to be made available, of course, there's no reason why women wouldn't be able to excel at wrestling or boxing, in competition with one another or even with men.

MASS: Most of the members of the New York Wrestling Club are gay. But on the basis of what you've said, I don't imagine that you consider yourselves to be a movement group.

HANDLEY: That's correct. As individuals, we feel enthusiastically pro-movement. But our organization is foundationally devoted to the art and sport of wrestling. We've co-sponsored events with some of the bars, but we haven't been political in other ways— endorsing candidates, for example, or participating as a group in marches or boycotts.

Nonetheless, one of the strongest and most consistent achievements of the New York Wrestling Club is the opportunity it offers gay men to explore and more fully realize their masculinity through competition they would otherwise avoid. What results is a powerful increase in self-esteem. Despite feminist rhetoric to the contrary, my experience has been that the strengthening of one's masculine identity results in a parallel strengthening of one's pride in being gay.

In fact, many gay men have come out of the closet because of their involvement in the club. This is facilitated by our multi-level membership structure. Here's how it happens. A man may join us initially by subscribing confidentially to our photo newsletter. There he sees and reads about men he wishes to meet. He then decides to go the next level and receive our membership directory— without his own address included. After several meetings at his own initiative, he becomes sufficiently self-confident to request full membership. At this point, he's no longer afraid—indeed, he's proud—to include his name and address in our directory. In effect, the New York Wrestling Club has brought this man out of the closet. *That* is our contribution to the movement. We are quiet about it, but very effective.

MASS: Besides sexual preference and an interest in wrestling, are there other factors your fellow club members have in common?

HANDLEY: Not really. There's such a diversity of ethnic backgrounds and professions. And not all members are gay.

MASS: Like boxing, wrestling is a physical combat sport that involves pain, dominance and submission. Are there philosophical rather than merely structural differences between boxing and wrestling?

HANDLEY: In boxing, the main objective is to knock your opponent out. In wrestling, you want to overcome his resistance without causing physical injury. That's not to say that pain isn't an important aspect of wrestling. It's just not an end-point. After a *fight*, boxers usually need a period of time, say one or two weeks, to recover from the kinds of injuries they regularly sustain. In a wrestling *match*, the opponents are far less frequently and certainly less seriously injured. And when they are injured, it's usually unintentionally. In collegiate and professional wrestling, intentional injury is actually a violation of the rules. Those who are squeamish may choose a fantasy wrestling style in which roles are acted with minimal force, and in which the chance of even accidental injury is almost nil.

MASS: How did you first become involved in wrestling?

HANDLEY: As a boy of six or seven, I first saw wrestling on TV. I was smitten. Around the same age, my father began teaching me how to box. My mother was also an influence. She liked boxing and was a big fan of Joe Louis. Somehow, all of this got worked in with playing cowboys and Indians, which I loved.

MASS: Were you a cowboy or an Indian?

HANDLEY: I was never an Indian. The Indians were always the ones that got shot, the bad guys. The irony is that I'm now more often identified with the so-called bad guys. I can really enjoy seeing an all-American rookie type get beaten by a "villain."

MASS: Are you different from most wrestlers in this regard?

HANDLEY: No. If you watch competitions on television, what you usually see is a "hero" being pitted against a "villain." This gets established by the opponents' looks, the way the match is announced, the opponents, gestures, but mostly by the audience's expectations and reactions. It has nothing to do with the relative skills of the opponents.

MASS: In pro-style wrestling, is the "good guy" usually the underdog?

HANDLEY: For the spectators, yes. Because he's the young, inexperienced, full-of-fight wrestler. It's good vs. bad, young vs. old, skill vs. experience, heavyweight vs. lightweight, race vs. race. Equals are rarely matched in pro-wrestling because they don't satisfy anyone's fantasies, straight or gay. Virtually all spectators at pro matches see in each wrestler what they want to see, knowing that reality is another matter: *fantasy*—before the matches, during the matches and after the matches.

So the "bad guy" is the one who is disliked by the majority of spectators. They want him to lose for all kinds of reasons that have nothing to do with the sport. Like all spectators, however, I root for the wrestler that *I* want to win. And in many cases, he's the "villain."

Generally speaking, those who are implicitly identified by the promoters and spectators as "good" I find less interesting. That's why many spectators, myself included, find collegiate wrestling, where both opponents are "good guys," where so many restrictive regulations are so rigidly enforced, boring. Unlike most spectators (but like many competitors), I would identify almost exclusively with the power and skill of the victor. The more palpable the sense of conquest, the greater is the intensity of this identification.

MASS: The spectators, like children, are still identifying cowboys and Indians. What made you realize that being a cowboy was less important than being a winner?

HANDLEY: Everyone likes a winner, myself included. In today's sports, unfortunately, it's not so important how you win, only that you win. We live in a win-oriented society where losers are accorded little respect.

MASS: We've established that as a competitor, you are relatively unconcerned with the human or political values that spectators like to attribute to their opponents. There are, then, differences between opponents and spectators. You argue that on the field of competition, there are no significant differences between straight and gay opponents. But are there significant differences between straight and gay spectators?

HANDLEY: Yes. There are differences, I think, between gay and straight *responses* to sports competitions. The sexual motivation or quality that some would attribute to the wrestler, particularly the wrestler who is gay—a motivation I claim is *not* characteristic of competitive wrestlers, straight or gay—does, I think, influence many spectators. What the spectator sees on the mat may "show up" later in his sexual fantasies.

MASS: Does this quality have any influence on which opponent a gay spectator would tend to favor?

HANDLEY: Yes. The gay spectators more often prefer to see the rookie/underdog type get trounced. But not for the same reasons that many wrestlers (including me) may enjoy or prefer such matches. I'm not sure why this should be so. But I suspect that it may have something to do with the fact the one getting trounced, often the younger and more physically desirable, becomes analagous in fantasy to the one who has always been so resistant, so inaccessible in reality. The identification might be something like this: I've beaten the one I've always wanted into submission. He's now mine to do with as I please. I think this kind of direct, sexual fantasy identification often characterizes the gay spectator.

Another difference here is that the gay spectator is often strikingly less demonstrative about his loyalties. These differences wouldn't be very noticeable at a golf tournament where the atmosphere is so much more conservative. But at a wrestling match, the straight spectators scream and stomp in a way you'd almost never see among the gay spectators.

MASS: Why should this be so?

HANDLEY: Perhaps because the experience is related to sexual fantasy and therefore more personal for the gay spectator we're stereotyping. But I think there's a more persuasive explanation: that gay people, generally speaking, are simply more cautious about their behavior in public, especially their enthusiasms.

MASS: We were talking about your childhood interest in male-to-male physical competition. As you got older, how did this interest develop?

HANDLEY: Nothing much happened until I entered the service. The army decided that I should be trained as a military policeman. Part of this training included Judo, which I loved and at which I quickly excelled. Because a number of the men in my outfit liked to wrestle, there was a kind of natural transition between the two sports.

MASS: At what age did you first become aware of your attraction to men?

HANDLEY: From my earliest childhood. I can remember having this awareness back to my fifth year.

MASS: As you matured, did you ever connect your attraction to men with your interest in wrestling?

HANDLEY: Yes, but only at the spectator level. Occasionally I would be aware that an individual wrestler was sexy, perhaps in a particular hold or posture. The wrestling situation has touched my fantasy life. But my fantasy life has nothing to do with the actual toil, concentration and perseverance — the *discipline* — of my athletic endeavors.

Personally, I don't get aroused by pretending to be in physical competition with the man who turns me on.

MASS: Do most of your fellow club members feel as you do? That is, do you think their interest in wrestling is nonerotic?

HANDLEY: Since we don't have a person's sexual preference on our application forms, we certainly don't attempt to screen their minds. Some members may relate their wrestling to extra-competitive, erotic activities more than others. It's difficult to say. In any event, I'm convinced that these associations, even where they exist, have little or nothing to do with the actual nitty-gritty of developing and wielding competitive skills.

What you seem to be trying to get at is the similarity between physical competition and the dominance-submission aspects of the sexual act. In this sense, I think the key word in relating sex to wrestling is submission.

MASS: To your knowledge, have self-identified sadomasochists shown any kind of definable interest in combat sports?

HANDLEY: Not to my knowledge. I wouldn't expect them to have much interest because in true sadomasochism, physical combat is virtually always a matter of fantasy. The action is staged so that it can be controlled. What primarily distinguishes sadomasochism here is that its roles are predetermined. Dominance and submission are invariably decided upon beforehand rather than determined by combat.

MASS: So you think that in true S/M the roles don't shift?

HANDLEY: What you're getting at is the love and power the sadist and masochist exchange in allowing one another to fulfill fantasy roles. If the masochist submits to the sadist, it's more a gift than a conquest. That's what people mean when they say, as they often do, that the masochist invariably controls the action. The masochist, in other words, is also and actually the sadist. Even so, the partners in a sadomasochistic relationship, to my limited knowledge, generally prefer and invariably assume predetermined roles. They don't very often alternate these external roles, whatever shifts may be taking place at subtle psychological levels.

MASS: Do you think it's a truism that the greater the resistance of your opponent, the greater your satisfaction (your sense of triumph, your pleasure) in his submission?

HANDLEY: Yes. The more effort you put into anything, the greater your satisfaction. Whether you've "won" or "lost."

FIVE INTERVIEWS FROM THE FIRST TWO YEARS OF THE AIDS EPIDEMIC (1981-1983)

[Ed. note: At the conclusion of my interview with him, John Money defined the sexual revolution as "a great tide of history" that was spawned by the effectiveness and accessibility of modern birth control technology and planning and that has welled with such interrelated developments as the evolution of civil liberties for women, children and sexually variant persons, the movement for sex education and the control of sexually transmitted diseases (STDs). There can be little doubt that this has been a true, trans-cultural revolution, like the industrial revolution, bigger and more important than any of the countless, recurrent STD epidemics it promised to alleviate, no matter how serious in time or place.

As the various STD epidemics of the 1970s did grow more serious, however, it became increasingly clear that the theorists of the sexual revolution—from Wilhelm Reich in 1936 to John Money in 1980—had not articulated and probably never anticipated just how elusive the control of STDs would actually prove to be. Even with the advent of new and very effective treatments for syphilis and gonorrhea, these two most prominent STDs in recorded history continued to be sporadically epidemic, especially in minority and underserved populations. And now, alongside them, among sexually active heterosexuals and bisexuals as well as among sexually active gay men, there were a number of other STD epidemics. In the United States, herpes, hepatitis B and amebiasis were the most serious and prevalent of these other disease outbreaks during the decade that preceded the first reports of the AIDS epidemic in 1981.

The problem of STDs turned out to be more serious than anyone had anticipated. In 1981 as today, however, it seemed important not to abandon the affirmations of sexual knowledge, freedom and fulfillment that were such fundamental tenets of the sexual revolution, as Money talked about it. Quite the contrary. In the *long range* preventive medicine of AIDS and other STDs, upholding the need for sex-positive sex education, reproductive freedom of choice, antidiscrimination legislation and sex (and STD) research seemed to be just as important as minimizing risk behaviors, the only other preventive measure we've had in the absence of a cure and/or vaccine.

It was with this viewpoint that I undertook the depressing task of informing the gay community and indirectly (I hoped, somehow) the world at large, of the very serious reality of the newest STD, AIDS. STD research, education and services had been going on in the gay community under the auspices of a small, dedicated group of mostly gay and lesbian physicians and other health care professionals for nearly a decade, but no physician had ever written regularly for the gay press. Nor was there, at the time of the first reports of Kaposi's sarcoma and *pneumocystis carinii* pneumonia, any regular coverage of gay and lesbian health issues in the gay press. In 1981 I became that physician and began that regular coverage. And with the appearance of the article from which the interviews with Drs. Friedman-Kien and Mildvan were taken, which was the first feature article on the epidemic to appear in any press, I became the first reporter to cover the AIDS epidemic on a regular basis. In 1981 I also became a co-founder of Gay Men's Health Crisis and a co-vice president, with Barbara Starrett, of New York Physicians For Human Rights (NYPHR). My coverage of the epidemic and my work for GMHC and NYPHR continued until the spring of 1983, when I was hospitalized with a major depression.

Predictably, news of the epidemic created factions of every outlook within the gay community. Generally speaking, these factions divided into two camps. In addition to Larry Kramer's, the most prominent voices on the "right" (politically conservative or reactionary) side of the issues — in the sense of indicting gay promiscuity as *the* cause of the new diseases — were those of Dr. Joseph Sonnabend, one of a handful of physicians in New York who were known within the community to be gay and whose practices were

mostly devoted to treating gay men with STDs, and two of Sonnabend's patients, Michael Callen and Richard Berkowitz. Unlike
Sonnabend, Callen and *New York Native* publisher Charles Ortleb,
however, Larry Kramer never became deeply, personally committed to a particular viewpoint about the precise cause(s) of AIDS;
that is, about whether the epidemic was actually being caused by a
single agent (in which case promiscuity was a very serious but secondary issue), or by multiple agents and infections (in which case
promiscuity, rather than the agent, became the overriding issue).
By contrast, Sonnabend, Callen and Berkowitz were consistently
outspoken in their certainty that "promiscuity," as opposed to "the
killer-virus theory," as they frequently referred to it, was the causative factor. As Callen and Berkowitz explained in a communiqué
in 1983, "It is the killer-virus theory which raises the specter of
quarantine and which permits blood donor programs to stigmatize
all gay men and all members of the affected groups with 'bad blood'
status. . . . Those who fear linking promiscuity with the present
epidemic should consider the far more dangerous implication already circulating in the national media: that gay men are carrying
and spreading a fatal, cancer-causing virus."

The same communiqué concluded that "While we cannot afford
to close our minds to any possibility, we must proceed with great
caution before allowing any one particular theory to eclipse all others in discussions; and we must remain mindful of the political consequences which would result from a premature endorsement of a
theory which subsequently may be proven to be incorrect." In treating the single agent hypothesis as "the killer virus theory" rather
than as a likely explanation independent of political consequences,
Callen and Berkowitz (and Sonnabend with them), it seemed to me,
were not really following their own excellent advice. Although I
was increasingly convinced that a single, transmissible agent, probably a virus like hepatitis B, was the primary etiologic agent in
AIDS, I can now see, in retrospect, that some of the earliest risk-
reduction recommendations I prepared endorsed this communiqué's
conclusion more wholeheartedly than they should have; that is, with
too much of the kind of "great caution" Callen and Berkowitz were
talking about.

In the risk reduction guidelines we published in the second *Newsletter* of Gay Men's Health Crisis (January 1982), there was a sepa-

rate question and answer called "Is AIDS caused by a single infectious agent or by multiple factors?" that gave equal credibility to both theories and sensibly concluded that:

> in each of the major theories — single agent vs. multiple factors — AIDS is believed to be caused, to a greater or lesser degree, by infectious processes. All theories thus agree that the greatest risk factors for AIDS are sexual contacts with many different gay or bisexual male partners, and the use of shared needles for the injection of drugs.

And in answer to the question "How can the risk of AIDS be lowered?" I wrote:

> Although no *conclusive* evidence exists, so far as we know, to lay *direct* blame on any infectious agent, drug, activity, place of residence or other factor as the cause or causes of AIDS, virtually all leading observers currently believe that the greatest risk factors for AIDS are: (1) sexual intimacy with many different gay or bisexual male partners and (2) the use of shared needles for the injection of drugs.
>
> Physicians are currently advising their gay patients, especially those who live in urban centers with large gay communities, to limit their sexual activity by having fewer partners and by selecting partners who are known to be in good health and who are themselves limiting the number of different partners with whom they have sex. One implication of this information at the present time is that, apart from abstinence, monogamy represents the lowest risk potential. It is the increasing number of *different* sexual partners, not sex itself, that apparently increases the risk of developing AIDS.
>
> If you are known to be immunodeficient, you should protect yourself and others by abstaining from sexual contact with new partners until you are advised otherwise by a knowledgeable health care provider.

What's wrong with these questions and answers and recommendations is what they don't say. After giving all due to the promiscuity/multiple factors theories and theorists, what these conclusions and recommendations *might* have said was something like the following (based on the information we did have at that time — winter 1982):

> We don't yet know what's causing AIDS, whether it's one disease or several different diseases, whether it's caused by a single agent or multiple factors. UNTIL WE DO KNOW WHAT CAUSES AIDS, however, it seems wise to err on the side of caution and CEASE ANY AND ALL SEXUAL OR OTHER INTIMATE CONTACT that might result in the transmission of a causative agent.

If I really believed in the single-agent-plus-cofactors hypothesis — which I did from the earliest months, albeit insecurely, like every other physician and researcher who favored this hypothesis during that period — why didn't I simply urge everyone to stop having sex altogether, as Larry Kramer wanted us to do? Why didn't I insist on a recommendation like the hypothetical example above?

At the time, such an approach seemed a lot more than sex negative or excessive or simply a matter of giving too much credibility to a theory that might later be proven to be incorrect. It seemed very dangerous in the sense of risking panic, a complete loss of credibility — if we turned out to be wrong — in the sexually active community we most needed to reach. Worse, there was the specter of Draconian public responses and public health measures against a community that was without protection of its civil liberties and that would almost certainly just be driven further underground during a period when ultraconservative forces were sweeping the country. There was much talk of concentration camps, which were in fact eventually set up in Cuba and openly endorsed on propositions in the United States. In retrospect, would the possible saving of lives, even hundreds or thousands of lives, have been well worth the price of civil liberties? In retrospect, it may seem relatively easy to say yes.

For me, the bottom line wasn't political, but scientific — what we knew with relative certainty versus what we didn't know with any certainty at all, and sounding the alarm for every gay man to instantly "stop having sex" — any and all intimate contact with any and all other persons — seemed much too big and vague a step in view of the limited information we had. In any event, I wasn't a public health official, nor was I an epidemiologist, virologist or infectious disease specialist. Much more important than my thinking or Kramer's, it seemed to me, was the fact that no federal or local health officers or other leading observers of the epidemic were making such sweeping recommendations. Dr. James Curran, who headed the AIDS Task Force of the Centers for Disease Control (CDC), wasn't. Nor was Dr. Dan William, who was considered to be a relatively conservative gay community health expert. Nor, publicly, were Drs. Alvin Friedman-Kien or Linda Laubenstein. Nor was New York City Health Commissioner Dr. David Sencer. Not even Callen, Berkowitz and Sonnabend were recommending that everyone "stop having sex." No such guidelines were being published in the *Morbidity and Mortality Weekly Report* (MMWR), or even in any of the leading medical journals. The only explicit recommendation we received from any organization of health care professionals we immediately published in leaflets and, in large print and boldface, at the conclusion of our risk-reduction recommendations, quoted above, in that second GMHC *Newsletter*:

RECOMMENDATION—WHAT YOU CAN DO
(This recommendation is made by New York Physicians for Human Rights—the organization of 175 gay doctors in New York, and also by the New York City Department of Health.)

We don't yet know what causes AIDS.
Until we do:

CUT DOWN THE NUMBER OF DIFFERENT MEN YOU HAVE SEX WITH. PARTICULARLY WITH THE MEN WHO ALSO HAVE MANY DIFFERENT PARTNERS.

Gradually, over time, our "minimum risk," then "safe sex," then "safer sex" guidelines became increasingly specific, based on the accumulation of reliable data, and even included a boldface warning that "AS SEXUAL EXCITEMENT INCREASES, SO MAY DISINHIBITION." Before late 1983, however, the epidemiology was such that no leading health care officer would state publicly that he or she believed that the disease was transmissible by a single sexual encounter, and no one was publicly saying that gay men should stop having sex altogether, except Larry Kramer and a fictional character in his 1984 play, *The Normal Heart*, named Dr. Emma Brookner.

In Act One of *The Normal Heart*, Ned Weeks asks Dr. Brookner "What is it exactly you're trying to get me to do?" To which she replies, "Tell gay men to stop having sex." Even with the very first reports of the epidemic, which made it clear that this disease was probably not airborne or otherwise casually transmissible, however, the issue wasn't whether or not to tell gay men to stop having sex but *exactly what* to tell them to stop doing. Should the new pro-scriptions include "wet" kissing? Protected sexual intercourse? Frottage? "Stop Having Sex" (Just Say No) was just as unaccep-tably general and vague a recommendation then as it is today. From the beginning, there were a lot of intelligent, decent and extremely concerned members of the gay community who wanted to know specifics, who wanted to do the right things and urge others to do the same, though you could never imagine that such persons existed from Ned's generalizations about the gay community in the play. In Act One, for example, he says "Dr. Brookner, nobody with a brain gets involved in gay politics. . . . It's filled with the great unwashed radicals of any counterculture. . . . Do you realize that you are talking about millions of men who have singled out promiscuity to be their principal political agenda, the one they'd die before aban-doning?"

Throughout his career, Larry Kramer has used hyperbole for ar-tistic as well as political purposes and often with great success. In today's perspective, there can be no doubt that Larry Kramer is not only *the* great hero of the AIDS epidemic, but also one of the most charismatic and important leaders in the history of the gay liberation movement and of our time. Throughout the epidemic, Kramer, who was the principal and spiritual founder of both Gay Men's Health Crisis and The AIDS Coalition To Unleash Power (ACT UP), has remained a friend, mentor and ally. But Larry was also on the "right" side of these issues, in the sense of blaming gay promiscu-ity — a word I avoided more than I should have because of its vague-ness and exploitability — for an epidemic that was probably caused by a virus like hepatitis B and that involved a rapidly growing num-ber of heterosexuals who weren't promiscuous.

Gay culpability (as opposed to responsibility) became a real issue of contention between us. For example, I was initially, defensively uncomfortable with the name Gay Men's Health Crisis. Throughout history, syphilis had been variously labeled "the Jewish disease," "the Spanish disease," etc., depending on which group seemed to be carrying or otherwise causing it. AIDS was probably the same thing, it seemed to me — an STD that was prominent among sexually active gay men in urban centers in America in the 1980s but otherwise wasn't any more a "gay disease" than syphilis was a "Jewish disease." On the other hand, I also recognized that there were some very real political advantages to designating this crisis as ours (which it certainly was) and to designating our organization and its achievements as "gay," so I supported this nomenclature. Thus far, I believe the disadvantages of the name GMHC contributing to the stigma of AIDS as a disease of gay men have been substantially outweighed by advantages in community affirmation and respect.

As Larry Kramer saw it, the gay community had caused the epidemic and was responsible for it. In his hyperbolic analysis, not just a subset of urban gays but the entire gay community was immature, sex-obsessed, promiscuous and pathetic. "We don't deserve our civil rights," he told the *New York Times*. "We have not fought for them." As many in the community read it, he was right in at least one sense. Prior to the AIDS epidemic, *Larry* had never been a member of a gay organization or participated in any of the gay community's demonstrations or other battles for civil rights. Unlike a growing (if still pathetically small and hopelessly inadequate) number of self-affirming lesbian and gay community participants, *Larry* wasn't out there fighting for *anybody's* civil rights.

The fledgling community, as it existed then, was extremely distrustful of Larry, whose commercially successful novel, *Faggots*, admired and quoted by homophobic enemies like Midge Decter and discussed on national television, was seen as a devastating betrayal of the gay liberation movement. As a gay rights worker in Chicago put it, "It would be as if James Baldwin were writing what was expected to be the definitive novel of emerging black consciousness in the early '60s, a book that would finally and for the first time tell a large, commercial public that black is beautiful, and the novel turned out to be a black comedy about welfare chiselers along the Mississippi and was entitled *Niggers*."

I confided this reaction of the gay rights worker in Chicago to another gay friend who disagreed. An English professor whose domestic life with a long-term lover and an adopted son many heterosexuals might emulate for its maturity, wholesomeness and stability, he had enjoyed *Faggots*, which he had deconstructed as "really very sweet." When I asked him what he meant, he said something like this: "The whole book is based on a naive, childlike assumption of the relative maturity, wholesomeness and stability of heterosexuality and monogamy. The sweetness, poignancy, and often unintentional humor of *Faggots* lie in this belief in the goodness of straight grownups and traditional marriage. There's no consciousness that these were the same grownups in the same traditional marriages who had tormented Larry throughout his childhood for being a sissy."

Larry often pointed out that the so-called "gay community" wasn't a real community at all. But whatever it was, this community's reaction to *Faggots* was one of angry and almost unanimous outrage, not because it couldn't take any criticism (though in those days it couldn't take much) or because there wasn't truth in *Faggots*. Nor was it because *Faggots* didn't reveal talent. (Personally, I thought isolated passages of *Faggots* contained some of the most powerful and stylistically impressive writing, bar none, I had ever read.) The community was offended by *Faggots* because, unlike Andrew Holleran's *Dancer From The Dance*, which was also critical of gay life but much better received, *Faggots* seemed filled with and motivated by vindictive hatred of the gay community (even if it was possible to interpret that hatred, as I did, as the reaction-formation of rejected love). Unlike *Dancer*, *Faggots* seemed to be yet another altogether negative portrayal, filled with caricatures, of a community whose fragile organizations were all founded on the hope of finally beginning to change these pervasive, relentless stereotypes. The gay and lesbian community understood that because Larry was nationally known as the co-producer and screenwriter of the highly acclaimed, Academy Award-winning film, *Women in Love*, *Faggots* was likely to be more widely read and more likely to have negative political consequences than *Dancer*. Finally, as had always been the case with the most negative of these attacks on gay life, *Faggots* had come from *outside* the community, from someone who — again, unlike Holleran — had never been known to participate in community endeavors. To the gay and lesbian community, especially in New York, where Larry lived, it was clear that what Larry so bitterly complained was missing from gay life — maturity, stability, individual and collective responsibility — in *Faggots* wasn't missing from the aggregate community's life nearly so conspicuously as from Larry's own.

During those first few months, there was one enormous difference between the factions on the far "right" (gay promiscuity is *the* cause of this plague, our just desserts), of which Kramer's and Callen's were the loudest, and those on the far "left" (to take the epidemic seriously is homophobic), like Michael Lynch, a writer for *The Body Politic*: Kramer, Callen and Berkowitz took leadership positions in the earliest community efforts to raise money and otherwise help out. From the beginning, it was clear that these people cared very deeply, whatever their "motivation." (In Larry's case, everyone I knew suspected that the intensity of his involvement, contrasting as it did with his noninvolvement in any other past or concurrent gay community crisis, was a way of saying *Itold-yaso* to the community that had rejected *Faggots*.) In real contrast, there were no prominent voices, early on, even from the more moderate "left" — from those who acknowledged the gravity of the health crisis and got involved but were reluctant to renounce, without qualification, "the sexual revolution" — except those of Edmund White and my own.

I offered my "Basic Questions and Answers About AIDS," which had appeared in the first two newsletters of Gay Men's Health Crisis, the organization I co-founded with Larry, Paul Popham, Nathan Fain, Paul Rapoport and Edmund White, to *The Village Voice*, *The Body Politic* and *Gay Community News*, as well as *The Adovcate*, but none of their editors thought it important enough to run. Eventually, *The Advocate* began its own initially sporadic coverage. (Most of these pieces were by Nathan Fain, who covered the epidemic longer than any other reporter except Randy Shilts. Fain died from complications of AIDS in late spring, 1987.) Months before they ever published any clear, educational information, however, *Gay Community News* and *The Body Politic* ran angry denunciations of the homophobic white middle-class male panic-mongers (Larry Kramer, Nathan Fain, Dan William and I were singled out, among others) in New York who were trying to return to the medical model of homosexuality-is-a-sickness by making such a fuss about this so-called new epidemic, which hadn't even caused the tiniest fraction of deaths that result annually from auto accidents or cigarette smoking or alcoholism.

I answered these critics in letters that were published in *Gay Community News*, *The Body Politic* and *The Advocate*, and later in a piece in the *Native* (January 17, 1983) called "The Case Against Panic." Here, I tried to defend my "centrist" position, to show with examples how it's possible to be highly aware and critical of pseudoscience and homophobia throughout the history of medicine and science, while at the same time respecting that, whatever the political obstacles, our understanding and control of the epidemic must eventually come from within mainstream medicine and science. That is, your doctor may be homophobic and the health care system he works within may be a nightmare, but the penicillin he's recommending for your case of gonorrhea is nonetheless the most effective treatment there is. It's him you'd go to for your case of "the clap," not a faith healer, even if that faith healer (like today's Louise Hay) is ostensibly a lot less homophobic and more politically acceptable, though not cheaper, than your doctor. (Of course, in the absence of a cure like penicillin, the situation *can* be reversed. That is, the homophobic doctor can do more damage than the faith healer.) "I have had to be the messenger with the bad news," I concluded in "The Case Against Panic." "Will better messengers make the news better? Perhaps, but there aren't many instances in which no messengers would be better than imperfect ones."

Unlike *Gay Community News* and *The Body Politic* prior to 1983, *The Village Voice* finally evinced some interest in what was happening and commissioned me to do a piece. From the beginning, *Voice* feature columnist Arthur Bell had known how serious the epidemic was—Larry Kramer and I spoke to him daily about it—but he thought the *Voice* should wait a while, until more information was available, before doing any sort of feature. As time passed, Arthur would mention the GMHC benefits and other items pertaining to the epidemic in his weekly column, but he wasn't getting very involved, not because he didn't care but because there was something else going on with Arthur. He was dying of complications of diabetes. By the time I finally got the commission from the *Voice*, Arthur was already working on a major piece about his impending blindness (and tacitly, his impending death) called "Slow Fade To Black." As important as the epidemic clearly was, and even though he began to fear that the cause of his deteriorating health might actually turn out to be "the gay cancer," as he was the first to call it in his column in the *Voice*, he would not divert his primary energies from what he probably knew, at some level of consciousness, might be the last major work of his life. As a result, the commission from the *Voice*, and Arthur's willingness to help me with it, didn't come until the winter of 1982, much later than it should have.

Arthur had always felt that my writing was too academic, too "highbrow." As I worked on the commission, he gave me some very sound advice, but the intensity of some of his criticism seemed to be coming from elsewhere. "You've got to write so that even someone as dumb and unintellectual as me can understand it," he'd shriek, as he carved giant X's across page after page of my manuscript. Eventually, we got the piece into a shape that he reassured me he found comprehensible and powerful, if still a bit too academic in spots for his tastes, and submitted it to senior editor Karen Durbin. Even though we were already into the spring of 1982, this piece, which was entitled "The Most Important New Public Health Problem in the United States," would have been the first feature piece on the epidemic to appear in the mainstream press in New York (Donald Drake had already written several big pieces in the *Philadelphia Enquirer*). It opened as follows:

> It hasn't gone away. On the contrary, federal health officers began describing it as epidemic in December. By that time, it had claimed more lives than the combined tolls of toxic shock syndrome and Legionnaire's disease; today it is being widely recognized as "the most important new public health problem in the United States."

More than three weeks after submitting it, Karen Durbin finally returned my calls. The decision was: "It's not a *Voice* piece." When I pleaded that it was extremely important that the information contained in the piece get to the public, no matter what the form or "style" or under whose byline, there was dead silence at the other end of the phone. I called my friend, *Voice* senior editor Richard Goldstein who blamed his editor-in-chief, David Schneiderman, for the decision, which Goldstein claimed he was not involved in and had no influence to change. The same half-hearted disclaimer came from Arthur. The *New York Native* ran the piece intact in their next issue under the front page, banner headline "The Epidemic Continues" (March 29, 1982). It would be months before *The Village Voice*, the *New York Times* or any other mainstream New York publication would run a major piece that would prominently feature essential, educational information for the general public about the epidemic.

In addition to its emphasis on the nuts and bolts—the basic information, numbers and recommendations—of what was happening, "The Epidemic Continues" tried to engage larger questions of what the epidemic meant. In doing so, it presented a concept I felt strongly about, a concept that, to this day, virtually no one else has directly promoted, neither in the gay press nor in the mainstream press: the insistence that civil liberties legislation for gay and lesbian persons—legislation that would include affirmation of gay and lesbian domestic partnerships—must be an essential consideration in the long range preventive medicine of AIDS and other STDs. "In what has to be the definitive example of Catch-22," I argued in the piece the *Voice* rejected, "gay people are denied the theological, social and legal opportunities to establish the very relationships they are regularly being punished and stigmatized for not having." In other words, you can't say to a population, on the one hand, that the most important risk-reduction recommendation we have is to try to establish or maintain a monogamous relationship with a low risk partner, and on the other, to tell that population that it must be denied the legal and cultural means to do so because its members have heretofore appeared to be promiscuous and incapable of establishing such relationships.

Whatever its deficiencies, most of my writing on the epidemic, in those first weeks and months—as well as today, in the GMHC publication I prepared from "Basic Questions and Answers About AIDS," and which I periodically revise, called *Medical Answers About AIDS*—was concerned with reporting the facts about the epidemic as accurately as possible, but in a sex-affirmative context.

The following question and answer, I think, exemplify this writing. They follow the risk-reduction recommendations quoted above in the second GMHC *Newsletter* (1/83):

> Q: What can be done about feelings of guilt, panic, 'sin' and fear in relation to this epidemic?
> A: Do not waste valuable energies on these negative reactions to sex. Now more than ever, ignorance, arrogance and hypocrisy about sex are to be repudiated. If anything, be even more genuinely affirmative about your sexuality. At the same time, you can recognize without contradiction that we are experiencing a public health emergency in the form of a serious, apparently new disease that appears to be sexually transmitted. This, on top of the epidemic spread of too many other sexually transmitted diseases. There's nothing "immoral," or "sinful" about celebrating your enjoyment of swimming in the ocean. If, on the other hand, your favorite beaches have posted undertow or oil spill warnings, it is prudent to avoid swimming in those areas as long as the signs are up. Like heterosexual men and women who are sexually active with many different partners, many gay men are having to face certain health risks that are increasingly associated with our sexual or lifestyle preferences. In the interest of public health, it is important to know what those risks are and how they can be minimized.

That first article in the *Native* ("Cancer In The Gay Community," July 27, 1981) from which the interviews with Drs. Friedman-Kien and Mildvan are excerpted, was accompanied by a second feature article, one I had been working on at the time of the first CDC reports of Kaposi's sarcoma and *pneumocystis carinii* pneumonia outbreaks in Los Angeles and New York. It was entitled "Chemical Castration" and dealt with the growing use of "anti-sex drive medication" (antiandrogen therapy, mostly medroxyprogesterone acetate), alongside such other forms of aversion therapy as shock treatments, to treat suddenly, exponentially growing numbers of "sex offenders." Predictably, this Orwellian strategem was being carried out with the collusion of mainstream American psychiatry. A large percentage of these persons, who were being characterized as "homosexual pedophiles" with "unconventional sexual desires," were apparently ordinary gay men who had been entrapped with undercover teenage hustlers. The struggle with medicine and psychiatry to depathologize homosexuality remained in the forefront of concerns as the epidemic, and my coverage of it, unfolded.]

Alvin Friedman-Kien

Dr. Alvin Friedman-Kien is professor of Dermatology and Microbiology at New York University Medical Center. He is the Principal Investigator of the *Morbidity and Mortality Weekly Report* study from the Federal Centers for Disease Control in Atlanta (July 3, 1981), "Kaposi's Sarcoma and Pneumocystis Pneumonia among Homosexual Men In New York City and California" [on which the first mainstream media news report of the epidemic was based — "Rare Cancer Identified in Homosexuals" by Lawrence K. Altman in the *New York Times*, July 5, 1981].

MASS: How does the KS that is being described among urban homosexual males differ from the types of KS observed among other groups?

FRIEDMAN-KIEN: There is an indolent type of KS that occurs in elderly males, usually of Jewish or Mediterranean extraction. The lesions in these patients are characteristically found on the lower extremities. Patient survival is usually eight to thirteen years. The KS that we've been seeing in young adult male homosexuals is most similar to the type we've observed in patients receiving immunosuppressive therapy for kidney transplants and other diseases like lupus. It also shares some features with the other type of KS — an often fulminantly malignant variety that is endemic to young black males (who are not, incidentally, homosexual) in Equatorial Africa (Uganda).

MASS: Why should immunosuppression be such a prominent feature in these cases?

FRIEDMAN-KEIN: In all of the homosexuals with KS that we've studied, there has been direct proof of, or strong evidence to suggest, past or active infection with CMV. CMV not only produces infection; it has also been shown to have an immunosuppressive effect on the host. Another cause of immunosuppression is repeated bouts of other infections—viruses, bacteria, parasites. Most (but not all) of the homosexuals in our study admitted to having had multiple sexual encounters with different partners, and to having had a variety of past infections—amebiasis, giardiasis, hepatitis, CMV, HSV (CMV, incidentally, is a member of the Herpes family of viruses), gonorrhea and syphilis most commonly among them. There was a recent study in the *Journal of Infectious Diseases*, based on statistics from a VD clinic in San Francisco, that demonstrated much higher CMV [levels] among gay than among control group males. What this means, it should be stressed, is that sexual frequency with a multiplicity of partners, rather than homosexuality per se, may be a risk factor in the transmission of CMV and, ultimately, in the acquiring of KS. Most of our patients, in fact, did report having had multiple sexual encounters on a given occasion— say, in a bathhouse—up to four times a month or more.

MASS: Was there any evidence that any of the individuals afflicted with KS had had contact with one another?

FRIEDMAN-KIEN: No.

MASS: Besides CMV, what are some other causes of immunosuppression that might be operating in these cases?

FRIEDMAN-KIEN: There's some evidence from animal studies that nitrite derivatives such as amyl or butyl nitrite may be immunosuppressive. But this hasn't been adequately researched. We just don't know what the long-term effects of some of these drugs are. And if there were carcinogenic or immunosuppressive characteristics, they might be due to the impurities in a specific brand rather than to the drug itself. Even if the nitrites are shown to be immunosuppressive, however, they would be only part of the greater immunosuppression that we know is caused by CMV and also by repeated bouts with the more common infections mentioned earlier. As you know, cancer cells are occasionally produced in all individuals. In those with healthy immune systems, these cells are quickly destroyed. In the others, the cancer may flourish. Suddenly, multiple tumors begin to appear all over the body. This is a different process from metastatic spread, where cells from a primary tumor spread via the bloodstream and lymph systems.

MASS: What do you make of the frequent history of amebiasis among the patients in your study?

FRIEDMAN-KIEN: Most of these patients have actually suffered *repeated* bouts of amebiasis and have been treated with a variety of medications, including flagyl, humatin and diodoquin. As you may recall, flagyl has been accused of being carcinogenic, specifically of causing hepatomas (cancers of the liver). It's now being used less and less, but *many* of our patients were in fact treated for their episodes of amebiasis with flagyl. Flagyl, incidentally, is structurally similar to Immuran, which is an immunosuppressive agent.

MASS: Some immunosuppressive steroids are used by bodybuilders. Was there any evidence of steroid use among the KS victims [*sic*] you studied?

[Ed. note: Like everybody else, including persons with AIDS (PWA's), I used the word "victim," prior to 1983. With the advent of the PWA movement, which rejected the term victim as a label of self-defeat, I respectfully abandoned the use of victim in any and all references to persons with AIDS.]

FRIEDMAN-KIEN: We never asked that question, but it's a good one. I'd have to say that it's my impression that most of these patients were not bodybuilding types.

MASS: If someone finds out he has KS, where should he go for treatment?

FRIEDMAN-KIEN: Right now, we're working on a protocol and are trying to determine the best treatment regimen, depending on the severity of the disease. Drs. Linda Laubenstein (an internist-hematologist) and Franco Muggia (Director of Oncology here at N.Y.U.) have developed the regimen we are currently using.

We feel it's wise for all patients in the area to be treated by the same team, in order to provide the best statistical analysis, treatment and follow-up. It's best to avoid shots in the dark. One of our patients went to Houston. Ironically, Houston then called us to find out what we were using for treatment!

The drugs we are using include vincristine, vinblastine, Adriamycin, as well as an experimental drug that, interestingly enough, is a derivative of pdophyllin (which is used to treat anal warts) and has been especially effective in treating tumors of the skin. Thus far, several patients who have had this treatment are currently in remission.

MASS: What can we say about prognosis?

FRIEDMAN-KIEN: It depends on how quickly the patients get to us and how quickly they get treated. Some patients have gone into total remission. Nine have died. Beyond this, the only thing we can say is that at this time it should be considered a potentially fatal disease.

MASS: What can you tell us about the experimental uses of Interferon in these cases?

FRIEDMAN-KIEN: Interferon is totally experimental. As a virologist, I can tell you that its effectiveness with any tumors is inconclusive at best. It has been badly misused by many scientists in many institutions. I think extensive news hype raised a lot of false hopes. In fact, Interferon has been used to treat two KS patients, with no anti-tumor effect. I do not recommend the use of Interferon for this disease at this time.

MASS: How is the Centers for Disease Control planning to continue this investigation?

FRIEDMAN-KIEN: The CDC is trying to help as much as possible. They're sending out surveillance people, they've made their laboratories available, and they're alerting physicians around the country. They are trying to help and guide us in countless ways. I want to say that the CDC staff is a magnificent group of people with whom I'm proud to be associated. And I've never encountered even a hint of prejudice against homosexuals (or any other group) from them. Any of the epidemiologic studies they perform — on this disease or any others — are done with absolute confidentiality, protecting the individual from any possible public exposure.

MASS: If an individual location is believed to be a source of a disease, it could be declared a public health menace and shut down. Do you see any such developments for any gay establishments?

FRIEDMAN-KIEN: I don't think we can be sure until proper epidemiologic studies are completed. Not unless it could be shown that there were a specific communicable disease being spread from a specific location. The frequent sexual exposures that may take place at some baths or bars with back rooms are unquestionably a factor in venereal disease transmission. But the location itself is not the issue.

MASS: How would you advise the gay community to respond to this news? What can we do to help prevent, treat and better understand these phenomena?

FRIEDMAN-KIEN: Every gay male who suspects that he has KS or suspects that he is immunodeficient because of repeated bouts of various infections should be carefully examined by a physician. And make sure the physician is informed about KS! Here at the Skin Cancer Clinic of NYU Medical Center we have a large number of staff physicians who will be happy to evaluate any patients for suspicious skin lesions. We'd rather see them and say there's nothing wrong than not see them at all.

The sudden appearance of this disease suggests that it may be the beginning of a significant epidemic among the gay subpopulation. But it should be stressed that there's no reason to panic, to respond to this news with alarm. The situation appears to be under good control. The finest scientific and medical minds are working together to keep it that way.

There's even an optimistic perspective here. This unique emergence of this particular tumor in the gay subpopulation may give medical researchers the first clue as to the possible interrelationship between viruses and/or environmental factors as a cause of cancer.

[Ed. note: Boxed within the interview with Dr. Friedman-Kien was a plea for donations for "Kaposi's Sarcoma Research" at New York University Medical Center, c/o Dr. Friedman-Kien. This was the first public appeal for funding in connection with the AIDS epidemic, and, indirectly, the first appeal for the research, information and service foundation we decided, as of January 1982, to call Gay Men's Health Crisis.]

Donna Mildvan

[Ed. note: The following short interview with Dr. Mildvan begins with a discussion of amebiasis, which was the most serious STD epidemic in the gay community after hepatitis and prior to AIDS. At the time of the first reported cases of AIDS (at the time of this interview), the epidemic of amebiasis in urban gay communities in America was at its apex.]

Dr. Donna Mildvan is Chief of the Infectious Diseases Division of Beth Israel Medical Center and is Associate Professor of Clinical Medicine at the Mount Sinai School of Medicine. In her work with Dr. Dan William and other New York area physicians, Dr. Mildvan has helped the gay community to better understand the implications of infectious disease outbreaks. She is an authority on what has been called "the gay bowel syndrome" (*Emergency Medicine*, February 1978).

MASS: Before we talk about KS and PCP, I'd like to ask you about another recent (and ongoing) scourge of the gay community: amebiasis. In what ways is the amebiasis currently being seen among gay males in American urban centers different from that which has long been a global (and especially a third world) problem?
MILDVAN: The most striking difference is in the prevalence of the disease. That is, amebiasis appears to be much more frequent among gay males in certain urban centers than it is in the general population. Another difference is that among gay men, it appears to be a less severe disease than the fulminant amebiasis we see, for example, in Mexico. In the gay community, we haven't seen the hepatic abscesses and other extreme manifestations of the disease. What we are seeing among gay males is a spectrum of diarrheal illness, sometimes without any symptoms at all.
MASS: Why, then, should amebiasis be so difficult to treat?
MILDVAN: That brings us to a major point. The reason it has been

so difficult to treat is that, often, it is not the only organism causing symptoms in the gay males who have amebiasis. These patients may also have giardia, shigella, or other enteric pathogens. It has been my experience, and also Dan William's, that one must consider the strong possibility that there will be simultaneous or sequential infections in a given patient. Then there's the whole problem of reinfection.

MASS: Are there any foreseeable breakthroughs in the diagnosis and treatment of amebiasis?

MILDVAN: First, I think the most important thing to emphasize about amebiasis is the way it's transmitted. The most likely means of successful treatment will probably be to break the lines of transmission and to treat sexual partners. Formerly, amebiasis wasn't considered a sexually transmitted disease. Today, this is a critical consideration. So sexual partners should be tested and, when appropriate, treated. As for new drugs, I'm not aware of any important developments.

MASS: Why don't hosts build up immunity to this disease?

MILDVAN: The immunologic response to amebic invasion of tissue has not been well characterized. The role of immune mechanisms in the prevention or healing of amebic disease is unknown.

MASS: Why should immunosuppression be suspected in cases of PCP but not in cases of amebiasis?

MILDVAN: We don't know. That's one of the exquisitely peculiar aspects of this puzzle.

MASS: If someone has a chest cold, how do they know it's not PCP?

MILDVAN: PCP is a severe, fulminating pneumonia. With PCP, symptoms of shortness of breath, high fevers and weakness are very striking.

MASS: What are the implications of these infectious disease phenomena among gay men for the population at large?

MILDVAN: The higher prevalence of amebiasis among gay males has been known for some time. Thus far, a higher prevalence of this disease, as well as the other diseases we're talking about, has not, however, been documented in the general population.

MASS: In what ways would you guide the gay community in responding to this information?

MILDVAN: I'd emphasize the importance of staying informed. Up-to-date information must reach the gay community in order to be translated into the best patient care. The medical community has learned that it must work closely with the gay community in agreeing upon and planning the most effective strategies.

MASS: Although your group did not have KS patients, you did have some cases of PCP, which was reported — like amebiasis — to be a concommitant or past infection in a number of the KS cases. What are your thoughts on the interaction of these diseases?

MILDVAN: The immunosuppressive nature of CMV, a virus that has a prevalence of over 90 percent among gay males in New York City (as compared to a 50 percent prevalence among controls) should be mentioned. But why CMV should be causing such serious illness in a small group of individuals continues to be a subject for speculation. There could be a genetic predisposition or some other vulnerability among selected individuals. However, none of this explains why this should all be happening right now.

MASS: What do you think is the answer?

MILDVAN: I don't know. Dan William believes that it has to do with the bombardment, the clustering of a whole range of infectious diseases among these patients which may be exhausting their immunodefensive capacities. Perhaps this is happening in ways that are without historical precedent. Homosexuality may have been just as prevalent 20 years ago, but homosexuals may never have interacted with one another to the extent they now do. Likewise, they may never before have experienced this confluence, this sequence, of so many infectious diseases. That's what's unique. But all of this — Dan's thinking as well as mine — is still speculative.

Donald Krintzman

[Ed. note: In this piece for the *New York Native*, which was entitled "Cancer as Metaphor," Donald Krintzman became the first PWA (person with AIDS) to be interviewed in any press. (At that time, the term AIDS did not exist and there was no certainty that persons with KS, like Donald, had the same underlying disease as persons with PCP.) Donald Krintzman was a fundraising executive with the Joffrey Ballet. His lover, Paul Rapoport, who died of AIDS in 1987, was a co-founder of Gay Men's Health Crisis.]

What does it feel like to be young, attractive and gay, to have a lover and a successful career—and to suddenly face a potentially fatal cancer? To find out, Lawrence Mass, M.D., interviewed one of the nearly 40 gay male Kaposi's sarcoma victims [*sic*] recently diagnosed in the New York City area.

MASS: How did you find out that you have cancer?
KRINTZMAN: Back in January I noticed a lump in my neck. When it didn't go away after a week or so, I made an appointment with my internist. At that time, I had no other symptoms.
MASS: What was the diagnosis?
KRINTZMAN: "A swollen lymph gland . . . probably a virus . . . in any event, nothing worry about." Well, it persisted. Finally, in June, I decided to get another opinion. I went to [a major Manhattan medical center] where they took a biopsy. The diagnosis was Kaposi's sarcoma.
MASS: Had you ever heard of it?
KRINTZMAN: A friend from Fire Island had been suffering from a rare cancer which they eventually said was Kaposi's. I noted the coincidence but didn't think much about it at the time. Then I saw the article in the *New York Times*.
MASS: What was your reaction?
KRINTZMAN: Actually, my first, my strongest reaction was to the

character of the article itself. I thought it was negatively edged. It raised a lot of questions in ways that seemed prematurely insinuative, given the few facts available. If you're going to talk about a disease that appears to have sociological associations or implications, I think it's crucial that you be real clear about your terms.

MASS: But if so little is known, how much clarity can there be?

KRINTZMAN: My point is that there's so much room for hysteria in a situation like this. I think it's incumbent upon a leading periodical like the *Times* to take a leadership role in directing appropriate concerns while discouraging unwarranted alarm.

MASS: Exactly how might the *Times* report have been different?

KRINTZMAN: There might have been some acknowledgment of New York's gay community—one of the city's larger constituencies and one of the *Times'* larger readerships. There might have been some appeal for calm, perhaps even a suggestion of compassion. No gay spokespersons were interviewed for their responses. Nor were any of the patients. The fact that this news tragically postscripted gay pride celebrations, that it followed a number of setbacks gay people have suffered in their quest for fundamental civil liberties, were affirmative observations that could have been expressed without violating journalistic neutrality.

[Ed. note: With characteristic insensitivity (or worse), the July 5 *Times* report by Lawrence Altman, "Rare Cancer Identified in Homosexuals," appeared opposite a 5 column "Sing out for Independence!" ad for Bloomingdale's. The ad was additionally and especially hurtful in view of yet another recent defeat of the New York City gay civil rights bill.]

MASS: Earlier, you said that the *Times* report seemed "prematurely insinuative." What were you referring to?

KRINTZMAN: Even though they didn't precisely state that all or most of the victims [*sic*] were promiscuous to the extremes that *were* stated, the implication was there. As one of the victims [*sic*], it made me feel terrible, as if I had been doing worse things than normal or respectable people do, as if I had gotten my just deserts. And that's just not the case. I've intermittently enjoyed recreational sex, just as I've occasionally taken drugs. But I also have a lover and I'm a fully employed, tax paying, law abiding contributor to society.

Look, if rimming makes you more likely to get hepatitis, OK. It's a risk. But going into the subway during the winter flu season, traveling to Mexico and eating the vegetables there, these are similarly risky. Taking a lot of sun increases your chances of getting skin cancer. Alcohol probably accounts for more diseases and death than any other single factor in human existence. Smoking causes lung cancer. Do you see my point? There's a fine line between fact and speculation that is not clearly identified as speculation, and judgment. I think it's going to be a real challenge to discuss these matters with true objectivity. But it's a challenge I believe we can all meet.

Let me ask you a question. Is this the first time a cancer has been linked with a venereal disease?

MASS: No. With the exception of breast cancer, cancer of the cervix has probably caused more female deaths than any other malignancy. More than 10,000 cases are reported each year in the United States alone. This cancer has a thoroughly documented association with the herpes simplex virus. Herpes, of course, is as much a venereal disease as syphilis and has for some years now been designated as epidemic among sexually active heterosexuals. It can also cause severe, sometimes fatal infections in the newborn of genitally infected mothers. Cancer of the cervix is more commonly observed among the lower socioeconomic classes. Does this mean that women from the lower strata of society are, generally speaking, less moral than those from the higher strata? Are the gay males who are getting these diseases, generally speaking, less moral than those who aren't? Does this, in turn, mean that gay people, generally speaking, are less moral than nongay people? The answer to these questions, in my opinion, is not a matter for speculation.

KRINTZMAN: I think it's important for gay people not to fall into the self-hating guilt trap that we, like other minorities, have always "fallen" into in the past. If certain sexual activities are more risky than others, then *that's* what should be initially dealt with, not hysterical speculations about the relationship between those activities and morality.

I may have the cancer, but I haven't the slightest doubt that I'm a lot more moral than many people, gay and straight, who have no diseases.

MASS: As a cancer patient, I'm sure you have many needs. First, you need to get well. You need to feel confidence in your physicians. As an intelligent person, you want to be persuaded that you are getting the most effective treatments available. What other needs do you feel?

KRINTZMAN: I think I'm speaking for my fellow patients when I say that we share a great need for psychological support, both at the individual and group levels. I think we KS patients urgently need to get together. We need to share our questions, our feelings and our pain.

MASS: You're getting at something I'd really like to ask you about: your new identity as a cancer patient. Is it as distinctive as your other identities—for example, gay, male, American, Jewish, New Yorker and so forth?

KRINTZMAN: Indeed. But I think my new identity as a cancer patient is less powerful than my new identity as a man who may be facing death. I've become very close with one of the other patients whose disease is more extensive. I really feel I understand what he's going through in a way that those who haven't been in this situation can't. Our communication has meant a lot to both of us. I'm sure it's going to have a positive influence on our getting well. Hope, the will to live, these are important aspects of the healing process. As more of us come together, the more positive that influence will be.

MASS: If you feel this way, why have you asked to remain anonymous?

KRINTZMAN: I have no qualms about having my name published. But right now, I need all my strength to fight this illness. I also want to join and help organize a support group of fellow patients. This is currently being pursued through hospital channels. At the same time, I just don't have the energy reserves to handle much else— phone calls from distant acquaintances, from community organizations or healthy people who want general information about KS.

[Ed. note: At Donald's funeral service in November 1981, none of the speakers, at least one of whom was gay, used the word gay or acknowledged that Donald was gay or that his lover was Paul Rapoport or that he had died of a disease that was decimating the gay community and that had already been characterized as the most serious epidemic disease in the U.S. since polio.]

MASS: In your most private thoughts, has this experience ever made you regret being gay?

KRINTZMAN: No. I've *thought* about it. I've once or twice fantasized what it would be like to be straight, to be surrounded during this period of such need by an idealized nuclear family. But I can't regret being gay any more than I can regret being Jewish, American or human. Gay is what I *am*!

MASS: What good do you think can come of all this?

KRINTZMAN: A lot. For myself, it's an opportunity to reevaluate my life, to identify which people and which things are truly important. It's also an issue that, I hope, will galvanize the gay community to reevaluate its priorities. My biggest fear is that gay people will perceive what's happened as a scourge of God, as punishment due, rather than as a disaster that has struck close to home. If we embrace the community concept, if we can engage our collective intelligence, courage and maturity, our emphasis will be on the overcoming rather than on the suffering of this disease. They're saying that the KS outbreak represents a unique opportunity to study the causes of cancer. Who knows? Perhaps these positively directed energies will help us, as members of the greater human community, to overcome all cancer.

In every person, gay or straight, there is both the child and the adult. My hope is that the adult present in everyone will respond affirmatively to this issue.

MASS: I've always been impressed, often bemused, by the Catch 22 situation that American society offers homosexuals. It says that because homosexuals are promiscuous, immature and incapable of forming stable relationships, they are therefore forbidden the legal, theological and social opportunities to establish them. What effect do you think a greater social sanctioning and integration of homosexual couplings would have on the stability of gay lives?

KRINTZMAN: It might have an effect, but I know you'll agree with me that change will have to come from within as well as from society. Certainly, the greater society is complicitous in many of the problems it accuses gay people of having. But gay people are going to have to demonstrate that they *want* more stability and more structure.

MASS: What I've often observed is that many of the straight people who decry promiscuity are equally contemptuous of gay love relationships that are monogamous. They don't draw distinctions.

KRINTZMAN: It seems to me you're talking about prejudice. We both know enough about prejudice to know it's irrational. But regardless of prejudice, gay people in America and across the world now have the option of responding to this epidemic in one of two ways. If it's seen as the scourge of God, it's certain to set back, to dismantle the many gains that have been achieved. On the other hand, if we act like adults — if the attitude is that these diseases have hit our community and we must do something about them — then I think the wonderful progress we've made in recent years will continue to evolve.

[Ed. note: Boxed within this interview was the first published call to action by Larry Kramer, which he asked me to edit. As edited by me, it was entitled ''A Personal Appeal From Larry Kramer'' and appeared as follows:

It's difficult to write this without sounding alarmist or too emotional or just plain scared.

If I had written this a month ago, I would have used the figure ''40.'' If I had written it last week, I would have needed ''80.'' Today I must tell you that 120 gay men in the United States — most of them here in New York — are suffering from an often lethal form of cancer called Kaposi's sarcoma or from a virulent form of pneumonia that may be associated with it. More than thirty have died.

By the time you read this, the necessary figures may be much higher.

The men who have been stricken don't appear to have done anything that many New York gay men haven't done at one time or another. We're appalled that this is happening to them and terrified that it could happen to us. It's easy to become frightened that one of the many things we've done or taken over the past years may be all that it takes for a cancer to grow from a tiny something or other that got in there who knows when from doing who knows what.

In four months, the number has risen to 120 of us stricken and 30 of us dead.

The majority of the Kaposi cases are being sent to at New York University Medical Center. The doctor who is most on top of this situation is Dr. Alvin Friedman-Kien. He and his staff are passionately determined to help take care of us and to find out what's going on here.

Money is desperately needed, both for their research, which is going on around the clock, and for the treatment and chemotherapy of many of the patients who have no money or medical insurance.

I hope you will write a check and get your friends to write one too. This is our disease and we must take care of each other and ourselves. We have often been a divided community in the past; I hope we can all get together on this emergency, undivided, cohesively, and with all the numbers we in so many ways possess.

Your check should be made payable to "New York University Medical Center." You may label it specifically "For Kaposi's Sarcoma." Please mail them to me, Larry Kramer, at 2 Fifth Avenue, New York, New York 10011.

Thank you.]

Dan William

At the international workshop on AID [*sic*] that was held at Mount Sinai Medical Center on July 13, presentations were given by three openly gay physicians: Drs. Roger Enlow, Dan William and myself.

[Ed. Note: This was actually the first international conference on AIDS. The new nomenclature — AIDS instead of AID — became official in the late fall of 1982. Because it gives such an authentic sense of the limitations of knowledge and vocabulary of the time, the usage of AID has been retained as it appeared in the original text of this interview and of my presentation to the conference.]

Enlow, who is assistant professor of medicine at Mount Sinai and an attending immunologist at Beth Israel Medical Center and the Hospital for Joint Diseases, summarized the findings of a study of young men with persistent lymphadenopathy (enlarged lymph nodes) and laboratory evidence of immune deficiency. Of 46 such patients who have been followed for periods ranging from five to fifteen months, five have developed Kaposi's sarcoma. Unfortunately, these data strengthen the hypothesis that persistent lymphadenopathy may be an important co-predictor of AID progression.

Enlow is a member of the National Gay Health and Education Foundation, Inc., and has been a regular physician volunteer at the St. Mark's Clinic. Working closely with his Beth Israel colleagues, Dr. Donna Mildvan and psychiatrist Dr. Stuart Nichols, he has been a leading interpreter of the current epidemic. Because of his special involvement in so many aspects of AID management, he was recently asked, together with NGTF co-founder Dr. Bruce Voeller, to corepresent the gay community in the special hearing on issues of blood banking and donor policies that took place on July 27 in Washington D.C. Gay political and health leaders had been concerned that new policy decisions might indirectly result in new stigmas for gay people. Responding to this threat, Manhattan internist and NGTF board member Dr. Terry Fonville quickly mobilized the ad-hoc task force on AID that elected to send Enlow and Voeller to Washington.

[Ed. note: As characterized in my report of the symposium in the *New York Native* (August 2, 1982), "A particularly disturbing question — a 'Pandora's Box,' as Dr. Dan William put it — was an inevitable consequence of this new information [about the first reported cases of AIDS in hemophiliacs]: Exactly how should the policies for screening and selecting blood donors be altered to exclude the new groups that have been characterized as especially susceptible to AID? Virginia Apuzzo, executive director of the Fund For Human Dignity, who attended the symposium, was among the first to point out that gay health and community representatives must take it upon themselves to advise their constituents on these important health matters. She emphasized, however, that we cannot risk a return to the bad old days of not so long ago, when a recurrently scapegoated minority could be sweepingly restigmatized for the taint of "bad blood." Apuzzo's concern is hardly overstated. At the symposium, one physician was overheard confiding to another that he would no longer dine in Manhattan restaurants because, as everybody knows, all New York waiters are gay."]

Enlow and Voeller apparently made quite an impact because they achieved exactly what they had set out to do. Emphasizing the need for more information about the exact nature of AID transmissibility, they influenced the assembly, which included the National Hemophiliac Foundation, NIH, NCI, FDA, CDC and other representatives, to indefinitely postpone making any major recommendations for policy change.

[Ed. Note: Back in New York, Enlow and Voeller worked with Apuzzo, Larry Kramer, Dan William, myself and other members of the ad-hoc group we had formed called The AIDS Network to immediately finalize and disseminate guidelines to the community urging any and all gay community persons who knew themselves to be at risk or who had reason to believe they might be, from donating blood. At that time, we were loathe—and I still believe our judgment was sound—to sanction any national or other official policy that would sweepingly exclude any and all persons who were known or believed to be homosexual.

As published in the *New York Native* (August 2, 1982), the following is the statement, alluded to in the opening paragraph of this interview, I presented to The First International Symposium on AID at Mount Sinai Medical Center in New York City. The subject and title of the statement is "Candidate Etiologies."

Three major categories of primary etiology have been explored: viruses, drugs and autoimmune mechanisms. But only that of viruses would seem able to provide a unitary hypothesis that could explain the sudden appearance of AID in a growing number of distinctive populations.

In the category of drugs, popular suspects have included nitrites, marijuana and intravenously injected narcotics.

Nitrites are unlikely to be the principal etiologic candidates for several reasons. First, nearly a third of the victims claim never to have used these drugs. Second, many individuals who have used nitrites, even in substantial quantities and over many years, remain healthy. Third, aromatic amyl nitrite has been used by cardiac patients in significant quantities for many decades, but the literature has not cited immune disturbances in this population. Finally, as epidemiologists have pointed out, it is exceedingly difficult to disentangle nitrite use from such other risk factors as the frequency of sexual encounters and the multiplicity of sexual partners.

Another intermittently suspicious recreational drug has been marijuana. Like the nitrites, marijuana is believed to be at least potentially immunosuppressive. But marijuana has been used by approximately 55 million Americans and has been popular for decades. Why marijuana should suddenly produce profound immune-deficiency in four relatively small, highly distinctive subpopulations, some of whose members claim never or seldom to have used it, remains critically unclear.

Since intravenously injected narcotics have only been used by a minority of AID victims and since narcotics have been abused by large numbers of individuals for many decades preceding this epidemic, a principal etiologic role for intravenously injected narcotics seems even less persuasive.

Sperm antigenicity would seem unlikely as a primary etiologic candidate for similar reasons. Digestive and parenteral exposure to ejaculate may well have become more common in recent years among a percentage of sexually active gay men in some urban centers. But the practices of fellatio and even traumatic anal intercourse are by no means limited exclusively to homosexuals or to this particular period in time. Any serious exploration of this theory must explain why the phenomenon isn't being observed in sexually active females, especially prostitutes, and why AID has never been observed in these groups before. Finally, how would exposure to sperm account for immune deficiency in the substantial and growing percentage of the epidemic's male heterosexual victims?

It could not. Unless, of course, we are dealing with a number of superficially similar epidemics, each with its own primary etiology.

I would like to take this opportunity to share with you a different perspective of candidate etiologies, one that emphasizes the transmissibility of AID, but one that has not yet been engaged in the medical literature or in medical forums on AID.

Some people have asked: Why are some gay men so promiscuous? Ironically, these are sometimes the same individuals who wittingly or unwittingly support the theological, social and legal proscriptions that prevent gay people from establishing the very relationships they are regularly being cited for being unable to establish.

If the increasingly important perspective of *preventive* medicine is to be most efficiently directed, it must begin to give due consideration to the potentially affirmative impact of destigmatization. To date, it has not done so. But if the otherwise extraordinary sensitivity to issues of stigma that has been demonstrated by every physician and researcher in this auditorium is any indication, the passage of civil rights legislation for gay people will begin to be seen as a critical cofactor in the preventive medicine of sexually transmitted diseases, which probably include AID.

This was yet another of my appeals for civil rights legislation and the sanctioning of domestic partnerships for lesbian and gay persons as an essential consideration of the preventive medicine of STDs and AIDS. If this concern appears obsessive, the reader is reminded that at the time of these appeals, neither New York City nor New York State, to say nothing of the federal government, had any such legislation.]

Dan William is a New York City internist with a private practice specializing in sexually transmitted diseases in gay men. He was a co-founder of New York's Gay Men's Health Project, a VD screening and research facility, and is on the board of directors of New York Physicians for Human Rights. He is a past director of research for the New York City Bureau of VD control. Fifteen of his patients currently have AID-associated diseases.

MASS: There was an interesting mini-dispute, if that's what it was, during the morning session—"Epidemiological Perspectives"—of the recent Mount Sinai Medical Center Symposium on AID. For the first time in public, Dr. James Curran, coordinator of the Task Force on Kaposi's Sarcoma and Opportunistic Infections for the federal Centers for Disease Control (CDC) in Atlanta, explicitly urged physicians to advise their gay male patients to limit risk by having fewer sexual partners. As moderator of this session, however, New York City health commissioner Dr. David Sencer, who is a former director of CDC, later expressed skepticism that such measures would have a decisive impact on the eventual curtailment of this epidemic. Were these positions in conflict?
WILLIAM: Yes and No. Dr. Sencer's skepticism may be based on many of the failed historical examples of attempting to control disease by changing patterns of social behavior. At the same time, I think he was emphasizing that the final solution to this epidemic will be technological—the identification of the factor(s) responsible, the development of a vaccine, effective treatments, etc.

But changes in behavior, however slow, *can* influence disease control. A good example of this is the American diet. I think there is solid evidence to suggest that a growing number of Americans are now more aware of many aspects of nutritional health. This has already been reflected in a lower prevalence and later age-of-onset of such diseases as arteriosclerosis (hardening of the arteries) and high blood pressure, which are the principal causes of heart attacks. Smoking and drinking are other examples. It's possible that miracle cures could be found for lung cancer, emphysema and cirrhosis of the liver. But you and I both know that the real solutions to these diseases are preventive.

MASS: But we're speaking here about what's probably an infectious disease. Although most of the reported cases of AID have been in sexually active gay men, a growing proportion of the epidemic's victims are heterosexual. Even if every gay man were to abruptly stop having sex, can we be sure that such a preventive measure could decisively influence the spread of this disease?

WILLIAM: We can't be absolutely sure. AID will probably continue to strike new populations. The gay cases could become a minority. This may have been Dr. Sencer's main point. On the other hand, the agent that causes AID is almost certainly sexually transmissible and the number of cases in gay men continues to grow. The *eventual* solution to AID may be technological—a preventive vaccine, for example—just as the eventual solution to hepatitis B may be the new hepatitis B vaccine. At the individual level for each and every one of us *today*, however, the decisions we make about our sexual behavior could determine whether or not we acquire immunodeficiency, just as similar decisions may have influenced our potential exposure to any sexually transmitted disease.

MASS: Until recently, the AID epidemic had been largely limited to two groups: sexually active gay men and intravenous drug abusers. The new groups are Haitians and hemophiliacs. What are the implications of this information?

WILLIAM: It strengthens our argument, already quite solid, that AID is caused by an infectious agent. Again, the epidemiologic model for AID is hepatitis B. Sexually active gay men, intravenous drug abusers, patients who receive blood products, and individuals such as refugees who have been living in crowded and unsanitary conditions have been among the highest risk groups for hepatitis B. Using our analogy to this disease, it was predictable that AID would be seen in hemophiliacs and other recipients of blood products and in environmentally disadvantaged groups like the Haitian refugees. *MASS*: I would question one area of this analogy. Medical personnel who are frequently exposed to the blood of patients with hepatitis B are at risk for this disease. Despite rumors to the contrary, CDC has not yet reported any cases of AID among the physicians, nurses or lab technicians who have been handling the blood of AID victims.

WILLIAM: Unlike influenza, tuberculosis and Legionnaire's disease, AID does not appear to be spread by airborne droplet exposure. Like hepatitis B, however, it seems to infect people primarily through sexual contact or parenteral exposure to infected blood, [by injection or] often via tiny sores or cuts on the skin.

Hospital workers who are not frequently in contact with the blood or serum of hepatitis B patients are actually at relatively *low* risk for developing hepatitis B. The risk in this group, as in the general population, appears to be similarly low for AID. Even those hospital workers who *do* regularly handle infected blood products are only at intermediate (as opposed to high) risk for developing hepatitis B. So you wouldn't expect to see many cases of AID in this population. Our analogy still holds.

MASS: This business of exactly how and to what degree AID is infectious is important. At the symposium, one physician was overheard confiding to another that he would no longer eat in Manhattan restaurants because all the waiters are gay.

WILLIAM: That's foolishness. Again, AID, like hepatitis B, does not appear to spread by casual, nonsexual contact. Incidentally, CDC has no specific recommendations even for chronic carriers of hepatitis B virus regarding the handling of food. The risk to the general public of catching AID from food handlers is probably negligible. If that weren't the case, it would probably have already shown up in the statistics.

MASS: Why are we now seeing AID in Haitians?

WILLIAM: The analogy of hepatitis B transmission to AID transmission is again useful. We've already pointed out that intravenous drug abusers and sexually active gay men in urban centers are at high risk for developing hepatitis B. So are those populations who live in close quarters and unsanitary conditions. It's this latter group to which the Haitians probably belong. In fact, the poverty and poor living conditions of Haitians in Haiti have been described as among the worst in the western hemisphere. Recently, an outbreak of tuberculosis has also been reported among Haitian refugees. An increased incidence of other communicable diseases would not be surprising. We already have evidence from a physician in Haiti to suggest that KS and perhaps AID may have been endemic there for years.

MASS: Do you know if the type of KS that has been seen in Haiti is the same as that which is being seen in AID victims in the U.S.?

WILLIAM: We don't yet know, but it may well be the same disease.

MASS: Throughout this epidemic, we have been suggesting that AID is a new disease. But what we're really saying is that the U.S. is dealing with a newly documented disease.

WILLIAM: That's correct. Chances are that this disease has existed in other parts of the world for some time.

This phenomenon of "new" diseases that aren't really new is constantly repeating itself. Cholera, for example, was recently reintroduced into the Gulf states after being absent from the U.S. for decades. Dengue fever has reappeared in the Caribbean. In fact, three of my patients recently acquired this disease while on Caribbean tours. Lassa fever is another example. Closer to home, venereally transmitted amebiasis was extremely rare in the U.S. before the mid-Seventies. Now it's widely prevalent among sexually active gay men in large cities.

MASS: Perhaps prophetically, you were among the first physicians to document this prevalence of sexually transmitted amebiasis. Are you suggesting that AID may have been sexually transmitted to Americans from contacts with Haitians?

WILLIAM: Perhaps yes. Haiti has been a popular tourist resort for many, including gay men. One possibility is that gay men vacationing in Haiti acquired AID through sexual contacts with Haitians. Another possibility is that Haitians brought this disease to the U.S. during recent immigrations.

MASS: If the greatest endemic focus of KS, if not AID, has been Equatorial Africa, are we also suggesting that AID may have spread from Africa to Haiti?

WILLIAM: That's another possibility, but we don't yet know much about the connections, if any, between these two parts of the world.

MASS: In this conversation, we've been assuming that we're dealing with a single, probably viral disease that has only recently been described in the U.S. But we both heard considerable disagreement on this point at the recent Mount Sinai symposium. Do you think that those people [Dr. Joseph Sonnabend and his patients, Michael Callen and Richard Berkowitz, outstanding among them] who believe we are dealing with a number of superficially similar epidemics, each with its own primary etiology, could be right?

WILLIAM: No. I think they're dead wrong. In medical school, we learned a simple rule that I've often found useful. Generally speaking, if you can find one process to explain several disease phenomena, it's more probable than explanations that require multiple hypotheses. To reiterate, I believe we are seeing the same disease phenomena in all four groups.

MASS: On the other hand, you do believe that other factors [cofactors] could influence one's susceptibility to AID?

WILLIAM: Of course. It may be the drug use, other infections, poor nutrition, genetics, etc., may play secondary roles.

Here's an example of what I mean. Two men are exposed to hepatitis B virus. One is in excellent health, the other is an alcoholic with advanced liver disease. The great likelihood is that the alcoholic will develop a far more serious hepatitis infection.

As you know, there's great variability in the severity of many infections. This is especially true of hepatitis B. For reasons we don't fully understand, some individuals with hepatitis B have no disease symptoms while others get very sick. In a small minority of cases, in fact, hepatitis B is a lethal disease. A similar variability in severity may also be true of AID.

In this sense, then, recreational drug use may be somehow contributory in some cases. But even in these cases, the primary cause of disease would be the infectious agent, not the drugs.

The role of nutrition in AID is another important issue. People are taking vitamins and a wide variety of dietary supplements, hoping to fortify themselves against this disease. There isn't an iota of evidence, however, to suggest that we're dealing with any kind or any level of dietary nutritional deficiency. Certainly, a balanced and varied diet is a cornerstone of good health. The irony is that gay men, including many of the gay men in this epidemic, could serve as models of nutrition for the rest of the nation.

MASS: Do you think that we are wasting valuable resources studying poppers, genetics, etc.?

WILLIAM: My own feeling is that most of these hypothetical agents will turn out to be "red herrings." I doubt that such studies will add much to our understanding of AID. But I think it's important to test these other theories with quality research. It could have important benefits. For example, before this epidemic, the long-term effects of poppers were untested and unknown. Now, we will finally have some answers to a question we've been asking for years: Are poppers safe?

MASS: At the symposium, infectious diseases expert Dr. Michael Lange suggested that simply being a gay man and living in New York at this time would place one at higher risk for AID. Is this a simplification of the issues?

WILLIAM: I think he was emphasizing that the principal risk factors for acquiring any epidemic infectious disease can be defined by time, place and susceptible population. We mustn't forget that more than half of all reported cases of AID have been in New York City. If, by contrast, you're gay and live in Australia, your risk—at least for the time being—is going to be much less. New York City in 1982 is where the agent appears to be most prevalent.

MASS: Since we're proposing, with the model of hepatitis B, that AID is parenterally transmissible (from exposure to the blood or blood products of an infected individual), and since AID has now been identified in several hemophiliacs, what advice should gay people be given about donating blood?

WILLIAM: This is a very difficult question to answer. Obviously, most gay men don't have AID and it would be totally inappropriate to stigmatize the entire gay [and lesbian] community as at risk. Since we don't yet have a way of screening blood for the agent that causes AID, other markers for high risk donors must suffice. I think I would advise promiscuous gay men with a prior history of multiple sexually transmitted diseases not to give blood until more information is available. This is especially important in New York City,

Los Angeles and San Francisco. What needs to be emphasized is that homosexuality per se is *not* a risk factor.

[Ed. note: At a press conference on January 17, 1983, spokespersons for The AIDS Network, including Virginia Apuzzo, Larry Kramer, Roger Enlow and Ron Vachon, issued a statement, in agreement with a consensus of blood industry and other AIDS observers, and answered the questions of reporters. The statement urged the following:

- Every effort be made by the blood industry to test blood and blood products for agents which indicate a current or past infection, e.g., hepatitis B, which may also indicate a high risk for AIDS.
- Funds be made available to government agencies, medical institutions, and voluntary community groups, to research the cause(s) — which remain unknown — effects and cure of AIDS as well as to offer patient services to those suffering from this disorder.
- All individual blood donors screen themselves, recognizing that in giving the "gift of life," there is the responsibility to give the safest gift possible.
- The medical and scientific community acknowledge what has been known for many years: that the direct or indirect questioning of donors is an inadequate safeguard to the quality of blood; moreover, a policy to exclude any group from blood donation, whether mandated or voluntary, would be both ineffective and inappropriate.]

MASS: When it became increasingly clear that AID was parenterally transmissible, some observers began to express concern about the new hepatitis B vaccine. Since it was developed with the blood of many gay volunteers, some observers wondered whether an AID-causative infectious agent, like hepatitis B virus, that we don't yet know how to detect might be a contaminant of the new vaccine. What are your feelings?
WILLIAM: I don't think there's much to worry about. In order to inactivate hepatitis B virus, the developers of the new vaccine used methods that kill every other known virus. The likelihood that an

AID agent could survive such thorough processing is, I'm convinced, very remote. Also, each lot of hepatitis B vaccine is safety tested in chimpanzees for months prior to being released. Therefore, I have no hesitation about recommending the new vaccine to all appropriate candidates.

MASS: How safe are the baths?

WILLIAM: Deep in my heart, I'm a civil libertarian and I take great pains to be consistent in that viewpoint. But I do think the time has come for gay physicians and public health officials to advise the general public about the health hazards of sexual activity with many anonymous partners. It may even be appropriate to mandate warnings, as we do with cigarettes. I would support an individual's right to smoke cigarettes, but I also believe that it is our duty to properly inform the cigarette user of associated health risks.

Here's another analogy. Restaurants are now required to post signs describing the Heimlich Maneuver, a simple, easily learned technique for saving the life of someone who is choking on food. Perhaps baths should post signs that warn their customers of health risks and advise them about precautionary measures. Incidentally, a significant proportion of the gay male AID victims had attended bathhouses prior to the onset of their disease.

Eventually, some restrictive measure may have to be imposed. Just as we can't allow motorists to speed down city streets at 90 miles per hour, we may have to look for ways to limit disease transmission. Obviously, the gay community must be actively involved in formulating any guidelines.

What I would like to see is some kind of compromise solution, balancing personal liberties with public health priorities. Perhaps bathhouses could evolve their environments to minimize the amount of interpersonal sexual contact allowable. They could retain their special character as gay meeting establishments. Perhaps there could be more in the way of gym facilities, game rooms and so forth, and less in the way of private sex areas. This would require cooperation and some truly creative thinking on the part of the health representatives and bathhouse promoters.

MASS: You've already pointed out one indirect benefit of the epidemic: that we will finally know more about the relative safety of

poppers. In what other ways has this experience impacted affirmatively?

WILLIAM: I've never seen the gay community so together on anything. People are concerned, supportive and involved in a way that
has been very inspiring.

The same has been true of the medical community's response.
It's extraordinary to see so much cooperation among so many diverse disciplines, and otherwise rival physicians and medical institutions.

I think everyone will benefit from the greater sophistication
we're gaining about sex and health, and about the relationship between immunity and disease.

It is ironic that a sexually transmitted disease is bringing people
together in a way that sex itself seemed unable to do.

David Sencer

[Ed. note: The *Native* entitled this interview "Health in a Society of 'Significant Others.'"]

Dr. David J. Sencer is a past director of the federal centers for disease control (CDC) and is currently commissioner of the New York City Department of Health. The following interview with him was conducted [in his Worth Street office] during the second week of January [1983].

MASS: At the Workgroup to Identify Opportunities to Prevent AIDS that was held at the CDC in Atlanta last week, you stated that in your opinion, the evidence is nearly overwhelming that AIDS is being caused by a sexually and parenterally transmissible agent. But one of the other panelists responded that because we still know so little about risk factors among the Haitians, and because the evidence for sexual and parenteral transmission (while impressive) remains circumstantial, we can't be sure that AIDS is a new disease — or that we are seeing the same disease in the same high risk groups. Can you give some additional perspective on where this debate now stands?

SENCER: This assessment is based on all of the epidemiologic evidence we've accumulated thus far. It strongly suggests that we are dealing with an infectious agent that is transmitted in much the same way that hepatitis B is transmitted: parenterally [from exposure of the blood stream via contaminated needles or via the transfusion of contaminated blood or blood products] and sexually [from exposure of mucosal surfaces to contaminated blood or secretions].

I think we can make this assessment even though we don't yet have much information about the risk factors in the Haitian cases.

MASS: Are efforts underway to obtain more information about risk factors in this group?

SENCER: Yes. Locally, Jim Monroe [who has been serving as liaison between the Department of Health and gay community representatives] is now also working with representatives of the Haitian community.

There has been a lot of conjecture that the Haitian cases might have been caused or at least facilitated by malnutrition. This supposition is based on the fact that many native Haitians have lived in conditions of extreme poverty. But that would not necessarily explain the clusters of recently reported cases of Haitians who have immigrated to the U.S. and who have been residing in this country, in some cases, for more than two or three years.

MASS: At the CDC meeting, I believe you also recommended that the Workgroup not delay publicizing risk-reduction guidelines. How, when and where will these guidelines be published, and are these guidelines likely to include any recommendations that have not already been widely and publicly (if generally) discussed?

SENCER: Risk-reduction guidelines are currently being formalized by the Public Health Service and will soon appear in press releases and in medical publications such as the *Morbidity and Mortality Weekly Report* [MMWR]. But a number of organizations, such as Gay Men's Health Crisis, in the highest risk communities have already issued risk-reduction recommendations. These include or will soon include the general recommendation that individuals who know they are at high risk — intravenous drug abusers, Haitians, and persons who have been sexually promiscuous — voluntarily abstain from donating blood. In this sense, I think Gay Men's Health Crisis continues to be an excellent example of concerned individuals assuming responsibility within their own communities and not necessarily waiting for a "Thou-shalt-not" to be issued by a government agency.

MASS: In the highest risk areas, such as New York City, San Francisco, and Los Angeles, there is growing pressure to pre-screen all potential donors with sexual histories and to exclude any male who admits to being homosexual. Where do you personally stand on this issue?

SENCER: I personally feel that screening for sexual orientation is neither a practicable nor a desirable thing to do. I think there are better ways than this kind of open questioning of obtaining the same results. We've already mentioned voluntary abstention as one approach. Others include concentrating on questions that are already asked during the routine screening of potential blood donors. Unexplained fevers, unexplained weight loss, unexplained lymph node swelling—these are symptoms that suggest risk. Individuals who have such symptoms, even if the symptoms are not thought to be related to AIDS, should not be donating blood.

MASS: At least one public health official—yourself, I believe—has said that AIDS is perhaps the most serious epidemic of a new infectious disease in this country since polio. If AIDS is that serious, why has CDC waited so long to publicly recommend risk-reduction measures?

SENCER: Since I currently represent the New York City Health Department, rather than CDC, I cannot speak for them. But I think the delay in making specific risk-reduction recommendations has been due (until recently) to the lack of more solid information about risk factors. To make recommendations before there is sufficient evidence to support them is at least as bad as not making any recommendations.

MASS: At least one gay community physician [Dr. Joseph Sonnabend] has publicly stated his belief that the single agent theory has more dangerous implications for gay people than other theories. He believes that this theory implies a greater risk to the general public and a greater likelihood of anti-minority discrimination and violence. In the worst scenario, he believes that the single agent theory will raise the issue of quarantine. When I myself asked one CDC official [Dr. Harold Jaffee] about this issue some months ago, he reassured me that such drastic measures were highly improbable because AIDS is still overwhelmingly limited to high-risk populations and continues to spread at a relatively slow rate. Do you agree?

SENCER: Yes. As in the case of hepatitis B, I think AIDS is likely to remain predominantly in the high risk groups already designated.

Generally speaking, quarantine has never worked. During the great flu pandemic of 1918, one of the islands in the Pacific avoided this disease by not letting any foreign ships land. Otherwise, I can't think of a single example of an infectious disease that has been effectively controlled or eradicated, since the 1600s, by methods of quarantine.

MASS: Dr. Dan William has compared to the posting of speed limit signs on highways with the encouragement of restrictions on public access to casual sexual activity. Within the gay community, many of us are asking what we can do to help. Are certain establishments significantly contributing to public health risk? And if so, in what ways can we all work cooperatively to minimize this risk?

SENCER: I think what you're getting at is similar to the issue of quarantine. If you're talking about bathhouses, would these include those which cater to orthodox Jewish men? In other words, where would the lines be drawn? How, exactly, would you define which establishments are dangerous? Some people now use radar detectors as a way of circumventing speed limits. I think the same kind of thing would happen if you tried to close bathhouses.

Unless a person is himself or herself convinced that a behavior pattern is dangerous to his or her health, any measures we attempt to implement or enforce are not likely to work. The programs in alcoholism and drug abuse that have worked have all been self-help programs. That's the basis of their success. Generally speaking, you can't force society to change. But individuals within society can change themselves.

MASS: At the Mount Sinai symposium on AIDS last July, you said that behavioral approaches to the control of AIDS were likely to be relatively ineffective. As was the case with polio, the real solution will be a preventive vaccine or its equivalent. Am I accurately describing your thinking about AIDS?

SENCER: Let's go back to polio. We recognized early on that the method of spread was oral-fecal. An individual could do certain things to minimize his or her risk. They could stay at home, they could avoid communal swimming, crowded places, etc. Individuals may have minimized their risk in some cases with such measures. But the real control of polio came with the development of a preventive vaccine.

MASS: Although billions have been spent on cancer research, cancer remains a major health problem. I think many people have the impression that more funding would guarantee a quick and simple solution to AIDS. If unlimited funds were suddenly to be made available, earmarked for AIDS research, what would be done with that money that is not currently being done?

SENCER: Additional funding could be helpful in various ways, but I think that the most important research is already underway and has been for some time.

On the other hand, I am increasingly convinced that the solution to AIDS will be based on a collaborative approach, rather than from the work of a few individuals. The individual approach is one that would involve, for example, pursuing a specific area of research with a grant from the National Institutes of Health. The collaborative approach emphasizes the working together of many individuals from many areas of medical research and practice. I guess I'm an optimist, but I believe that the collaborative direction we're moving in now will yield important results even sooner than many of us had hoped.

MASS: It's wonderful to hear such optimism.

SENCER: I've been wrong before. I was wrong about the swine flu epidemic. [As director of CDC, Dr. Sencer had, in 1976, concluded that there was a significant possibility that swine flu might produce a pandemic with the lethal proportions of the 1918-19 flu pandemic. With this concern, President Gerald Ford was persuaded to approve a $135 million innoculation campaign. The deadly pandemic turned out to be a false alarm. At the same time, it was under Sencer's directorship that CDC had one of its most spectacular successes: determining the cause of Legionnaire's disease.]

But I am optimistic that we're approaching a major breakthrough on AIDS. And I believe one of the reasons we are close to a major breakthrough is because of the tremendous cooperation and responsibility the gay community has shown throughout this epidemic. I think that everyone has developed a new and special respect for the gay community as a result of this experience. And I think that this involvement has been critical in keeping negative, pejorative, and irrational public reactions to a minimum.

MASS: Would you say that it's true that a gay man could significantly reduce his risk of acquiring sexually transmitted diseases by having one mutually monogamous partner, as opposed to having many casual partners?

SENCER: Yes. But I would add that this risk-reduction measure, generally speaking, would apply equally to all people, regardless of their gender or sexual orientation.

MASS: Would you agree that it would be prudent for everyone to support a simple, victimless, cost-free means of at least facilitating this risk-reduction measure?

SENCER: I don't know what you mean.

MASS: Why don't our most credentialed and respected public health leaders — individuals such as yourself — strongly urge the passage of civil rights legislation for gay people and legislation that would support the right of gay people to legitimize their relationships?

SENCER: I fully support the right of *all* people, including gay people, to conduct their personal and private lives as they see fit, without interference or penalty from society. The privacy of an individual's home should always be respected, regardless of that individual's sexual orientation. But the issue of legalizing relationships in this country has become very complicated, and that complexity is just as applicable at the present time to heterosexuals and bisexuals as it is to gay people. The complexity I'm referring to has to do with legal contracts, insurance, etc. Whether the partners are homosexual, bisexual or heterosexual, the basic problem has been to define the rights of what sociologists call "the significant other." This is what we need to clarify and support because we are increasingly becoming a society of significant others.

Protecting Lesbian and Gay Youth

A Conversation with Damien Martin and Emery Hetrick,
co-founders of the Harvey Milk High School,
the first school in history for lesbian
and gay youth

[Ed. note: Following my burnout as a writer and activist, which culminated in my being hospitalized for depression in the spring of 1983, I resumed writing about homosexuality and sexuality. As I had perceived it during the first few years of the epidemic and have continued to understand it since, AIDS is only one chapter in the evolution of the gay liberation movement and in the much vaster developments of what John D'Emilio and Estelle Freedman call the sexual revolutions, albeit an all-important and profoundly tragic one for our time. In 1984, the year of the premiere of Larry Kramer's play, *The Normal Heart*, however, it was even more challenging to assert this perspective than it is today.

In *The Normal Heart* there is a character based loosely on me called Mickey Marcus. Mickey, Larry wrote me, is named after an American Jew, Colonel David Marcus, who became an Israeli war hero. (Colonel Marcus's story is depicted in a Hollywood film called "Cast A Giant Shadow" with Kirk Douglas.) As Larry acknowledged it to me in his letter, the character is "a composite," combining elements of a number of persons and characters, fictional and nonfictional. Despite the allusion to Colonel Marcus, and although the character is referred to as "our first hero" and says two or three sympathetic and even powerful things before being carted off to the hospital to be treated for exhaustion, I was more disturbed than flattered by Larry's characterization, as I perceived it, and for several reasons.

First, the character, who was a reporter and community volunteer, was not a physician. One of the messages I read into the play, whether intentional or not (it is not something anyone in the play actually discusses or that Larry has ever discussed) was that the Emma Brookner character was the only real physician around. In denying the reality of Mickey's status as a physician, there seemed to be a tacit indictment of me as someone who turned out to be this gay activist/sexual revolution person instead of the tough, responsible, conservative physician who was needed.

As a physician, I did not have the credentials or the status that Dr. Linda Laubenstein (who was the inspiration for Dr. Brookner in the play) had in the medical community, or that Dan William had in the gay community, and I have never been very good at panels or public speaking. In addition, as Larry Kramer knew, I was in the midst of a personal crisis as a physician and writer who needed to be able to be both full-time. Notwithstanding this dilemma, however, I was a physician (all of my AIDS pieces were written with the by-line, Lawrence Mass, M.D.), as I remain today, and took my responsibilities very seriously. To imply that the advice I was giving the community was somehow less medical, less physicianly, than Dr. Brookner's, seemed homophobic at best. That is, it "proved" Larry's hypothesis that the community was nothin' but a buncha nincompoops and sissies. The real doctor, predictably enough (from Larry's perspective), had to come from outside the community. The gay community had no such person. In view of the fact that Dr. Laubenstein's public advice in those days was no stronger or more specific than my own (at her first few appearances on community panels, she showed a slide of my *Native* feature, "Cancer in the Gay Community"), changing Mickey's role from physician (the only physician who was a co-founder of Gay Men's Health Crisis) to generic community volunteer seemed at worst to be mendacious.

As this book will, I hope, make clear, my belief in the values of the sexual revolution, as Money talked about it (as opposed to Larry Kramer's use of the phrase to connote nothing more than sexual license) and my pride in being a member of the gay community did not render me incapable of giving competent, medically authoritative advice, based on what knowledge we had, to the community about what to do and what not to do in the face of the AIDS crisis. But you would never know that from the *wimper*ings of Mickey Marcus in *The Normal Heart*. In the second act, Mickey sobs to Ned: "I love sex! I worship men! . . . I don't know what to tell anybody. And everybody asks *me*. . . . I feel so inadequate! How can we tell people to stop when it might turn out to be caused by — I don't know! . . . And I've spent fifteen years of my life fighting for our right to be free and make love whenever, wherever . . ." As extensively reviewed and discussed in the editorial note that introduces the *Five Interviews from the First Two Years of the AIDS Epidemic*, the information and advice we did and did not give people was a lot more substantial and complex than anything even hinted at by this play's caricature of the gay community as personified by Mickey Marcus.

The proverbial last straw came in Act II, when Ned says: "Mickey, why didn't you guys fight for the right to get married instead of the right to legitimize promiscuity?" As readers of these interviews and conversations will appreciate, I had been fighting very hard alongside many other people in the gay community for precisely that right. Adding insult to injury, it was a right that Larry, who was not known ever to have sustained a domestic partnership with a lover, had himself never fought for. When I complained bitterly about this to Larry the day after the premiere of *The Normal Heart* (I had walked out of the play at that point, though, with my lover's help, I managed to regain my composure and return a few moments later), he decided to add a new line. In the published version of the play, Mickey responds to Ned's accusation by saying "We did!"

Later, my pain and concern about the garbled history of GMHC and the unfolding of the epidemic *The Normal Heart* was perpetrating were heightened when I read, in Andrew Holleran's introduction to the published version of *The Normal Heart*, the following summation: "*The Normal Heart* is, after all, a history play. . . . It is a play which relies, to an extraordinary degree, on what actually happened and what actually was said." Whatever my misgivings, I nonetheless admired *The Normal Heart*, which rang true, often and more loudly than anything else around. Much more immediately important than any quibbling over facts and details was the fact that at the time of its premiere, *The Normal Heart* was the only real alarm being sounded before the general public. Another play, *As Is* by William Hoffman, dealt movingly with the human faces of AIDS, but did not go near the medical or political crises that were raging around the epidemic. And although *Night Sweat* by Robert Chesley, the other "AIDS play" that preceded *The Normal Heart* (*Night Sweat* has the distinction of being the first play in this genre), did deal with the political implications of the epidemic for the community as well as for the public at large, it was not commercially successful and not widely enough seen and discussed. By the time of the premiere of *The Normal Heart* in 1984, I was in full agreement with Larry that total, all out alarm was necessary, and I did everything I could to support this extremely timely, necessary work of political theater. For *The Advocate*, I made the following statement, which was published in May 1985:

As a co-founder of Gay Men's Health Crisis who has known Larry Kramer for nearly twenty years and as one of the models for a composite character in the play, there's no way I can be truly objective about *The Normal Heart*. But here's what I would say. As an historical documentary that purports to detail exactly how GMHC evolved, what this organization has or has not achieved, what other organizations did or did not do, and the complex role Larry Kramer actually played in it all, *The Normal Heart* promulgates a number of sometimes patently self-aggrandizing, sometimes stridently polemical distortions, simplifications and untruths. *However*, while broadcasting just how serious this epidemic is and how much worse it's going to get, *The Normal Heart* speaks more persuasively than any other book, film or play of recent years about such longstanding and entangled crises as gay self-hatred, the closetedness of powerful homosexuals, the dearth of visible gay leadership, and the underlying homophobia of society at large. As a semifictional docudrama that reveals, sometimes unwittingly, the most devastating truths about the state of our so-called community today, *The Normal Heart* is, I think, explosively powerful and uniquely important.

In October 1985, Larry wrote me:

> What constantly surprises me is how you refuse to see the
> character of Mickey Marcus as the hero I intended him to be.
> . . . Mickey is a sympathetic character and is viewed as such
> by everyone but you. I am not condemning *you* for not educat-
> ing the world. Why are *you* taking it so personally? . . . We
> were always very close, and I admire the enormous contribu-
> tion you made in those early years. . . . The line in the play
> that Emma says is: 'Why aren't you telling them bluntly stop?'
> And this holds true. But, again, the play attempts to dramatize
> how difficult it was for anyone to say this. Again, why are you
> taking all of this upon your own individual shoulders. There
> were many of us, most, in fact, who couldn't say this . . . only
> you seem to see Marcus as a character being criticized, not as
> the character who breaks everyone else's heart, because he is
> so moving, so true, so complicated, so torn by the struggles of
> the community . . . You were the only one out there and the
> work you did was scrupulous. Nowhere have I said otherwise
> or indicated otherwise that I feel differently to this day.

Larry wrote this letter to me in response to the interview which
follows with Emery Hetrick and Damien Martin. Clearly, this letter
is loving and supportive. I wept when I read it, as I wept several
years later when Larry acknowleged me at a Human Rights Campaign Fund Dinner and in his book, *Reports from the Holocaust*. In
1985, however, all this love and support seemed inconsistent with
my absence among the persons who are thanked in the acknowledg-
ments in the published version of *The Normal Heart*, including Drs.
Roger Enlow, Alvin Friedman-Kien, Frank Lilly, Joseph Sonnabend, Norman Levy (to whom the play is dedicated) and Linda
Laubenstein (to whom Larry gave "special thanks and tribute"),
just as this professed love and validification seemed likewise inconsistent to me with the actual impression "Mickey Marcus" makes
in the play.

In "Protecting Lesbian and Gay Youth," the first piece from this
period (and the first interview I published following the premiere of
The Normal Heart in Spring, 1984), I was at pains to address the

less measured critics of the community, especially Larry Kramer. In an interview for the Long Island *Connection* (May 21, 1985), Larry had progressed from the "distortions, simplifications and un-truths" of *The Normal Heart* to baldfaced lies, e.g., "You must use the word 'contagion'; you must use the word 'epidemic'; neither of which GMHC will use. It's as simple as that. . . . GMHC are murderers, bluntly, because they are not telling people to cool it."

But even more disturbing than the gross hyperbole, it seemed to me, were Larry's ongoing assertions that "the sexual revolution will be the death of us." In my opinion, then and now, he couldn't have been more wrong.]

The Institute for the Protection of Lesbian and Gay Youth (IP-LGY) [which is now called the Hetrick-Martin Institute] was co-founded five years ago [by Emery Hetrick and Damien Martin] to provide services for gay and lesbian youth in need of help. The organization was catapulted into the national spotlight when the *New York Times* and other newspapers ran front-page stories about a special school for lesbian and gay dropouts in their June 6 [1985] editions. The existence of the Harvey Milk School—named after the openly gay San Francisco City Supervisor who was assassi-nated, together with San Francisco Mayor George Moscone, by ho-mophobic ex-City Supervisor Dan White in 1978—caused a furor that continues as of this writing. IPLGY is intimately involved be-cause it helped to establish and provide supportive services for the special high school.

But the Institute also provides a number of other services. IPLGY now averages over 800 face-to-face contacts per month (or about 10,000 per year) in its Manhattan offices. This is in addition to many thousands of telephone contacts. In the last two years, IPLGY has trained over 3000 professionals via seminars conducted throughout the U.S.

IPLGY's officers include Program Director Joyce Hunter, a black lesbian, and Clinical Director Steve Ashkinazy, a gay man and orthodox Jew. The Institute's co-founders, Hetrick and Martin, are [life partners].

Before co-founding IPLGY, Damien Martin, who is associate professor of communications at New York University, was involved with Dignity, the national gay Catholic organization and, in the early 1970s, with the New York Political Action Committee. An expert sexologist, Martin has debated, among others, Dr. William Masters on the *Donahue* show, debunking the Masters and Johnson claims to have "converted" homosexuals to heterosexuality.

Emery Hetrick, M.D., is a charter member of the National Gay Task Force (NGTF), a co-founder of the Association of Lesbian and Gay Psychiatrists (ALGP) and of Gay Psychiatrists of New York (GPNY), a co-founder of Senior Action in a Gay Environment (SAGE), and a founding member of New York Physicians for Human Rights (NYPHR). Based largely on his work with the lesbian and gay community, Dr. Hetrick was the first openly gay psychiatrist to be made a Fellow of the American Psychiatric Association. Among many publications, he is most recently the co-editor, with Dr. Terry Stein, of *Innovations in Psychotherapy with Homosexuals* (American Psychiatric Press, 1984).

[Ed. note: In early 1987, Dr. Hetrick died from complications of AIDS.]

MASS: How did the Institute get started?

HETRICK: We were at a meeting with [City Comptroller] Harrison Goldin. This was probably 1980. We heard about lesbian and gay kids who had been discriminated against, [and about some who] had even suffered serious violence in some very well known shelters. That's when Damien and I first expressed interest in helping out in these cases. In the beginning, we were really more of an ombudsman group for youth, challenging agencies that were discriminating against them and helping them to better negotiate the system. Two major things happened right away. First, we really did find discrimination, *appalling* treatment of these kids, on a much larger scale than we had feared.

MARTIN: We did indeed. But we also found a lot of professionals who wanted to work hard and help us develop programs. That was the second thing. The problem was that these people had no formal training in dealing with gay and lesbian youth. Nobody did. In attempting to get started, they had to deal with hostile administrations and community groups. They also had to learn how to handle the straight kids in the agencies who had been programmed to hate queers and faggots.

The professionals on the front lines welcomed us with open arms. It was incredibly moving. That they needed help was obvious, that they wanted it even more so. At first, I thought we should be an exclusively educational organization. Emery said we would have to provide social services as well, but I didn't want to get involved with the whole thing of fundraising and endless bureaucracies, so I initially fought him on this.

Emery turned out to be right. What finally convinced me was the vice squad. One night, in this very apartment, one of the officers came right out and said, "We don't know what to do with these kids. Why don't you provide social services?"

MASS: What was the vice squad doing in your apartment?

HETRICK: They were responding to complaints we had made to official agencies regarding the treatment of gay youth.

MASS: It was during this early stage of the Institute's development that you had to deal with the North American Man/Boy Love Association (NAMBLA). What happened?

HETRICK: Our committee meetings had been slowly evolving when the issue of NAMBLA erupted. We had to confront this organization and take a strong stand. We decided that we could not have people who were actively involved with NAMBLA or in promoting certain NAMBLA points of view, either on our board of directors or in any other way connected with the Institute. We felt from the beginning that NAMBLA's goals and priorities were antithetical to the needs of lesbian and gay youth.

MASS: Could you be more specific?

MARTIN: First of all, NAMBLA did not differentiate between the adolescent and the pre-adolescent. The second issue has to do with our firm conviction that this kind of intergenerational relationship— between an older person, an adult, and an adolescent or (especially) a pre-adolescent, is *not* favorable to the young person in the vast majority of instances, because it interferes with their social development. This is especially true of males. It's always a power issue. Regardless of the goodness of their intentions, the adults always manipulate and the kids, regardless of how responsive they are or how much fun they may be having or appear to be having, always learn to manipulate back. What we found, universally, is that such experiences are not positive for the young person. When we interviewed young gay and lesbian people, what we found is that what they really wanted was the opportunity to *speak* to lesbian and gay adults, without having to worry about whether or not they had to "come accross." Contrary to NAMBLA mythologies, these kids did not need or *want* adults to have easier access to them sexually, or vice versa.

HETRICK: From a professional point of view, we feel that what gay males and lesbians need first and most is the opportunity to interact amongst themselves, with others their own age. Unless they can first find ways to interact socially among themselves, any question of freedom of choice when it comes to interacting with adults is a closed point. They can't have freedom of choice without freedom of socialization. And, in our society, without a chance to meet young or adult gay people in other than sexual situations (Times Square, adult bookstores, etc.), they cannot be said to have any kind of freedom of choice.

MASS: Where sexual interactions have taken place, aren't these young people more likely to conceptualize their gayness more exclusively in terms of their sexuality?

HETRICK: Yes. In fact, generally speaking, gay youngsters are socialized to hide in the closet. As a result, they tend to identify being gay or lesbian solely in terms of eroticism and not to see its connection with the rest of their lives.

MASS: However indirectly, does this imply that most gay and lesbian youngsters are sexually exploited by adults?

HETRICK: No! The overwhelming majority of gay and lesbian youngsters grow up without having *any* contacts with adults who are self-identified as gay or lesbian. But because of the closetedness of young and adult gays, whatever explicitly cross-generational interactions do take place are more likely to be primarily sexual, or at least covertly erotic.

MARTIN: True. But the primary problem underlying all others is the need to hide—from parents, teachers, friends, everyone. This need to hide is the major problem affecting gay and lesbian youth, just as it continues to be the major problem facing adult gays and lesbians, and it has both created and aggravated the specific problems we see at the Institute. The kids all feel isolated. They have no way to know what their burgeoning sexual feelings mean. What does it mean to be gay? Who else is gay? Virtually all gay youngsters continue to report that they thought they were the only ones "like that."

MASS: If this isolation of the gay and lesbian child is still so universal and more likely to result in an overemphasis on the erotic, doesn't this lend support to the contention of critics who say that the gay community has defined itself almost exclusively in sexual terms?

MARTIN: No. Despite the isolation, most of us have developed age-appropriate social behaviors. Most older gay men are no more or less interested in the erotic than most older heterosexual men. That's why you don't see them so much in the bars or the baths. And lesbians have never defined themselves with a primary emphasis on the erotic. There are some, of course, who still try to maintain at 40 and 50 the behaviors that were so exciting and releasing at 20. I would have to agree with critics to the extent that many of us begin with an exaggerated sense of the importance of the sexual. As we said before, this is virtually mandated in a sexist, erotophobic and homophobic society. Even so, and even in the sexual '70s, we were a sizable, diverse community that included all types.

HETRICK: That's one area where I tend to agree with some of these critics: gay publications. On the one hand, we're trying to let the kids know that being gay is a lot more than fucking and, especially today, that sex demands a lot of responsibility and is associated with serious risks. In this sense, it's problematic to leave even the best of our gay community publications around for the 13-and 14-year-olds, because of the pervasive emphasis on hedonistic sex that interlaces the medical and news reports and literary pieces, which are often erotica. Adults may be able to reconcile this dichotomy, but it's a lot harder for kids.

MASS: It sounds as if the Institute is acknowledging what writer Larry Kramer has been saying for years, that the gay community defines itself almost exclusively in terms of sex.

HETRICK: No! There is a distinction we insist on making. What we say is that this emphasis on sex is what the majority of us — gay people like you and me—have overcome, despite the fact that straight society forces this emphasis on us. Despite this *straight*-jacketing, if you will, *most* gay people discover as they get older that they have other options. Some do not. Many gay people have never taken part in the Fire Island/baths subculture Kramer is still so preoccupied with. The people who think that everyone goes to the baths all the time because everyone they know does, have limited their social networking within the community.

MARTIN: It's interesting that straight society tolerates the Fire Island/baths world, but goes berserk when two gay teenagers try to attend a school prom together. The point is very clear. Homosexual sex is not so bad as long as one is stigmatized while doing it. Any attempt to be a social being that denies that sex defines your identity, however, will bring the wrath of society down upon you.

The gay community has, of course, internalized all this to a significant extent. Even so, we have a lot of kids who come to us who know they're gay or lesbian and have never had sex. One of the things we try to do at the Institute is to let them know they have options, and that one of those options is to postpone sex until it can be more satisfying emotionally, as well as a pleasurable physical experience for them.

MASS: In his play, *The Normal Heart*, Kramer (as the play's protagonist, Ned Weeks) says at one point: "Why didn't you fight for the right to get married rather than the right to legitimize promiscuity?" The truth is that we fought for *freedom*, not for marriage only or promiscuity only. This is ironic because, to my knowledge, Kramer has never before mentioned gay marriage, in print or anywhere else. By contrast, other gay writers, spokespersons and activists have gone on record repeatedly in support of efforts to legalize gay and lesbian marriages. Furthermore, I've urged public health officials to endorse the concept of gay marriage as an essential consideration in the preventive medicine of AIDS and other sexually transmitted diseases. Where does the Institute stand on the issue of gay marriages?

MARTIN: We all need ritual and legal protection. In that sense, we definitely favor "marriage." But many of us are already in committed relationships. *That's* what we're trying to get across to the young people. If you're gay, you don't have to be a blond, blue-eyed hunk to fall in love and establish a relationship. Being together is an option for us, just as it is for heterosexuals.

MASS: How much of a factor or problem at the Institute are issues of gender behavior?

MARTIN: We're finding tremendous variations in gender behavior, much of it connected to ethnic or cultural background. For example, some black and Hispanic kids are more likely to equate being gay with being female. This is because there's more of the hyper-macho thing and less tolerance of any kind of gender duality in certain black and Hispanic communities.

But it gets very complicated. Gender-deviant behavior on the part of any individual may be connected with any number of cultural variables, none of which may be connected with homosexuality. We have kids at the Institute who say that if they act the way faggots are supposed to act in their ethnic neighborhoods (i.e., effeminate), they run less risk of getting beaten up. We have other kids, who have been prostitutes, who say: "I'm not butch enough for the customers who want the butch kids, so I make myself more swish for the customers who want that." In other words, "cross-gender behavior" is determined by a combination of factors, including economic.

HETRICK: There's another aspect to all this. There's the kid who will cross-dress as a camp — that is, as a way to make fun of himself and the world in which he finds himself. This is typical minority group behavior. It's a little like the way a minority group develops its own language and own brand of self-deprecating humor. The group will take on the characteristic that is assigned to it and show it up in spades.

MARTIN: This gender behavior business gets even more convoluted by another factor. Gay and lesbian kids begin to avoid certain involvements with their peers because they don't want to be perceived as different. Take baseball, for instance. The straight kid who makes a mistake is better able to laugh about it, or otherwise brush it off. The gay kid, by contrast, will attribute the same mistake to the fact that he's "different." This is what happened to me. I was a good pitcher, but an inexperienced catcher. Whenever I'd drop the ball, I'd get humiliated out of all proportion to what had happened. Instead of working hard on my catching, I stopped playing baseball.

HETRICK: Similarly, I tried out for track and made the team, but decided not to stay on because it meant an involvement with other boys, some of whom I was afraid would find out I was different. I dropped out of broadjump for the same reason. I was turned on by the other guys and was afraid it would show and that I'd be humiliated. It never occurred to me that I might laugh off erections in the shower, the way all the other boys did.

MASS: How do you regard sexual orientation at the Institute? Do you see it as something fixed from earliest childhood? How do you feel about psychiatrists, sex therapists, psychologists and others who still maintain that change in sexual orientation is possible?

MARTIN: Emery and I agree that there is no possibility of change in sexual orientation. On the other hand, any one of countless kinds of pressures may influence people to transiently modify their sexual *behavior*. People like Masters and Johnson and Helen Singer Kaplan have been able to get a few people who have internalized society's homophobia to perform sexually with the opposite sex, usually with their eyes closed and the lights out. But true change in sexual orientation has never been documented. Not once. In addition to being unscientific, of course, this charlatanry is unethical. Failures of this kind of approach have been and remain universal, but it still goes on and still is of great concern.

HETRICK: What we see at the Institute is more subtle. For example, the liberal, urban social worker, psychologist, or other professional interacting with the gay or lesbian adolescent, who says to the kid who is talking about homosexual feelings or experiences, "Oh, that doesn't mean you're homosexual," or "Keep your options open." The subtext, of course, is "Let's hope you're not homosexual. You still have a chance to turn out all right." Can you imagine the same therapist saying to adolescents who are discussing heterosexual fantasies or behavior, "Keep your options open. Lots of people feel that way but it doesn't mean you're heterosexual"! It's sad to have to admit that there are plenty of gay psychiatrists and therapists who do this as well.

MASS: Did you see the television movie *Consenting Adult*? Laura Hobson told me how thrilled she was with the adaptation of her novel, and I missed my chance to tell her how disturbed I was by the program's "updating" of events to include AIDS, while simultaneously showing a conversion-type psychiatrist. In so doing, the program suggested that the drama was contemporary, rather than from the 1950s and '60s, and suggested to a television public of many millions that this kind of therapy is approved of by mainstream psychiatry today.

HETRICK: Yes. If they were going to mention AIDS as a contemporary problem, they should have made it clear that mainstream psychiatry (the American Psychiatric Association) officially declassified homosexuality as a mental disorder in 1973.

MASS: We've been talking about unethical treatment of gay and lesbian youth by mental health care professionals. As co-founders and officers of IPLGY, what other kinds of issues will you be speaking about?

HETRICK: Although advocacy is a part of our mission—indeed, is stated as one of our purposes—we do not see speaking out about specific political injustices as our major purpose.

MARTIN: The point Emery's making is that we are not taking on psychiatry as a primary objective. To be an ombudsman for gay and lesbian youth was and remains the Institute's first goal. We begin by trying to help the kid who is caught up in the system and we still do that. We advocate for the kids with welfare, with immigration, and with legal aid. We see to it they get the services to which they have a right. Our kids come in with a multiplicity of problems and we've had to set up a multiplicity of programs to deal with them.

As we said earlier, the major problem these kids have is isolation. They have no information about what it means to be gay and no one they can confide in and share their feelings with. When they do dare to confide, they are often betrayed. A young man or woman tells a friend at school that he or she is gay, the confidence gets betrayed and life becomes hell. For the other gay and lesbian kids at the school, the lesson is clear—stay hidden! Therefore, one of our key initiatives is our socialization program, where we give these young people a chance to interact with others their own age, to share their feelings, and where we can provide them with information about what it means to be gay. Do you know that it was a major event for many of them when I put Emery's picture on my desk? They had never seen that before. They were very interested in the fact that we have been together ten years.

Members of the gay and lesbian community are the only minority group persons who run the risk of being rejected by their own families, simply because of who and what they are. You don't get thrown out of the family for being black or Jewish, but you do if you're gay or lesbian. Gay and lesbian people are the only minority group who don't begin assuming their social identity as a minority until they reach adolescence.

Our socialization program includes a drop-in center, film clubs, dances, and other activities where young people can come in contact not only with their peers but also with older gay and lesbian people who can be perceived as role models.

MASS: You bring up this issue of role models. In a recent interview, Larry Kramer said, "The only people who come out to be [our] leaders are people that the majority can't follow, because they're too radical, or too fanatical. They're a leather queen, they walk around with pierced nipples, lesbians with truck driver hair. I mean the majority of gay people are not like that and don't want to follow those people." Apart from the issue here of what might be interpreted as homophobia, is there any sense in which this observation is true regarding gay and lesbian youth?

HETRICK: I simply don't understand.

MARTIN: Neither do I. I'm not apologizing for anybody's appearance, but the majority of people I've worked with, and even those in the movement I've fought with, do not fit this description.

MASS: What Kramer is saying is that he wants nothing to do with our so-called movement when people like Sister Boom-Boom show up on TV. It's a little like wanting nothing to do with being Jewish when Meir Kahane or an ultrafundamentalist Hassid appears in public, or wanting nothing to do with being American when they show people like Ronald Reagan or Jerry Falwell.

MARTIN: This is one aspect of the isolation of gay men and lesbians we talked about earlier. The media would rather have a Sister Boom-Boom because he is more colorful, more what middle America thinks of when it thinks of gay people. At the Democratic convention in San Francisco last year, when Sister Boom-Boom got all that media attention, there were plenty of active, professional, relatively conservative gay people who were more than willing to speak with the media, but the media wasn't interested. Kramer should go after the media more than he has, not this nebulous group he's pejoratively stereotyping as "our leaders."

This is part of the self-hatred that often comes up in a minority group. It's called blaming the victim. One blames the members of the group for what has happened to them, and this blame usually comes from group members themselves. It's definitely true that gay and lesbian kids don't get the role models they should have, but the major reason for that is *not* because we don't have stronger, more conservative-looking leaders, and *not* because gay and lesbian persons can never get their act together. The reason they don't get the role models they need is that *society* makes it so difficult for people to come out. *Many* people should be caring more and fighting more, but we are not responsible for the gigantic right wing movement that is wreaking such havoc on *all* minority groups.

HETRICK: The problem of visible role models is complicated by another factor. Gay men and lesbians are scared to death of gay and lesbian adolescents. The reason for this, of course, is that the most effective charge that has ever been brought against us (as well as against other minorities), now more than ever, is that we are a danger to children, either as child molesters, poor role models, or poor influences. The "recruitment" issue is still big for most of the straight world, even among so-called liberals. As a result, most adult gays and lesbians run from our adolescents. And as a result of this, our youth become the most underserved subpopulation in the community. Less money comes to organizations serving gay youth than to those serving other parts of the community. People feel more comfortable supporting a political group, or a social service agency like SAGE, because older people are "safer" than adolescents. Gay and lesbian adults reflexively bend over backward to prove they are not interested in kids. Isn't that sad?

MASS: In the current political climate, you can hardly blame gay people for being hypersensitive about these things. How is the current wave of reported child abuse crimes, investigations, and media discussions affecting the Institute?

MARTIN: Have you already forgotten that our kids are the most likely of all children to be abused as adolescents? We're finding a much higher rate of reports of sexual abuse, of both males and females, in our population than one would expect. Like most victims of such abuse, they blame themselves, rather than the person who abuses them. What we're also finding is that the adult who abuses them sexually is usually straight — that is, it's the father or the married uncle, or the older brother who later gets married and despises fags.

We think it occurs more than usual because the gay kid is spotted as different, is more likely to be isolated, and is therefore singled out. Those who are more vulnerable, for any number of reasons, are the ones who get molested in general. But it's not just sexual abuse. One third of those who come to the Institute have suffered violence of one kind or another. Almost 50 percent of that violence comes from the family, because the kids have been recognized or discovered to be homosexually oriented.

MASS: What about the kind of abuse sexologist John Money talks about, the punishment or other prevention of the child's naturally developing sexuality?

HETRICK: That is a serious problem for *all* children and adolescents, but it's ten times as bad for our kids. Society at least allows heterosexual adolescents to mingle openly with their peers. Our kids are terrorized into hiding and never being able to ask *any* questions about their sexual feelings. This is one of the most cruel and widespread abuses inflicted on our young people.

MARTIN: Let's go back for a moment to the issue of the gay and lesbian adults who are afraid to be out. I'm not attacking them for being afraid. As we said earlier, you can hardly blame them. But we do have an obligation to fight that fear, to be there for the gay and lesbian kids who need us.

HETRICK: Look, we keep talking about the gay and lesbian community. If we have any future at all, it is in our young people. Yet that is the one group we ignore above all others. If that continues, our movement, our community, is doomed. It's absolutely essential that we let young gay and lesbian people know that we're much more than sexual beings. They must learn that their lives, our lives, have to do with relationships, with jobs, with everything else in the world. They need to see older, adult lesbians and gay men who have been successful in doing that. What we're really fighting — above, beyond, and beneath everything else — is ignorance.

MARTIN: The saddest part is that this ignorance is pervasive even among our peers. I'm constantly amazed by the people who have never heard of Barbara Gittings or Frank Kameny. So many people don't realize that our movement is well over 100 years old, that people like Magnus Hirschfeld and Karl Ulrichs were fighting the same battles in Europe, were having to deal with the same preposterous charges, back in the 19th century. Did you know that studies have found that 20 percent of gay men attempt suicide before the age of 20? There's this big to-do in this country right now about teenage suicide, but how often have you ever read or heard of homosexuality playing a significant part in it?

MASS: You're right. I didn't know that, though it's certainly not surprising. Of course, this is never mentioned in the mainstream media.

MARTIN: Homosexuality is a major risk factor in teenage suicide throughout the country, yet even our own community ignores this actual physical danger. For all the need that exists, the Institute is the only organization of its kind in the country.

MASS: We've been talking about global problems affecting gay and lesbian youth. What about more specific issues of health and safety, like AIDS and teenage pregnancy?

HETRICK: We're trying to deal with the AIDS crisis in an integrated and systematic way.

MASS: (sarcastically) "Integrated and Systematic"!? We've got an absolute public health crisis/emergency on our hands and you're talking about "integrated and systematic"!? Some people would say we should just stormtroop in, grab these kids by the collar, and tell them "never, ever fuck or you'll die!"

HETRICK: That simply won't work. You have to have a better plan than simply scaring the shit out of people, especially young people. Scare tactics get some people to modify their sexual behavior, but it should not be completely ignored that these tactics will also increase anxiety and fright around sexuality and increase the problems young people have in accepting their sexuality. I don't know if you remember what it was like when you were an adolescent, but kids think they're immortal. Death has little meaning for them. Most of them would just ignore a scare campaign.

MASS: (sarcastically) Then maybe we should lock them all up, in their own best interests.

MARTIN: Look, do you remember when being caught being queer meant getting beaten up, humiliated, thrown out of school, discharged from the armed forces, going to prison and going to hell? I was scared to death of all those things. So were you. But we still fucked. Do you know of anyone, anywhere, who isn't already scared about AIDS? You have to present these kids with a lot more than just fear and risk and dread, especially those kids for whom sex is the only way of making emotional and social contact. As Larry Kramer correctly points out, that's what so many of *us* learned. We made contact with our group by fucking first, getting acquainted later. That's why it's so *fundamentally* important for gay and lesbian kids to have a chance to learn more about who they are, a chance straight society has never really allowed us to give them.

HETRICK: At the Institute, we give them an opportunity to learn how to form more meaningful and stable relationships, how to date, etc. Many of our kids have learned in a more natural way how to say, "I'm not ready to have sex yet. I need to get to know the person first." We feel that in the long run, affecting the total lives of these youngsters is going to have a greater impact than any kind of scare tactics.

MASS: And in addition to this, you do, of course, tell them the truth about AIDS, about risk factors, etc.

MARTIN: Of course. We're not denying the unprecedented seriousness and importance of AIDS. But what we're saying is that responses have to be more complex than simple scare tactics. AIDS is not the only issue we have to deal with, not by a long shot. It's not even the only health issue. As you know, hepatitis B remains a serious health problem in the gay [male] community, and it may surprise you to learn that we're seeing a number of teenage lesbians who become pregnant, often as a means of hiding or trying to deny their homosexuality, or because of family pressures (the family would rather have an unmarried, pregnant daughter than a lesbian daughter).

HETRICK: True. These young women need health education and knowledge of family planning services and have a host of other needs. Our biggest problem is that we need more funding. It's a shame, too, because our program could serve as a pilot for programs all over the country. A small investment now could save the government and the nation millions later on in health costs, and could help thousands of kids in a number of other ways as well.

MASS: It sounds like the kinds of problems the Institute is having parallel those of the public schools in attempting to implement sex education courses. Prejudice and lack of funding. I donated tickets for *As Is* and *The Normal Heart* to the Institute. Did any of the kids go? What did they think?

MARTIN: They went and were extremely grateful, and their reactions were complex and fascinating. But the donation was of only two tickets for each show. Our kids can't afford such things and we needed to have a shared group experience in order for there to be a real discussion. But the idea is a good one. In the past, we've shown movies like *Boys in the Band* and gotten their reactions. It's possible, for example, to introduce health issues around the character who is promiscuous, ask questions like "What problems may come up if you go to bed with many people?" "What is this person's responsibility to his lover?" "Does he have a right to expose his lover to AIDS or other diseases?" Within this kind of context, you can make these dangers seem real to the kids without simply scaring the shit out of them, risking their denial of the seriousness of what you're telling them.

HETRICK: That's the worst danger of a simplistic fear campaign, especially with children. They'll simply deny. And, no matter how sincerely and thoroughly you advise people, there will always be those who resist. Just as there are countless millions of people who continue to smoke cigarettes, drink alcohol and otherwise knowingly expose themselves to serious risk, so some people will continue to deny the seriousness of risks they are taking sexually. Then there are unfortunately those people who reason, "I've already got the 'virus' so I'm going to die; I might as well go out having fun, so I'm going to continue to fuck whenever and with whomever I want."

MARTIN: That should not be a surprise. If you look at the histories of other epidemics, there were always a certain number of people who became even more irresponsible. There's always a range of behavioral responses to such catastrophes, and there must always be a range of programs to deal with them. One simplistic approach simply will not address everyone and everything that needs to be dealt with.

HETRICK: Unfortunately, people will often interpret what we're saying as a lack of concern. They'll say we're not as concerned as we need to be about the disease, about the fact that people are dying. They'll say we're irresponsible.

MASS: That's precisely what Larry Kramer is saying. Beyond the out-and-out lies that Gay Men's Health Crisis refused to tell the community that AIDS was contagious, refused to use the word "contagious," refused to publish information about symptoms, etc., Kramer insists that if it weren't for a few individuals, like Mayor Koch, and groups — people who fought for sexual freedom, the board of GMHC, etc., all of whom he repeatedly calls "murderers" — we would have no epidemic. When you pick a small, relatively defenseless minority and scream at the public, "*They* are to blame for all our troubles," isn't this classical scapegoating?

[Ed. note: My first GMHC communique was a letter that was called "Late Evidence on Contagious Causes," which was distributed at the time of the first GMHC benefit, "Showers" (April 1982). Like every other GMHC *Newsletter*, leaflet and booklet that we published, it contained detailed information about symptoms. And the first GMHC *Newsletter* (July 1, 1982), included the following question and answer in a section I prepared called "AID and What To Do About It" (which was the first version of what subsequently became "Basic Questions and Answers about AIDS," and eventually, in June 1984, *Medical Answers About AIDS*):

> Q: Is AID contagious?
> A: There continues to be no incontrovertible evidence to suggest that AID is overtly contagious. Informed speculation, however, suggests that an infectious agent — perhaps a 'virus such as cytomegalovirus or Epstein-Barr virus — is at least a critical factor in the outbreak. Federal health officers are currently paying intense scrutiny to "clusters" of the syndrome, which seem to be appearing in coastal and Sun Belt cities more than in the Midwest and Northeast and Canada.

(It is a copy of this first GMHC *Newsletter* that the fictional Dr. Brookner throws to the floor — a gesture suggesting it is worthless and/or incompetent — in the first act of *The Normal Heart*.)

During the same time frame (fall 1982), Larry Kramer and I prepared a leaflet for distribution at the bars and baths called "AIDS: What You Should Know About Our Health Emergency." It concluded with the following question and recommendations:

> Q: Is AIDS Contagious?
> A: Not through simple social contact. But current opinion points to something like a virus that MAY BE transmitted sexually.

Two years later, I realized we had been using the word contagious much too casually. The fourth and fifth revisions of *Medical Answers* (1985 and 1987) thus included the following question and answer:

> Q: Do the terms communicable, contagious, infectious and transmissible all mean the same thing?
> A: The words communicable, and transmissible mean that the disease-causing organism may spread from person to person, without specifying the mode of transmission. An infectious disease is not necessarily communicable or transmissible from person to person but *may* be so — sexually, parenterally, and/or from casual or household contact. The word contagious, however, can imply disease transmission from casual or household contact . . . Therefore the word contagious (and contagion) should not be used to characterize PCP, HIV infection or AIDS.]

MARTIN: I think it's interesting that he is calling a number of gay people exactly what Paul Cameron is calling us: murderers. To call GMHC — a group of gay men from the community who are working as hard as they can under impossible circumstances — murderers is, at the very least, unfair. I think disagreement is good. I think criticism of our agencies is good. But I don't think calling each other murderers is simple disagreement. It's self-hatred.
MASS: On a recent episode of *Crossfire*. Cameron called not simply for the quarantining of all gays, but for their extermination. Is Cameron as dangerous as Anita Bryant was? More so?
MARTIN: Part of me wants to dismiss him, to say, "He'll hang himself." But remember, people said the same thing about Hitler. And remember also that Hitler's ascension to power took place

within the system. No. No matter how paranoid and insane he may sound, I don't take Cameron lightly.

HETRICK: In psychiatry we still don't have a full understanding of this kind of psychopathology. The grandiosity, the perversity, the extremity of the position often reflects an underlying theme that exists within the whole society, and therefore, unfortunately, the whole society can resonate to it. The Holocaust is but one example of this. Hitler would not have been able to do what he did if his position, extreme as it was, did not overlap to a certain extent with society's attitude toward those who were "different." I have to admit that I am likewise very frightened of Paul Cameron.

MASS: This kind of dread the two of you are expressing is not so different from the kind of dread Kramer aroused in his comparisons of today's gays with Jews in the early 1930s. But what he's additionally saying is that we're all murderers, because we're not fighting harder to prevent the catastrophe he foresees.

MARTIN: I agree with him in the analogies between Jews and gays, but I don't think we're murderers. I'm no longer a Catholic. I no longer accept the idea that you get just punishment for your actions. Nobody *deserves* to be killed, whether it's by AIDS, by Hitler, by the hand of God, or whatever. The parallel between the Jews who did not recognize the danger that they and their brothers and sisters face is valid. Just as with the Jews in the 1930s, the belief that "it could never happen to me" is prevalent in the gay community today. But, as angry as I get at people who refuse to care, to participate, to acknowledge the seriousness of what's happening, I would never go so far as to say they *deserve* what they get. Even the gay people I know who voted for Reagan, and there were plenty, don't deserve to be murdered by fascists.

MASS: Kramer concludes from it all that our number one problem is the absence of great, powerful, selfless leaders, like Dr. Martin Luther King, Jr. Do you agree?

MARTIN: No. Our major problem is *not* a lack of charismatic leaders. I'd rather have a little less charisma and a lot more organizational and fundraising experience come out of our community.

[Ed. note: Boxed within the larger interview, "Protecting Lesbian and Gay Youth," was a second, smaller interview, conducted by telephone with Damien Martin, about the controversial new Harvey

Milk High School. It was entitled "Doing It All for That Kid in Altoona."]

MASS: How could such an important thing as the first school in history specifically geared to the needs of gay and lesbian students have been going on in our community for several months and escaped everybody's attention?

MARTIN: I think it has to do with the way the media pay attention to social service organizations in the gay community. We were not secretive. In fact, we were telling everyone in sight. *We* were the ones who approached the *New York Times* about doing a story on the school. This was just a few weeks ago. The attitude at first was that this probably wasn't much of a new story. We thought it would be a small item in the education or style section. Then it turned up on the front page.

MASS: How did the school come about?

MARTIN: We gradually began to identify a number of kids who were dropouts or chronic truants and who were having severe problems staying in school. We tried a number of things—working with teachers, finding alternative schools for them, etc. It was Steve Ashkenazy, in conjunction with Wayne Steinman in Manfred Ohrenstein's office, and a few other people, who first conceived of the idea of an alternative high school, and who first approached the Board of Education.

MASS: Exactly what is the connection between IPLGY and the Harvey Milk School?

MARTIN: The school is an official alternative high school of the New York City Board of Education. The Institute is a community organization that provides support services for the school. These range from our paying the school's rent and purchasing certain supplies to providing a social worker and counselor who offer individual and group counseling for the kids. We also find volunteer tutors for those who are having special problems in certain areas. We offer socialization programs at a drop-in center for the young people as part of our overall services. In other words, we take the services that we deliver to gay and lesbian youth in general and we make them available to the school, free of charge.

MASS: What does it mean that the school was established without a vote of the school board?

MARTIN: It doesn't mean anything. The school board does not have to vote on the establishment of an alternative high school. We followed all the appropriate procedures.

MASS: When interviewed on a recent TV news program, Dr. Robert Gould, a well-known specialist in adolescent psychiatry, raised the issue of such a school aggravating the idea of "difference" or "handicap" in these kids.

MARTIN: I think what Dr. Gould is pointing out is that one runs the risk here of having those people who see homosexuality as an illness now saying things like "See, here's further proof that they're different and that you have to treat them as different." Dr. Gould was talking about how this information might be misused, rather than about the school itself. I know this to be true because I spoke with him subsequently. Overall, he's very much in favor of the school.

MASS: If the gay kids are displaying "flamboyant behavior," as Schools Chancellor Nathan Quinones puts it, why aren't they being hustled into "gender reinforcement" clinics, to change their behavior — the kind of therapy many psychiatrists still support?

MARTIN: Because we're not interested in changing that kind of behavior *per se*. Our primary interest at this moment is to get them an education. Everyone is convinced that a high school education is a necessity for even the most basic jobs. You have to set priorities for those kids' problems, and our first priority is their education.

One point should be made here, however. Sometimes, certain kinds of so-called sissy behavior can in fact be a kind of hostile acting-out on the part of a youngster. Although our first priority, as I said, is not to change these kids' behavior but to educate them, we do try to help them understand that they have choices about at least some of their behavior in certain circumstances. Beyond all our legitimate concerns about homophobia and sexism, it's important for kids to understand, in the context of the real world in which they live today, how certain behavior will trigger certain responses in some people.

We don't see being gay or lesbian as an abnormality or special handicap that needs to be corrected so much as a special circumstance, like pregnancy, that justifies special educational arrangements. We don't tell our kids that putting on a dress or wearing make-up is bad. On the other hand, we do tell them that they have choices about these matters, choices that should be made with a realistic awareness of what the responses may be. An analogy can be made here with advising people about interviewing for a job. You and I may believe that people who don't wear ties to job interviews are no less worthy of consideration than those who do. Yet we may advise them, realistically, that they may better their chances of getting the job by wearing the tie.

MASS: Don't you think it's better to keep these kids in public schools, in the mainstream, when — and wherever possible?

MARTIN: Of course. One of the misconceptions that keeps coming up is what the school is. This is not a high school for gay and lesbian students. This is a high school for students who are drop-outs, who can't function in a regular school, because they happen to be noticeably lesbian or gay. We advise gay and lesbian students who are happy and well-adjusted in their current school situations to stay where they are. And one of our primary goals, of course, is to *return* those kids who do attend Harvey Milk School back into mainstream schools and back into the mainstream of society. Again, we are talking about only a subgroup of the larger group, who need these special, alternative school facilities.

MASS: If society were more tolerant of gay people, would there be any need for such alternative schools?

MARTIN: No one would be happier than I if there were no need for either the school or for the Institute.

MASS: Is there any difference between the basic curriculum of the Harvey Milk School and that of other public high schools?

MARTIN: The basic curriculum our kids study is standard and leads to a high school diploma.

MASS: One of the most controversial ideas for the public is this business of saying which famous persons were gay or not gay. Is it true that the kids are learning that "Shakespeare was gay"?

MARTIN: I disagree with Steve Ashkinazy about this. I don't think you can say Shakespeare was gay, but there *is* a lot of scholarly debate about the sonnets. Why shouldn't the students learn that this kind of debate is going on?

MASS: Why did you choose to name the school after Harvey Milk?

MARTIN: There's a marvelous line in the Academy Award-winning film documentary, *The Times of Harvey Milk*, where Harvey says he's doing it all for that kid in Altoona. We couldn't think of a more wonderful human being or better role model for the kids than Harvey Milk.

The Swastika and the Pink Triangle: Nazis and Gay Men

An Interview with Richard Plant

[Ed. note: A concern that reverberates throughout these dialogues becomes salient in these interviews with Richard Plant and Arnie Kantrowitz: that *some* homosexual and lesbian individuals have been, historically and today, so self-hating, so nonidentified as homosexual or lesbian, that they can espouse a fascistic politics that is openly committed to their own destruction. Otherwise, these discussions are related only at the level of appearances. Whereas the overriding concern of the interview with Professor Plant is to document the Nazi persecutions and mass murders of homosexuals, the latter looks at a contemporary issue that is at best tangential to (rather than consanguineous with) this subject — the implications of Nazi imagery in pornography.]

Richard Plant is well known to the gay community for his frequent essays, interviews and lectures on the subject of his book, *The Pink Triangle: The Nazi War Against Homosexuals* (A New Republic Book, Henry Holt and Company, New York, 1986, 257 pages, including Appendices with a Chronology, Notes, Selected Bibliography and Index, $19.95). Since emigrating to the U.S. in 1938, he has contributed numerous essays and reviews to many publications, including *The Advocate, Esquire, Christopher Street, The New York Native, The New Yorker, The New York Times,* and *Saturday Review.* He is also the author of a novel, *The Dragon in the Forest,* and coauthor of Jack Beeson's opera *Lizzie Borden.* He currently teaches at the New School for Social Research in New York City.

MASS: The Pink Triangle is essentially a history, framed by an account of your own experiences as a political refugee, of the con-

ceptualization, implementation and aftermath of the Nazi persecutions and mass murders of homosexuals. In your chapter on Ernst
Roehm, you state that the "Night of the Long Knives" (June 28-
July 3, 1934)—when approximately 300 of the S.A. militia and its
chief, Roehm, were assassinated by rival S.S. troopers under orders
from Hitler—was the signal that homosexuals would henceforth be
targeted by the Nazis: "Precisely one year after the Night of the
Long Knives, and shortly before the anti-Jewish laws were announced in Nuremberg, stringent new laws concerning homosexual
conduct among men were promulgated. [These laws amended and
expanded the scope of Paragraph 175, which had been part of the
German penal code since 1871, and which stated that any male over
the age of 21 "who indulges in criminally indecent activities with
another male or who allows himself to participate in such activities
will be punished with jail."] The date on which these new restrictions were made public—June 28, 1935-clearly alluded to the
Roehm purge of the year before. The crusade against those dangerous contragenics, the homosexuals, was on."

PLANT: Yes, the assassination of Roehm was the signal. And I
devote my next chapter ["The Grand Inquisitor"] to Roehm's
former subordinate and rival, Heinrich Himmler, who became the
architect of this crusade. In 1936, when Himmler was appointed
chief of all SS and police forces, he established the Federal Security
Office for Combating Homosexuality and Abortion, which was a
department of the Gestapo. There have been very few books about
Himmler, and I discovered that his obsessive rantings and ravings
about homosexuals as archenemies of the German race had never
been properly documented. Whether this neglect is itself more a
problem of homophobia than of Himmler's comparative lack of
charisma, I can't say. Some of his most homophobic speeches and
memoranda didn't surface until 1974.

MASS: You use the word "crusade" to characterize the xenophobia
with which Himmler pursued gays, but you also imply that his homophobia was less religious than military in character. What do you
mean?

PLANT: German homophobia wasn't really like that in America,
which derived from Puritanism, was fanned by the church, and reflected a negative attitude towards all things sexual. It wasn't de-

rived from the kind of religiosity that, in this country, led to prohibition. The Nazi hatred of gays was based on the fear that male homosexuals were racial degenerates who were incapable of fighting, and who would pollute and corrupt the real men who were doing the fighting. That's what Himmler believed. He wanted a race of soldiers that would make Germany more powerful than any other nation and that would conquer the world. In Himmler's ideology, homosexuals were like hens that couldn't lay eggs.

MASS: Nazi homophobia may not have been explicitly or consciously "religious," but whether religious or military, homophobia is inevitably masculinist. In this context, Himmler's preoccupation with male homosexuality is comprehensible.

PLANT: Lesbianism was never punished by law, even in the old German code. What this reflects, of course, is the ancient patriarchal attitude that women simply don't count. In 1937 an effort was made by the young Nazi lawyer Rudolf Klare, author of a book about homosexuality and the penal code [*Homosexualität und Strafrecht*] to try to extend the laws to proscribe sexual activity between women, but Himmler rejected these recommendations because he couldn't conceptualize how or why it would make any difference what women did with one another. They weren't fighters, they weren't going to corrupt the men, and they could always be *forced* to carry pregnancies. Despite the absence of stringent codification, some lesbians were persecuted by the secret police and in the camps, but very few.

MASS: Your book contains fascinating new documentation that just as Himmler ideologically distinguished male homosexuals from lesbians, he likewise distinguished "aryan" from nonaryan male homosexuals in his legislation.

PLANT: That was something really new. In Germany and in countries that were later to become part of the greater German empire, homosexuality was fully prosecuted. On the other hand, in Poland and Czechoslovakia, where the people were considered to be racially subhuman and where population increases were discouraged by a variety of means, the laws against homosexuality were sometimes softened. They didn't want homosexuals to corrupt *aryan* soldiers. This, however, is a minor consideration in the Nazi war against homosexuals.

MASS: The racial thinking was so convoluted. Why didn't they apply the same logic to the Jews? That is, why didn't they allow Jewish "race defilers" to flourish in occupied territories they considered to be nonaryan for the same reasons they tolerated "contragenic" gays?

PLANT: I haven't figured that one out, except to suggest that Hitler's hatred of the Jews transcended all other considerations. The Nazis had two goals. One was to conquer and rule Europe and the world; that is, to win the war. The other was to annihilate the Jewish race. But Hitler's obsession with the Jews was such that he sabotaged the war effort. When it became clear in '42 or '43 that they weren't going to win the war, Hitler concentrated on murdering as many Jews as possible. So there was a lot of illogical, interconflicting strategizing on many levels. But I think this distinguishing of aryan gays from contragenic gays was essentially just another of Himmler's little crackpot ideas. Incidentally, I found out that the Vichy regime also persecuted gays. This hasn't been adequately researched yet, but the evidence is there.

MASS: Let's go back to Ernst Roehm. In the conclusion of your chapter on him, you state that "the real meaning of the Roehm affair escaped even the most seasoned observers: namely, that under Hitler, wholesale murder had become a permissible principle of state." Weren't the Nazis under Roehm already murdering groups of people — the Jews — in the name of the state?

PLANT: Yes. I want to make this clear. The murder of Jews had already been sanctioned, but not the murder of their own troops. In the Roehm case, the lawyers declared that Hitler had acted legally to protect the honor of the Reich. This was a real turning point. Henceforth, dissenters would be prosecuted to the fullest extent of the law, which now extended to the murder of whole groups.

MASS: Now I'm confused. When you used the word "sanctioned," do you mean tacitly or legislatively? *Was* the Night of The Long Knives in 1934 in some sense the legal precedent for what became the Final Solution in 1942 (which was never explicitly legislated)? What I'm trying to get at is this. Were the mass murders of Roehm and his brown shirts legally sanctioned explicitly because of their homosexual crimes, and if so were these, then, the first murders of an unwanted minority group to become explicitly legal?

PLANT: These executions were sanctioned because the perpetrators were accused of having attempted an uprising against Hitler. That there were "homosexual deviants" among them was used to inflame the emotions of the folk. The main point was that the courts made the Roehm assassinations legal retroactively. But let's not try to find logic in Nazi legal thinking!

MASS: So dissension within the ranks, a power rivalry, rather than homosexuality, was the real issue in the Roehm case . . .

PLANT: Yes. Roehm had a sort of fiefdom of his own, a power base that was resisting Hitler's efforts to centralize the Nazi command. Himmler never really made it to a position of membership in Hitler's private court, by the way. He was very powerful but unlike his predecessor, Roehm, he never directly influenced Hitler's military decisions.

MASS: Are you implying that Himmler's obsessional homophobia was really based more on his power struggle with Roehm than on hatred of homosexuals?

PLANT: No. Himmler's homophobia was quite real. His obsession with homosexuality was a little like Hitler's obsession with the Jews. Coincidentally, this homophobia proved to be a convenient weapon to use in the power struggles that were going on between Hitler, Himmler and the SS on one side, and Roehm and the SA on the other.

MASS: You talk about Himmler as a character who was so bizarre that not even a Dickens could have invented him. You also said that he was a drab person.

PLANT: Yes. Himmler was both deadly and colorless. I've given this aspect of his character much space in my chapter 3 ["The Grand Inquisitor"]. All this can be read in my attempt to make him more understandable.

MASS: One of the ugliest prejudices the gay movement has had to deal with is the mythology that homosexuals were pervasively involved in the hierarchy of Nazi Germany. Your book establishes that Roehm, who was eliminated in 1934, was the only prominent Nazi known to be homosexual, and that whatever the circumstantial or even enthusiastic participation of a relatively small number of individual homosexual German citizens, the overwhelming fact of the relationship between homosexuals and fascism in Nazi Germany was the victimization of the former by the latter. Is this correct?

PLANT: Yes. This notion that the Nazi leadership was riddled with homosexuals is wishful thinking on the part of those who are looking for easy scapegoats and simple explanations. Unfortunately, even some of our most authoritative observers, writing at a time when ignorance and prejudice about homosexuality were still pervasive, reflect this problem. For example, I don't want to take away from [William L.] Shirer's merits as one of the early American journalists to alert the USA to the dangers of the whole Nazi movement, but he didn't deal with the persecution of homosexuals at all [there is no listing of homosexuality in the index of *The Rise and Fall of the Third Reich*]. On the other hand, he hints, somewhere, that among Hitler's cohorts were thieves, thugs, criminals and homosexuals. This was an inaccurate generalization. Incidentally, my statements about the complete absence of known homosexuals from the Nazi ranks after the assassination of Roehm are not controversial. I know of no respected, contemporary observer who believes otherwise.

MASS: In your book, you cite examples of several films that have contributed to this prejudice.

PLANT: Yes, I cite Visconti's *The Damned* and Bertolucci's *The Conformist*, but they weren't the only ones. The lunacy that Nazi soldiers — in uniform! — would have publicly consorted with drag queens [as in *The Damned*] gives you some idea of the levels of distortion we're dealing with here.

MASS: Visconti and Bertolucci were proudly, self-assertingly communist. They were also admittedly gay, but apologetically so. In *The Pink Triangle*, you point out the Left's repeated betrayals of gays despite the official positions of support of homosexual rights the Bolshevik Revolution had established in 1917. It's discouraging to realize that homophobia is compatible with any politics that is masculinist, whether of the "left" or "right."

PLANT: Just before the Hitler-Stalin pact in 1939, the Russians made a movie called *The Traitors* by a German emigré communist named Gustav von Wangenheim in which the Nazi leadership was portrayed as gay. When the pact was signed, of course, the movie could not be released. I never saw it. Recently, it was supposed to be shown in Holland, but left wing groups prevented it from being distributed. In any event, this tactic of feminizing and homosexualizing the enemy is identical to that of trying to make him Jewish. Both derive their power from centuries old prejudices that are widely shared. If you want to really vilify your enemy, make him Jewish or effete. Now, nobody could say that the Nazis were Jews or communists, of course, since these groups were such well-known, principal targets of Nazi hatred and persecution. So what was left? Homosexuals. I think, unfortunately, that Shirer and other early observers shared a tendency towards this kind of scapegoating.

MASS: I think one area where confusion still exists is over the connection some people are tempted to make between the espousal of a homosexual identity and the subliminal homoeroticism that pervades all fascistic, militaristic and other masculinist phenomena. Or between a homosexual identity and the masculinist imagery that may seem to distinguish some homosexual, sadomasochistic pornography. It's probable that up until 1934, a number of homosexuals — closeted types who weren't active in the contemporary homosexual emancipation movement in Germany — were, like other German citizens, willingly involved in the Nazi cause. After 1934, some continued to pass. As you've indicated, we'll never know how many.

[Ed. note: At Professor Plant's request, the following passage was eliminated from this question in the published version of the interview that appeared in *Christopher Street*: "Even today there are a few deranged individuals who publicly identify themselves as 'gay Nazis' (as one person does in Rosa von Praunheim's film documentary, *Revolt of the Perverts*). But with the rarest of exceptions, openly, self-assertingly gay men, then and today, have clearly understood that their security as members of a sexual minority is not compatible with masculinist politics. Those types who were closeted or who were politically unconscious about their homosexuality, like Ernst Roehm (or like the Robert Baumans, Terry Dolans or Roy Cohns of today), are inevitably surprised when the masculinist politics they've espoused ends up betraying them."]

Incidentally, your book notes that Roehm wrote an autobiography. What's it like? Does he indicate any self-awareness as a member of a sexual minority?

PLANT: No. It's a rambling, artless, and completely undistinguished book. It has never been translated and never will be. He never even mentions his sexual preference, though perhaps there are some hints. We know from the scandals he was involved in that he was less closeted than many of his ilk, but the autobiography is that of a soldier and monarchist — loyalties he transferred to Hitler, not the biography of a gay man.

MASS: You point out that Roehm had a virtually unique closeness to Hitler, as a friend and supporter from the early days.

PLANT: Yes. When Hitler was discharged, Roehm, who was a regular army man, gave Hitler his first job. Roehm saw that Hitler was a good speaker and assigned him to speak to small groups about the need for Germany to rearm. Their friendship was such that Roehm was the only high ranking Nazi Hitler addressed with the informal "Du." The only other persons with whom he publicly used the familiar were his valet and a chauffeur, Maurice. Hitler knew about Roehm's homosexuality, of course, but chose to ignore it as long as Roehm was useful to him.

MASS: So with the Night of the Long Knives and the stringent amendments to Paragraph 175 in 1935, any and all homosexual inclinations had to go underground.

PLANT: Yes. As I've said, there were no high-ranking Nazis after Roehm who were known to be homosexual, though I might mention here the famous actor, Gustaf Gruendgens. Gruendgens was much admired by Goering's wife, so even though the bisexual actor's affairs were as notorious as Roehm's, Goering appointed him head of the State Theater and he quickly became head of theatrical life in the Third Reich. Grundgens, of course, is the subject of Klaus Mann's bitter satire, *Mephisto*. He had been married to Mann's sister, Erika.

MASS: In your book, you state that Klaus Mann, whom we know today to have been a very politically conscious and heroic gay man, wrote the book "to analyze the abject type of treacherous intellectual who prostitutes his talent for the sake of some tawdry fame and transitory wealth." I'm so glad you included that.

PLANT: Gruendgens was an example of the kind of bisexual or gay man who found a way to pass. As we know, the SS was a barbaric organization, divided into various subgroups. Some of these groups consisted more of businessmen than fanatics, and sometimes you could bribe somebody, if you were careful and knew the right people. Or if you were in the right profession, such as medicine or engineering. I met a gay physician who survived and described what his life was like. He said it was very Kafkaesque. He could never have sex, he had to get married and live with his wife, and, of course, he could never speak to anyone about his preferences. So many bisexual and gay men were able to pass, even though hundreds of thousands were arrested on charges of homosexuality.

MASS: And what happened to the thousands of male homosexuals who weren't able to pass or bribe their way out? In the camps, which you so vividly call "boomtowns of hell" in your book, what happened to them? First, how were they treated differently from other designated groups?

PLANT: All groups, of course, were treated badly. The professional criminals fared best. They were the ones with the green triangles. The other groups, especially the largest of them, at least tended towards some sort of self-regulation and organization. In some camps, brave Jewish inmates had managed to establish some sort of organization, so even though millions were killed, there was a certain coherence. But the gays were too scattered and few in number to have any kind of group identity. They didn't even know each other or if they did, they were distrustful. So they had no power in the camps. They were one of the smallest groups and were frequently selected for the worst tasks.

For example, one of the worst assignments for labor was in the quarries, where prisoners had to work with bricks, cement and impossibly heavy loads. These assignments had the highest mortality. If the camp were being "run" by the greens (the criminals) or the reds (the politicals), as many camps were, they would preferentially select from outside their own groups. Since the gays invariably had the least power of any of the designated groups, they often got the worst of these assigments.

MASS: According to your research, in fact, they had the lowest likelihood of survival.

PLANT: That's what my research has shown. When you speak of the Nazi concentration camps, of course, it's very difficult to say who was treated "the worst." In hell, these distinctions are relatively fine. But at the end of the war when the camps were liberated, the percentage of those survivors who had been designated as homosexual, those with the pink triangle, was the lowest of any of the groups.

MASS: Touching this issue is one of your most controversial findings — the much *lower* estimate of the total number of persons specifically designated as homosexual who died in the camps. Earlier estimates have been as high as hundreds of thousands, but your more conservative figure is fifteen to twenty-five thousand. Or is it five to fifteen thousand?

PLANT: I am not sure. I would *estimate* that around 15,000 died, but it may be closer to 20,000 or to 10,000. These numbers are derived, like so much of my information, from the research team of Professor Ruediger Lautmann of Bremen. But I must stress that *we do not know* the real numbers. There is important archival material in East Germany, Eastern Europe and Russia that has yet to be researched. The information is still altogether too incomplete. Like the greater discipline of gay history itself, the study of the Nazi persecutions of homosexuals is still in its infancy. We do know that in the years from 1933 to 1944 something like 50-60,000 men were arrested and charged with crimes of homosexuality. The documentation of that is in my Appendix.

I think I should say something here about this business of placing so much emphasis on numbers. It's unfortunate that some have chosen to interpret what happened to gays, Jehovah's witnesses, gypsies and other groups as something that somehow lessens the enormity of what was done to the Jews. I think we have to embrace the full scope of the Nazi horror and I'm proud that Elie Wisel — who is a very great man and a genius and who, after all is *the* spokesperson for the Holocaust — is preparing a conference on other victims of the Holocaust. I think this is a very significant development.

MASS: An article in a recent issue of the *New York Times* stated that the West German government will for the first time officially and formally attempt to compensate gypsy survivors of the Holocaust. Have any gay groups or persons, presenting themselves as gay and as having been persecuted by the Nazis for being gay, have any such groups or persons been formally compensated by the West German government?

PLANT: I'm not sure, but following Bitburg, Richard von Weizsaecker, the President of West Germany, mentioned that homosexuals were among the victims of the Holocaust who have not yet been sufficiently honored. I believe this was the first time that such a high level acknowledgment had been made.

MASS: When I began reading your book, I was brashly confident that I could handle the material. After all, I thought, apart from specific details of exactly which officer did exactly which atrocity to which ethnic, demographic, political, denominational, sexual or other subcultural group, is there really any major overview observation about the Nazi evil that hasn't already been widely assimilated? To my horror, I discovered the affirmative answer to that question in the conclusion of *The Pink Triangle*. Your suggestion that the twentieth century may have seen the most brutal mistreatment of minorities in history is extended to your book's final statement: "The specters begin to come to life whenever fanatical fundamentalists of any sect — religious or secular — take over a nation and call for a holy war against its most vulnerable and vilified minorities."

For you personally, how powerful are the parallels between what happened in Germany in the 1930s and what is escalating throughout the world today?

PLANT: They are powerful. I look at what's happening all over the world and I see that in the eighties, in so many spheres of life, the fanatics are pushing out the pragmatists. Look at what's happening in the Near East. What they're doing to each other is against all common sense. I think we're entering a new Middle Ages. Certainly, the Age of Enlightenment is over. What I'm saying now is, of course, personal speculation and outside the scope of my book. But I see this fanaticism all over, and it scares me, just as it scares you.

Nazis and Gay Men II

An Exchange with Arnie Kantrowitz

Writer and veteran gay activist Arnie Kantrowitz was vice-president of Gay Activists Alliance and a cofounder of the Gay and Lesbian Alliance Against Defamation. He is the author of *Under the Rainbow*: *Growing Up Gay*, an autobiography, and is currently completing a novel. A journalist since the early 1970s, he is also a poet and is associate professor of English at the College of Staten Island, City University of New York. The exchange which follows began with informal discussions in 1987 and was completed in 1989.

MASS: You and I have talked about the problems that we feel are raised by the eroticization of the swastika in commercially available pornography. We've always agreed that everyone should have the right to do whatever she or he wishes with Nazi or with any other paraphernalia in privacy. It's when that paraphernalia and/or those acts become public that controversy can sometimes arise. In the past, you've sent letters of concern to both *Manpower* and *Drummer* magazines regarding their use of the swastika and other fascist imagery or subject matter. Please tell us about these communications.

KANTROWITZ: In May, 1984, *Drummer* magazine published a story by Roy F. Wood called "The Conquering Strength," whose narrator, in order to obtain the sexual favors of a Central American military dictator, allows himself to become a tool in the enslavement of a people, even though it will cost him his own life. I wrote a letter protesting the promulgation of such a politically anti-democratic sexual object and the (obviously) nonconsensual involvement of a nation's people as the victims of repression, torture and murder, all for the sake of an orgasm. The letter was published without editorial comment. I also received an unpublished answer, which assured me that the story was not an endorsement of fascism, but a comment on the dangers of becoming fascinated with fascism, and that my response was in fact the desired one. I can only take the editor at his word, but I cannot be certain that *all* the readers were sophisticated enough to understand the message since it was never made explicit.

MASS: But did the story arouse *you* sexually?

KANTROWITZ: Certainly not. In a similar incident in February, 1986, I encountered a Colt publication called *Manpower: The Leather File*, already some years old at that time, in which several of the models wore swastikas on caps and jackets, one of them very prominent. Again I protested, stating that for me the swastika was a political symbol that reminded me of the Holocaust rather than an erotic symbol that aroused me. The responding letter contained several disclaimers: (1) The photographer was no longer involved with the studio, (2) The models wore their own clothing, (3) The swastika is actually an Indian design, (4) Colt studio never did and never will support Nazi politics, and (5) That issue of *Manpower* is the only one in which that symbol was displayed. The multiple excuses suggested to me that the magazine was indeed apolitical and that its publishers had low political consciousness and sensitivity. The notion that the swastika was an allusion to the Hopi symbol was patently absurd, since that magazine's readers are obviously aroused by storm trooper paraphernalia and not by the arcane spiritual symbols of a peace-loving Indian tribe.

Since those incidents, I have seen swastika tattoos on models in newsstand magazines such as *Honcho* and Nazi uniforms on actors in [commercially available] erotic videotapes, so it's clear that the eroticized swastika is becoming more common and, one assumes, more acceptable.

MASS: I think that's true. But the swastika is an ancient American Indian (and Buddhist) symbol and one that some gay men do find especially appealing, despite its associations with fascism. In *RFD* (Spring 1989), for example, there's a poem I showed you called "Swastika Lovers" by Mark Lind in which gay lovers are metaphorized "as two sticks-overlaid." Following the poem, there's a paragraph about the history of the swastika in which Hitler's desecration of this symbol of peace and a balance of forces is denounced as "a shameful crime." (The author and his lover are residents of Santa Fe and are at work on a book called *The (Complete) Swastika*.) Was this poem similarly problematic for you?

KANTROWITZ: Lind's attempt to connect with the swastika's original meaning as an ancient symbol of peace and harmony has a certain charm, which is more readily accessible against the background of Indian culture in the Southwest where he lives, but his attempt to reduce the effect of Hitler's appropriation of the symbol to an unfortunate but easily reversible fifty year interlude is dangerously naive. "To let it go on being misinterpreted would be more shameful," he concludes, apparently imagining that his good intentions are enough to neutralize the image Hitler branded into world consciousness and that his loving words can restore to its original benevolence the esoteric image created by ancient cultures. This is reminiscent of the fantasy of the Radical Faeries that they can reconnect themselves to cultural roots that weren't originally their own, which is just as far-fetched as the power fantasies reenacted by the leather community. Both extremes are out of touch with the pained responses of real people in the late twentieth century to this reminder of the worst evil perpetrated in human history and the hatred that survived it. The symbol I see crudely scrawled on bathroom walls and subway posters almost every day is surely no statement of peace and love. It is a sign that anti-Semitism is alive and well, and even if it died tomorrow, it would take at least several generations and the further spread of historical illiteracy to exorcise the evil of the swastika symbol — but that forgetting of history implies that the benevolent origins of the symbol will be even more fully forgotten in the West than they were before Hitler used it.

MASS: When I complained to a leathersex friend about the presence of swastikas in a leather issue of *Colt*, he said that, as he saw it, these images should have no more power to provoke or disturb than images of army or police uniforms. "It's just porn," he said. Should people be upset over such popular, commercial porn fantasies of Klansmen raping black women or black nationals raping white women or men in Russian military gear with hammer and sickle badges raping peasants? He didn't think so. Was he right?

KANTROWITZ: Any fantasy of power needs some specific embodiment in order to be acted out, and in that sense the images of police and army uniforms are merely symbols of authority, which the sexual participant consents to accept. Theoretically, it shouldn't matter what city the policeman's uniform is from or which nation the soldier represents. But to find historical oppressors romanticized into sexual objects, their images burnished with eroticism, is at least disquieting and possibly terrifying or enraging, which is why I wrote those letters of protest.

What I'm uncertain about is whether the use of such images suggests an unfeeling disregard or an enhanced respect for the pain of actual historical victims. I also wonder about the use of images so common that they have become trite. Why don't we see the Israeli dominating the Palestinian or the Yankee subduing the rebel? I suspect that many of us would be even more uncomfortable with those images. There is a positive side to seeing negative figures performing unpleasant acts, even if those acts are arousing to some observers.

The issue is the trivialization of evil, but it's not clear how concrete a problem that is. "It's just porn," suggests that erotic fictions have little or no bearing on nonsexual opinions or behavior. That may be true, and in any case, the depictions are certainly no more trivial than the portraits of bumbling, ineffective Nazis in such television sitcoms as *Hogan's Heroes*. At least one videotape, *Razor's Edge*, reverses the usual symbolism and presents a Nazi officer as the victim of a body shaving administered by a man in leather jeans; so the Nazi's authority can be overcome, which is at least historically accurate. The danger, of course, lies in not taking seriously the real dangers of fascism, but as far as I know, no connection has been demonstrated between erotic fantasy and political action.

The attempts of feminists to discourage sex objectification have clearly failed, and I think it is widely agreed that "politically correct" sex rarely leads to orgasm. Though we cannot expect to alter behavior which is based on deep-seated needs, it is not out of order to educate people about the implications of the imagery they employ and the valid reactions triggered in others when they make their private fantasies publicly visible. Since we cannot and should not police the imaginations of others, it seems pointless to get upset over their private fantasies, but it is somewhat disconcerting to see an era of sexual politics, which made sexuality part of history, give way to an era of political sexual fantasies, which reduces history to a sexual aid.

MASS: In 1987 you were made an honorary member of *Gay Male S/M Activists* (GMSMA). In a ceremonial tribute to you, David Stein made reference to an article you'd written for *The Advocate* about S/M and GMSMA called "A Minority's Minority Steps From The Shadows" (published 5/29/84, originally entitled "The Leather Lobby"). Five years later, have the views you expressed in this article changed in any significant way?

KANTROWITZ: I continue to support the rights of the leather community to dress as they please (*pace* animal rights activists) and to engage in consensual sadomasochistic acts. The main point of my article was that the fear and dislike suffered by the S/M community vis à vis the gay community is a nearly exact parallel to the fear and loathing suffered by the gay community vis-à-vis society at large. Part of the problem is that their external appearance and their visible behavior belie the sexual and political realities of their lives. What looks violent and fascistic is often a roundabout way of expressing erotic affection and political liberalism. Of course, there must be exceptions to this observation, which is anecdotal and not statistical, but I believe that viciousness and anti-democracy are no more common in the leather world than they are in the rest of society, whether heterosexual or gay.

MASS: I couldn't agree more.

KANTROWITZ: Early in 1989, I spoke to GMSMA on the topic of their taking their rightful place as a respected minority in the gay world. In that talk, I pointed out my personal reaction to the use of the swastika, explaining that I object to attacks on my self-respect as a Jew as much as I resent derogatory comments about my gay male identity. I stated that if I thought fascism were implicit in the real-world politics of S/M, I'd walk out.

Soon after my talk, I was contacted by a Jewish member of the organization whose desire to wear leather came into conflict with his identity as the son of concentration camp survivors, especially when a strange woman confronted him in the street for looking like a storm trooper. I don't pretend to be a psychologist, but it seems plausible to me that this man's family background had robbed him of a sense of strength, which was replaced by identification with the oppressor — adopting the appearance of those who had injured his self-respect. In public, however, his appearance had an unwanted effect on strangers, who had not consented to be the audience to his theater piece.

On other occasions, I've taken the role of the woman who confronted him. Once, an acquaintance insisted that I try on his leather cap to see how good I would look. I refused to do so until he had removed the small swastika pin from the hatband, explaining that to wear it would damage my integrity. I don't know whether he was attempting to bolster my ego with the cap or to make fun of me with the pin, but he did remove the pin. Another time, I was startled to see that the arm of a clerk who was waiting on me in a store was tattooed with the double lightning bolt of Hitler's *Schutzstaffel* (SS). I asked him directly if he were a Nazi, and he assured me that it was just a form of "punk" body art which he was about to have covered since it had drawn so much negative criticism. I don't think that either of these men was a Nazi, but even if one of them were, the victory was mine since they renounced any allegiance to the substance represented by their symbols.

MASS: I've had a number of similar experiences of being confronted with Nazi imagery that I did not solicit and which I regarded as extremely assaultive. These were situations in which I was not forewarned about the possible presence of this imagery. Nor was there any kind of reasonable expectation that such might be present. Several of these encounters are detailed in my book, *Synchronicities: Memoirs of Growing Up Gay, Jewish and Self-Hating in America*. As in the situations you've described, the persons involved disclaimed any associations with fascism, but my experiences didn't resolve so triumphantly. One involved someone showing up at a party wearing a leather costume that was highlighted by swastika earrings. The people at the party were not all leather people and weren't consulted about the costume beforehand. So far as I know, this person, who has been a leading spokesperson for the S/M community, was not asked to remove her earrings by any of the people at the party, despite their discomfort. But if she had been asked to do so, I wonder what she would have done.

KANTROWITZ: I hope she would have had the decency to remove them, and I wonder why no one asked her to do so, or at least mentioned the discomfort she was causing. Of course, some "fashion statements" are originally intended to be confrontations, but often they degenerate into mere fads, as in the case of the militant black Afro hairdos of the 1960s or the pro-Palestinian Arab *keffiyehs* of the 1980s or the nihilistic Hell's Angels, skulls and swastikas.

I suspect that the earrings in the case you mentioned were the statement of a sexual radical rather than a political reactionary and that her good taste had been left at home in her dresser drawer.

MASS: When Richard Plant's book was published, I told you of my concern with what I perceived to be the book's avoidance of the subject of the collusion of *some* homosexuals in the early Nazi movement. What I'm saying is very touchy but important, so let me make it as clear as I can, even though it will still be misinterpreted. It's absolutely correct to point out, as Plant does, that the *overall and overwhelming* fact of the relationship between Nazis and homosexuals was that of victimizer and victim. Homosexuals, like many other groups, were targeted victims of the Nazis. Like Jews, gypsies and political prisoners, they were severely persecuted and murdered, in the thousands. But it's also true that a small but noteworthy subset of homosexuals were enthusiastic about Hitler and Nazism prior to 1934. In fact, as Plant acknowledges, there was homosexuality in the ranks of the SA, the original Nazi elite that Roehm, who was widely known to be homosexual and who was Hitler's closest confidant and right-hand man, had built. Roehm and these "brown shirts," as they were called, were mass-murdered by the SS ("black shirts") in the infamous Night of the Long Knives in 1934. The pretext was homosexuality and thus did the SS become Hitler's elite. After 1934, there were no known homosexuals among Hitler's elite.

The problem with Plant's treatment of this information is not in its overview and conclusions so much as in its exclusion of any real discussion of this subset of Nazi and pro-Nazi homosexuals. Plant's perspective on Ernst Roehm is that Roehm was an anomaly, a man with no gay consciousness who became the sole homosexual in Hitler's elite. That's unassailably accurate. There were no other known homosexuals in Hitler's elite. But as Plant has also acknowledged, there were many gay and lesbian German civilians who, like most other Germans, were enthusiastic supporters of Hitler. So there were others *like* Roehm—profoundly homophobic men like Roy Cohn, Terry Dolan and Robert Bauman in our own time and place who had and have no consciousness whatsoever of being members of an oppressed minority and who have embraced a politics that is overtly committed to their own persecution.

The same perspective extends to Jews. Despite the overwhelming fact of the Nazi persecutions of Jews, it's also important to detail and try to understand the much less significant phenomenon of Jewish collaboration with the Nazis, and to contemplate their counterparts in today's world.

KANTROWITZ: It is clear that there were German homosexuals who supported Hitler's fascism, but despite the fears of some Jewish scholars, like Larry David Nachman, who, in his essay "Genet: Dandy of the Lower Depths" (*Salmagundi*, Fall 1982), actually equates homosexuality with fascism, I suspect that their numbers were few, since, aside from Roehm's brown shirts, there is no other known record of their active support. Without data this is a matter of pure conjecture.

MASS: But some data at least merit acknowledgment. The early Homosexual Emancipation Movement in Germany was essentially split into two groups. The one we always hear about and know best and identify with is the one that was led by sexologist Magnus Hirschfeld. The other, which was known as *Der Eigene* ("The Special") and which is not mentioned in Richard Plant's book, had more than a thousand adherents and published what became the first gay magazine in history. (The magazine was called *Der Eigene*.) Like the Nazis with whom they flirted (although the feeling wasn't mutual), "The Special" were anti-modernist, anti-urban, anti-sexological, anti-feminist and masculinist. (Information about *Der Eigene* can be found in *The Homosexual Emancipation Movement in Germany* by James Steakley, Ayer, 1975). What I keep wondering is to what extent the masculinist values of *Der Eigene* are re-emerging within the fringes of today's leather worlds.

KANTROWITZ: Except for supporting one gay rights petition in 1920, *Der Eigene* was an apolitical group which may have romanticized the Nazis' masculinity, but I don't believe that all masculinism is a form of fascism. In those cases where the two are linked in gay men, I think we need to ask if these people are fascist or sympathetic to fascism *because* they are gay or for some other reason. I agree that such a political stance, either in the Germany of the 1930s or America today, is probably a manifestation of internalized homophobia, but in that sense such people might be seen at least partly as victims, even though they became dangerous to other members of their social class. Any sympathy elicited by such an analysis must be set aside, however, when the well-being of the rest of the group is at stake. I have seen magazines published by a cadre of gay American Nazis in the 1970s, which focused on the theme of anti-Semitism as if they thought their hatred of Jews would make the Nazis embrace them and forget their homophobia. Those people are my enemies as a Jew, as a gay person, and as an American, and I would fight against their inclusion in a Gay Pride march. But today the threat of conservative gay Republicans seems more immediate than that of gay fascist extremists. I would have no compunctions about doing battle with a Dolan, a Cohn, a Bauman or anyone, regardless of sexual orientation, who actively works against the gay community.

The experience of the Jews does have parallels, not necessarily to be found in those who were pressed into service in the Judenräte (Jewish councils), since they were directly threatened with reprisals if they didn't facilitate the transport of other Jews to the death camps and they were deluded into thinking that they might actually help by reducing the numbers of internees. The parallel may be seen, however, in the case of Chaim Romkowski of Lodz, whose position elicited delusions of grandeur and power, leading him to betray his fellow Jews, and in the *kapos*, or barracks guards, some of whom were Jews who had internalized their anti-Semitism and willingly committed acts of violence against other inmates, thus becoming enemies of their own people deserving of censure and prosecution. However, as in the case of German homosexuals, the primary blame for the persecution of Jews must be borne by the Nazis.

As for any connections between the experience of some German gays in the 1930s and that of today's gay leather community, there appears to be an unspoken assumption in this analogy that leathersex people are covert fascists, but I haven't seen any evidence of actual fascism implicit in the gay leather world and I don't see any explicit organized leatherworld support for political causes that are fascist. So I'm not persuaded that this is a valid comparison.

MASS: First, let me make it very clear that I likewise do not believe that the leathersex community, certainly no leathersex organization I know of, is explicitly fascist. Furthermore, I think that to deny leathersex people their right of visibility is a form of homophobia. For example, there's a new book out called *After the Ball: How America Will Conquer Its Fear and Hatred of Gays in the '90s* by two gay men which sees drag, promiscuity and leathersex as detriments to the idealized, wholesome image of the gay community they want to project. That's homophobic. Also, in attacking the leather community, they perpetuate the error that Hitler's elite was "highly homosexual," mistaking the SS for the SA. This is the kind of serious misinformation that Plant was at such pains to redress. It would be extremely regrettable if what we're saying here somehow abetted such prejudice and distortion. Even at the risk of being misunderstood and misappropriated, however, I would maintain that it's still not illegitimate to speculate, as we've been doing here, about some of the social consequences, however unintentional, of flirting with fascism in public.

On the subject of parallels and self-criticism, let me add another convolution to our discussion. I think what happened to Plant's perspective is parallel to something I feel is true of the S/M subculture in general. Let me explain. In the early years of gay liberation, we were very resistant to say or hear anything critical of homosexuality and gay culture and for good reason. Prior to gay liberation, there were only negative and hostile images of gays and lesbians in the media. We were correct to insist on affirmative representations only. By the start of the next decade, however, health problems within our community were such that—*even though serious homophobic persecutions were ongoing*—not only could we no longer hide these problems from ourselves, we could no longer legitimately pretend that they didn't exist to the world at large. As I see it, the extremely defensive mentality that we all had about criticism of gay culture in the early years of the gay movement in America (in the early '70s), is what made Plant so reticent to deal in greater

depth with the reality of *some* gay enthusiasm in the early years of
the Nazi movement (even though the politically conscious gay
movement that *we* identify with, led by Hirschfeld, was never in
any way or at any time sympathetic to the Nazis). The information
about *Der Eiqene*, for example, is not information we need to hide
from or to obscure from public consumption any longer. A little bit
like our health problems, it's an unpleasant fact of our history that
we can acknowledge, even though it may appear to run the risk of
endangering the well-being of the community.

The same thing, I feel, has happened to the S/M subculture that
happened to Richard Plant's history. Our nation remains even more
phobic toward leathersex than it has been toward same-sex sex. In
reaction, the leather world, like gay people in the '70s, has become
defensively self-affirming, to the point of being hostile to any and
all criticism. This is certainly brave and has certainly been necessary. But the problems that more and more people in and on the
fringes of the leatherworld have been encountering in recent years
need to be more clearly and extensively addressed than is currently
the case. In *Urban Aboriginals* by Geoff Mains, for example, the
fact that serious injuries may result from fisting is acknowledged,
but the statistics on these injuries and information about where to go
and what to do about them is nowhere detailed. If this information
is widely available in another book or elsewhere in the leather
world, I haven't seen it. Mains's celebration of leathersex, like
Gayle Rubin's essay in *Coming To Power*, glosses over issues of
health risk by comparing leathersex activities to those of sports. But
if that's what these spokespersons believe, then they should be advocating that leathersex, like football, boxing and ballet, be included within the purview of sports medicine. To my knowledge,
no one is doing that. I certainly agree with Gayle Rubin's assessment of "the real danger . . . that the right, the religious fanatics,
and the right-controlled state will eat us all alive." At the same
time, however, I'm also suggesting that we're now at a point when
greater self-analysis and criticism in the leather world should proceed, despite the risks, in the interests of truth and growth.

KANTROWITZ: Of course S/M practices are not above criticism,
and I agree that constructive comments and *self*-criticism should be
encouraged, but the S/M world is constantly exposed to the criti-

cism of the heterosexual world and the non S/M majority of the gay world (which they defensively refer to as "vanilla"). Their primary effort, like that of the gay movement throughout this century, is to find a measure of self-respect in spite of the din of public opprobrium. The gay movement has secured at least some legislation to protect its rights and so may be more ready to be self-critical in public. The S/M community hasn't even progressed far enough to seek legislation and still doesn't feel safe enough to air its problems for fear they will be used against its struggle for respectability.

If the issue is truly one of sexual safety, you are correct in noting failures in this area. Obviously, practices such as fisting, flogging, electro-torture, etc., are fraught with peril. The equation of fisting with sports is clearly a whitewash, and sports medicine may be the wrong place to take these problems, but why don't the practitioners of sexual medicine include these issues in their work? Is it the same fear of endorsing publicly scorned activities that made prison wardens object to passing out condoms to their inmates for prevention of AIDS?

MASS: Quite the contrary. It's only in the medical literature that information about the diagnosis and treatment of fisting injuries has appeared, although I myself did a feature piece for the *New York Native* on this subject in 1981. Entitled "Handballing: High Risk Sport," it summarized the information on the commonness of injuries among (anal) fistfuckers (female as well as male) and included safety guidelines for people who want to continue fisting, knowing the high risks involved.

KANTROWITZ: Leather people may play with fire, but whatever the failures of some individuals, the organized leather community is highly conscious of the dangers it flirts with. GMSMA, for example, has devoted many of its meetings to instruction about safety measures, and warnings are frequently issued about the necessity of avoiding drugs and alcohol and establishing clear signals between partners so that reasonable thresholds of pain and responsibility may be observed. In fact, S/M fantasy is often touted as a form of safer sex in the era of AIDS.

MASS: I've certainly been impressed with GMSMA in this regard, and I quite agree with the idea of emphasizing the safer-sex advantages of S/M fantasy play.

KANTROWITZ: The sexual practices of the leather world, like those of the gay world, may seem bizarre to most of society, but that does not mean that the people who experience mutual fulfillment through such practices are quintessentially sick or evil. To suggest that there is complete truth in the popular stereotype of the sadomasochist as a brutal villain or a self-hating wimp doesn't do justice to this minority. Playing with swastikas doesn't make one a real Nazi any more than quoting the Bible makes one a good Christian.

"Sissyness" as Metaphor

A Conversation with Richard Green

[Ed. note: Of all the psychiatric allies (or ostensible allies) of the gay liberation struggle, Richard Green had always seemed the least accessible. When I tried to arrange for an interview with him in the early 1980s, admittedly during a time when I was questioning the ethics of his work with "sissy" boys in print (e.g., in the interviews with Pillard, Marmor, Szasz, etc.), he would not return my calls, though I was given a message that anything I wished to communicate to him could be put in writing. Feeling snubbed and defensive at the time, I abandoned the project. This time, my approach was a lot more politic. In fact, it was totally submissive, and I made it very clear to Dr. Green, in writing, that he would have full editorial approval of every word of content. Even so, this interview — the oddest in the collection — probably wouldn't have happened at all if it weren't for Gladys Topkis, Green's editor at Yale University Press, who went out of her way to act as intermediary.

"'Sissyness' as Metaphor" focuses on the "problem" of "effeminacy" in young boys in our culture. In doing so, it gives voice to a paramount concern of the sexual revolution, a concern that likewise shapes many of the interviews in this collection: the sexuality of children. As Wilhelm Reich articulated it in his book, *The Sexual Revolution*, in 1936: "Past experience shows unequivocally that any kind of hindrance of infantile and adolescent sexuality by parents, teachers or government authorities has to be eliminated. In what way this prohibition can be brought about it is impossible to say today. But *the necessity for social and legal protection of infantile and adolescent sexuality can no longer be doubted*."

More specifically with regard to homosexuality, "'Sissyness' as Metaphor" raises two related and very important questions: (1) How much of current psychiatric practice is devoted to treating the so-

213

called gender identity disorders of childhood? and (2) In view of the
fact that virtually everyone now agrees that sexual orientation becomes relatively fixed in early childhood and since the majority of
psychiatrists and sex researchers (including Bell and Weinberg,
who co-authored the Kinsey II study of homosexuality, *Sexual
Preference*) now believes that the most consistent predictor of a
homosexual or lesbian orientation in adulthood is "gender nonconformity" in early childhood, is American psychiatry simply engaged in a long, subtle process of reconceptualizing homosexuality
as a mental illness with another name — the "gender identity disorder of childhood"? These questions have not really been asked before and they are not satisfactorily answered elsewhere to my
knowledge or by Dr. Green in this interview.]

Richard Green is professor of psychiatry and director of the Program in Psychiatry, Law, and Human Sexuality at the University of
California, Los Angeles. (He will receive his J.D. from Yale in
June, 1987.) He is founder and editor of the *Archives of Sexual
Behavior* and was founding president of the International Academy
of Sex Research. His previous books include *Transsexualism and
Sex Reassignment* (coeditor), *Sexual Identity Conflict in Children
and Adults* (author), *Human Sexuality: A Health Practitioner's Text*
(editor), and *Impotence: Physiological, Psychological, Surgical Diagnosis and Treatment* (coauthor). His new book, *The "Sissy Boy
Syndrome" and the Development of Homosexuality* (Yale University Press, 1987) is the subject of the following interview, which
took place by correspondence during late winter, 1987. Although
Dr. Green is well-known to the gay community as one of the principal architects of the 1973-74 declassification of homosexuality as a
mental disorder by the American Psychiatric Association, and although he has been consistently, often outspokenly supportive of
sexual privacy rights, this is his first interview for the gay press.

MASS: In the first chapter of your new book, The *"Sissy Boy Syndrome" and the Development of Homosexuality*, you explain that in
our culture "sissy" is pejorative in a way that "tomboy" is not and
that you "do not use that term except to convey quickly the picture
of a cluster of behaviors that distinguishes these boys, as in the

book's title." If I'm not mistaken, the phrase "Sissy Boy Syndrome" is not actually used or cited in the text of your book. Where does this phrase come from and how did you settle on the title of your book? (Did you consider other title possibilities?)

GREEN: The title was conceived with two principal considerations: "sissy" epitomizes the stigma these boys suffer in consequence of a sexist society — pediatric and adult; "syndrome" says that these boys show a more complex set of behaviors than "garden variety sissies," boys who are tagged with this label merely because of their aversion to fighting or sports.

MASS: Your book contains very little explicit mention and virtually no discussion of the gay liberation movement and how it may have influenced the progress of your study. Although you collectively acknowledge "gay activist" responses to psychoanalytic and behavior modification "treatments" of "gender identity disorders" as "not cushioned" and "strident," and with the exception of Bruce Voeller's 3-line "endorsement" on your book's dust jacket, you do not actually or directly quote any gay community representatives or viewpoints. Incidentally, the dust jacket description concludes as follows: "Parents, teachers, mental health professionals, social scientists, and anyone curious about the development of his or her sexual identity will find this book unusually informative and provocative." Won't this information be of at least as much interest to the gay community, as a designated group, as to parents and teachers? In sum, do you think my perception that the gay community and gay perspectives have been eschewed in your study is misinformed or distorted?

GREEN: I have written at length about the politics of mental health and homosexuality. In 1972, I published a controversial paper, "Homosexuality as a Mental Disease," challenging psychiatry's view of homosexuality. I credited the "gay liberation movement" with forcing psychiatry to confront its biases and contradictions. By contrast, this new book is a research report.

As for the dust jacket description, this work should be of interest to the gay community (or communities). And, of course, there is nothing mutually exclusive about these communities and those of teachers, parents' mental health professionals, and social scientists, is there, Doctor?

MASS: No, but specifying "the gay community" wouldn't necessarily imply exclusivity from the other designated communities,
any more than specifying "teachers" and "parents" implies mutual exclusivity between those two groups. So I have to stand on
what I've said. In your chapter, "Psychotherapy and What It Did,"
you ask the questions "Should parents have the prerogative of
choosing therapy for their gender-atypical son?" and "Who is to
dictate that parents may not try to raise their children in a manner
that maximizes the possibility of a heterosexual outcome? If that
prerogative is denied, should parents also be denied the right to
raise their children as atheists? Or as priests?" The answer, you
seem to tacitly concur, is that "the rights of parents to oversee the
development of children is a long-established principle." So you're
willing to work with, to go along with long-established tradition
rather than to invest the bulk of your efforts in attempting to change
those traditions. Is this correct? Do you think parents should have
the right to circumcise their children? Do you think parents should
have the right to clitoridectomize them? Do you think that, in our
society, the fact that parents have the right to try to condition a son
to become a priest justifies the parents' right to try to condition a
son to become heterosexual, and for psychiatry to help them in this
endeavor?

GREEN: When the State invades the home and dictates the values
parents must impart to children, whether it be religious, political, or
sexual, democracy and personal freedom suffers, and we march in
lockstep to the State's cadence. To protect against this nightmare,
we must take the bad (values as perceived by some) with the good
(values as perceived by some).

MASS: In *The "Sissy Boy Syndrome,"* you present a pair of identical twin males both of whom are or have been functionally bisexual. However, since early childhood one twin was more behaviorally "feminine" and preferentially homosexual. While qualifying
your observations, you attribute the more "feminine" boy's comparatively dominant "femininity" and homosexuality to his having
been primarily cared for by his mother during a protracted period of
illness in early childhood, a situation that left his brother to develop
under the nearly exclusive influence of their father. You suggest
that these twins are "this study's metaphor" and that "the greater

degree of homosexual orientation in the previously 'feminine' twin demonstrates the influence of gender role behavior on later sexual orientation.'' In characterizing the case of the twins as metaphorical of the entire study, are you thereby indirectly implying that gender reinforcement therapy in early childhood might influence many more boys to become more "masculine" and preferentially heterosexual?

GREEN: The twin pair exemplifies, and the larger sample illustrates, the significance of early father-son shared time. The chapter on psychotherapy and what it did (and didn't do) describes the outcome of early therapist intervention. (The chapter was originally principally titled "Trick or Treat," but a humorless university press fainted dead away.)

The boys who had a lot of "gender reinforcement therapy" (from behavior therapists, among others) now have the same sexual orientations as the remainder of the group.

[Ed. note: At Dr. Green's request, the following question was eliminated because, as he wrote me, "it assumes facts not proven."

MASS: In the case of these identical twins, did you consider the possibility that the more "masculine" twin had learned, under the influence of his "dyed-in-the-wool conservative" father, to more deeply and homophobically repress what might otherwise be his more natural "femininity" and homosexuality?]

MASS: In your study, you cite the admittedly "spectacular finding" of Franz Kallman in 1952, that of 39 homosexual twins assumed to be monozygotic [genetically identical], all co-twins were also homosexual. You also cite a later study of 4 sets of identical male twins, in each of which only one twin was homosexual. How much do we really know about the nonhomosexual co-twins of the later studies? Is the evidence really convincing that they are preferentially, as opposed to functionally, heterosexual? How homophobic do you think these co-twins might have been, as medical study subjects during one of the most homophobic periods in American history? Finally, what's happened to these nonhomosexual co-twins since these studies were published?

GREEN: I have no idea.

MASS: In your chapter on the identical twins, incidentally, the following exchange takes place between yourself and the more "feminine" twin:

> *RICHARD GREEN*: To what extent are you interested in the leather/chain/jean/key ring type gays?
>
> *PAUL*: Leather?
>
> *RICHARD GREEN*: Yeah. Super macho ones with motorcycle and Nazi jackets?

Could you say something about what you think, in the context of this interview or elsewhere, about the leather world's use of Nazi symbolism and how you think this may relate to gay life or to the gay world of your client? [Do you refer to them as clients or patients?]

GREEN: I will speculate, not having studied that subculture. It may represent an adoption of a distorted image of "masculinity," perhaps analagous to the disfigured product of compulsive weight lifting. Both can be used to convince society and self that although homosexual, "I'm (very) 'masculine.'"

MASS: In a later interview with the same patient, he explains that he's been seeing a girlfriend who has become pregnant. Your response is "Congratulations!" Is this response an impartial expression of support for his freely chosen path, or is it a "reward" for his "achievement" of heterosexuality and manhood?

GREEN: Try sarcasm.

MASS: Your book's conclusion seems to be that under better family and social circumstances, many boys who are stigmatized as "sissy" or who are behaviorally exclusively homosexual would be less brittle (more fluid) in their gender identities and sexual preferences. That is, they would be more often, more comfortably "masculine"-identified and more heterosexually competent. Is this correct?

GREEN: To the extent that society currently directs that personal sexual scripts conform to the writing of others, less stigmatization and stereotyping would permit more editing of the dialogue.

MASS: You were one of the principal supporters of the 1973–74 American Psychiatric Association declassification of homosexuality as a mental disorder. In the gay community, you are less widely known as a principal architect of a more recently characterized (in DSM-III) "psychosexual disorder" called the "gender-identity disorder of childhood." Since most reputable studies, yours included, concur that gender nonconformity in early childhood is the strongest predictor of homosexuality in adults, is psychiatry wittingly or unwittingly in the process of trying to redefine homosexuality as a mental disorder of gender identity in childhood? In other words, DSM-III might permit most adult homosexuals to be considered "normal," but it would be classifying a significant percentage of those same persons, during their childhoods, as mentally disordered. Is this correct?

GREEN: The nuclear component of the gender identity disorder of childhood is the child's strong wish to be the other sex. Cross-gender behaviors (e.g., preferential cross-dressing, female role-playing) reflect that painful discontent. To the extent that children mature beyond that early pain, they do not have a mental disorder, be they heterosexual or homosexual. To the extent that they retain it, they have a diagnosis: transsexualism.

MASS: How are the classifications of "gender-identity disorders" and "ego-dystonic homosexuality" [which I understand will be deleted as such] evolving in DSM-IIIR and are you satisfied with these developments?

GREEN: A decade ago, I was a vitriolic opponent of including "ego-dystonic homosexuality" in DSM-III, unless it was complemented by a heterosexual disorder, such as in "Sexual relationship disorder: heterosexual pattern; homosexual pattern."

In response to the APA's recent, belated deletion of "ego-dystonic homosexuality," this letter [which was published] in the APA's *Psychiatric News* provides your answer.

Dear Editor:

As a primary advocate for not including the diagnosis "ego-dystonic homosexuality" in DSM-III, I am mostly pleased that it is deleted from DSM-IIIR. My displeasure is that the process all along has been political, where it could have been scientific.

Ever since American psychiatry disgraced itself as a science by referring to referendum whether homosexuals are mentally ill, it has been plagued by how to appease the interests of those psychiatrists dedicated to the "cure" of homosexuality, and those homosexuals, psychiatrists and others desirous of a clean bill of mental health.

The decision to include ego-dystonic homosexuality was a political compromise, there being the fear that, if it were not, the whole question of homosexuality as a mental disorder *per se* would be reopened. The scientific data of then are not different from those now. Homosexuals did not and do not satisfy the DSM criteria of mental disorder. Only today, the political gains made by American homosexuals, including psychiatrists, have taken a firmer hold on the conscience of the public — and our profession.

So now, ego-dystonic homosexuality disappears into the well-deserved abyss of the black hole of dead psychiatric diagnoses. Good. But too bad the right decision was made for the wrong reason.

MASS: How much of current psychiatric practice would you estimate is devoted to treating gender identity disorders of childhood and "homosexual dissatisfaction," to use Masters' and Johnson's term? Has malpractice litigation ever been instigated against practitioners of gender reinforcement and/or sexual orientation conversion therapies, and if so are any trends discernible?

GREEN: I don't know.

MASS: In your chapter, "Psychotherapy and What It Did," you conclude as follows: "Nor was anyone obviously *harmed* by treatment . . . The boys look back favorably on treatment. They would endorse such intervention if they were the father of a "feminine" boy. Their reason is to reduce childhood conflict and social stigma." Do you really think that the fact that "these boys look back favorably on treatment" is a legitimate justification for treatment? There are doubtless some African women who look back favorably on their having been clitoridectomized. Does this mean that the procedure is justified?

GREEN: Not in and of itself. On the other hand, had they disavowed therapy, that would be a compelling argument for a restraining order against child psychiatrists.

MASS: Have you read or heard about Walter L. Williams' book, *The Spirit and The Flesh* [about the American Indian *berdache*]? What it's saying is that in this society which recognized and respected gender nonconformity and gender variant persons, there's no such phenomenon as transsexualism and no gender or sexual orientation dysphoria. How do these findings complement or contradict those of your study? [Don't they suggest that the entire concept of cooperating with society to urge gender conformity is, at the least, misdirected?]

GREEN: How quickly they forget. In 1966, I authored a chapter in Harry Benjamin's *Transsexual Phenomenon*, reporting cross-cultural and historical aspects of cross-sex behavior. It included discussion of the berdache. With the Native Americans, as well as with other people and in other times, cross-gendered-behaving boys were granted a non-stigmatized role. Some later lived adult lives approximating what we now call "transsexualism." Some later lived as homosexuals. The lesson taught by these observations and records is that gender-nonconformity need not be punished in either childhood or adulthood. However, it does not refute the link between childhood gender behavior and adulthood sexual behavior.

MASS: In your book, you refer to your earlier study (*Sexual Identity Conflict in Children and Adults*, 1974) and quote from its "broader social view": "Treatment intervention . . . focused on helping these people adjust to their society. What can be done to help society adjust to these people? Can the behavioral scientist also be effective as a social activist? Can the researcher/therapist modify societal attitudes so that atypical sexual lifestyles which do not infringe on the liberties of others do not cause conflict for the atypical individual?" In the current study, you make no direct attempt to answer these questions? Why? Would you care to do so now?

GREEN: Actions speak louder than words. In June, I will receive a law degree from Yale University. My motivation for going "back to school" was to expand my activities on behalf of a person's right to sexual privacy. Previously, I was limited to my role as an expert witness on behalf of those oppressed by the public or the state for their sexual expression.

MASS: In your "developmental synthesis: clinical," you chart the "clinical" course of a "feminine" boy to homosexual adulthood. I really identified with the part where you note that "early heterosexual arousal receives little positive reinforcement." That was true of me, but I *always*, ever since I can remember, had a primary sexual attraction and feelings of limerence (falling and being in love) for men. In a less sexually pathological society, I might have been more actively or fluidly bisexual, but it's difficult for me to conceptualize that I would ever *not* have been primarily homosexual. Any comment?

GREEN: I never comment on individual psychodynamics unless I spend a lot more time exploring them with the person.

MASS: Are you one of these boys? That is, a "feminine" man who, after a period of considerable sexual identity ambiguity and conflict, managed to "achieve" a pattern, not merely of competent but of fully *limerent* heterosexuality?

GREEN: I never comment publicly on my own psychodynamics, even after having spent a lot of time exploring them with the person.

MASS: Last question. Isn't your study's approach inverted in the sense that all the time, energy, intelligence and money that have gone into this psychiatric work with "sissy" boys would be better spent on media and public education campaigns to reduce homophobia and sexism in society?

GREEN: My commitments to (research) comprehending and (political) understanding of the complexity of sexual identity are several. And they are not mutually exclusive. Statements by the boys (now men) in this study teach that sex role rigidity can puzzle and punish. But I am not primarily a political activist. I continue to be curious about the deviations and the derivatives of sexual identity. I know more than when I started about the childhood experiences of persons who fill out the sexual identity spectrum. Now, with my legal training, I hope to harness that knowledge as it plays out in the drama of human rights.

Keeping Time

A Conversation with Martin Bauml Duberman

[Ed. Note: The following paragraph of introduction has been updated for this collection.]

Martin Bauml Duberman, the noted historian, playwright, critic, essayist, person of letters, feminist, civil rights activist and humanitarian is currently Distinguished Professor of History at Lehman College, The City University of New York. His books include *Charles Francis Adams, 1807-1886*; *The Antislavery Vanguard: New Essays on the Abolitionists*, ed., *James Russel Lowell*; *In White America*; *The Uncompleted Past*; *The Memory Bank*; *Black Mountain: An Exploration in Community*; *Male Armor: Selected Plays, 1968-1974*; *Visions of Kerouac*; and *About Time: Exploring the Gay Past*. His biography of Paul Robeson was published by Knopf in 1989, and he is co-editor of *Hidden From History: Reclaiming The Gay and Lesbian Past* (New American Library, 1989) and most recently, he has completed *Cures*, a book about his experiences in therapy. Duberman is the founder of the Center for Lesbian and Gay Studies of the City University of New York. The following interview took place in Professor Duberman's home on October 31, 1986.

MASS: In what ways do the selected essays of Martin Duberman, which comprise the second half of your collection, *About Time* (Gay Presses of New York), complement the annotated historical documents of the first half? In what ways, in other words, do you feel that the two parts of this book belong together?
DUBERMAN: In a way, I think, those essays are themselves historical artifacts, like the documents. The first ones date back fifteen years. Since then, the gay movement and the issues have changed

so much that I think the essays involve a similar excavation of a time past.

MASS: So you're an historical figure who's also an historian examining historical documents which now include your own.

DUBERMAN: I guess that's one way to put it. These days I often think of myself as somebody examining his own life as well as other peoples' in order to come up with some information about gay issues, especially since I'm a gay man of . . . uh . . . a certain generation. I can explore what it was like to be gay in the fifties. That really is a historic time span. So I feel as if I'm using myself as another document in the collection.

MASS: How did you come to the decision to offer the historical documents to the *Native*?

DUBERMAN: I met Brett Averill [then Editor of the *Native*] at David Rothenberg's. I forget what the occasion was. David introduced us and said "Maybe Marty will write something for you." Brett asked me what I was doing, and I told him I had been collecting material for what I hoped was going to be a sort of one-volume narrative history of sexuality in America. But within two years of launching that project, I realized it was premature. In speaking with Brett, I suddenly realized that since I had stopped the history, all the documentary finds I'd already made were just sitting there. Then, when Brett suggested a column for the *Native* — it was his idea — I thought, "What a perfect way to get some of this stuff out into the world, and what a perfect audience for it." So no, I never even thought about offering the documents to anybody else because the connection with Brett and with the *Native* happened so spontaneously.

MASS: How did you come to the decision to make the *Native* column the basis of a book?

DUBERMAN: Felice Picano came to me with the idea of collecting the columns as a book for Seahorse Press/Gay Presses of New York. At first I hesitated, not convinced that the columns by themselves were sufficiently weighty to justify a volume. Then I got the idea to add a second half to the book — a selection of essays on gay themes which I'd written for various publications over the past dozen or so years. The two halves made a fat whole.

MASS: The second part of *About Time* is made up of a number of

your own pieces—essays, reviews, addresses, and correspondences. Your reminiscing about Brett and the early days of the *Native* reminds me that one of these pieces, your discussion of the Masters and Johnson study, *Homosexuality in Perspective* [in *The New Republic*], was the basis of our first communication—yours and mine. Although I was by no means convinced by everything the authors said, I was so grateful for the enormous damage their work would and did in fact wreak on the public credibility of tenacious medical and psychiatric prejudices that I took exception to your clarion denunciation of the study's inconsistencies. I think time has shown that I was wrong. Whatever the secondary benefits of *Homosexuality in Perspective*, it *is* riddled with heterosexist, monogamist, and pseudoscientific biases. The second half of this section in *About Time*, which is entitled "The Experts and Homosexuality," is devoted to the Kinsey Institute study, *Homosexualities*. While also critical of inconsistencies in the conclusions of co-authors Bell and Weinberg, you seem to be angrier about the monogamist assumptions of Masters and Johnson than about those of Bell and Weinberg. Am I correct, and, if so, why?

DUBERMAN: Well, the main reason is that the Masters and Johnson study is much less fundamentally sympathetic to gay people than the Kinsey study. It raised my dander that Masters and Johnson, who essentially view gay people as malfunctioning neurotics, would at the same time be lecturing us about lifetime monogamous pair-bonding being the optimal sign of mental health. In the Masters and Johnson study, those two messages come in tandem: that we gay people can never do more than approximate mental health because we can't "truly" pair-bond, like heterosexuals. Even though the Kinsey study likewise implied that monogamous pair-bonding—*closed-coupled*ness—was associated with optimum happiness and stability, I didn't find it to be so strongly moralistic. I was more tolerant of it, even though it may have shared some of the same failings of analysis or perspective that the Masters and Johnson study had.

MASS: These pieces were originally published in *The New Republic* and The *New York Times* respectively. Why haven't we been reading these big, substantial pieces of yours in these publications in the last few years?

DUBERMAN: Oh, my history with the *Times* is . . . complicated. There was a change of editors of the Sunday *Book Review*. Harvey Shapiro, the new editor, wasn't sympathetic to gay issues. I used to be able to just call the *Times* and say "There's a new book I've heard about . . .", and so long as I would swear I didn't know the author, I could pretty much review what I wanted to. When Harvey became editor, that stopped being true. I remember when Ann Douglas's book came out. It was called *The Feminization of American Culture*, and I had heard wonderful advance things about it. So I called Harvey Shapiro and proposed that I review it for the Sunday *Book Review*. Well, he just laughed at the suggestion as if it were manifestly ridiculous and then said, *very* condescendingly, "I really don't think so." Then I said, "Harvey, despite the title, this book isn't about what you apparently think it's about. It's not about gay life. It's about the alliance of protestant ministers with female reformers in the nineteenth century and the effect that they had on American culture." "Well," he said, "I think you've probably had your say on these issues, anyway." Not wanting to again subject myself to that kind of humiliation, I vowed never again to suggest to the *Times* books that I'd be interested in reviewing; and I haven't, though they called me when the *Book Review* editor shifted again, and last year I did a review for them on an unrelated topic.

MASS: And what happened with *The New Republic*?

DUBERMAN: I think it was pretty much the same kind of thing, a shift in editor from Jack Beattie, who had very sympathetic to gay issues. In a larger social context, of course, the editors only shift because the climate of opinion has shifted.

MASS: I know what you mean. In some ways the *Times* has improved. In others, however, this shift to the right is all too clear. For example, I thought Walter Goodman's review of the recent revival of your epic play, *Visions of Kerouac*, was homophobic, not because he didn't like the play or the production — he's entitled to that, I suppose — but because he didn't even mention, let alone examine or explicitly reject the play's historially important suggestion the Kerouac may have been preferentially bisexual. I guess this more tacit homophobia, of omission, is more characteristic of the eighties.

DUBERMAN: That's exactly what I thought was offensive about the review. What I was trying to do in the play was raise the issue of the emotional costs of growing up male, macho male, in our fierce culture. A man like Kerouac couldn't allow himself to even consider the possibility of exploring, let alone fully expressing, the deep love he had for Neal Cassady.

MASS: It's pretty clear that his friendship with Cassady was actually *the* love relationship of his life, isn't it?

DUBERMAN: Oh, I think so. Absolutely. Not incidentally, the character in the play who was meant to be Ginsberg—but called Irwin Goldberg in the play, which is the name Kerouac used for Ginsberg in his books—by way of contrast, is the only male in the play who emerges whole. He develops and flourishes, whereas the constricted macho men, terrified of their own feelings, progressively decay. I think that's true of the actual lives of these men. It's not something I've superimposed on them. Anyway, Walter Goodman in the *Times* refused to deal with any of this.

I don't want to go on too much, but I remember being stunned a few months ago when the *Times* gave Hilton Kramer a book to review on the radical left in the early part of the twentieth century. He murdered the book, of course, and it was clearly an ideological review. With Walter Goodman, it was the same situation. I mean, you don't send a neoconservative to review a play about the Beatniks.

[Ed. Note: This has since happened again with *Robeson*. The *Times* gave the book to a known neo-conservative, John Patrick Diggins, and, according to Duberman, even went so far as to edit out the letters of protest that came in from various people.]

MASS: It's the old *Times* philosophy of having Charles Socarides review the latest sex-research study of gay life. They feel it's somehow "balanced" to have the absolute archenemy of something, no matter how biased—or, as in the case of Socarides, even frankly disreputable—the person.

DUBERMAN: I remember when Charlotte Curtis was editing the Op-Ed page, they published a savage attack on gay people by a professor at Shippensburg State College in Pennsylvania. I wrote a letter of protest to Curtis who wrote back that the Op-Ed page "had

to publish all points of view." So I replied, "Do you publish
Hitler's point of view on the Jews?" She didn't answer that one.
The *Times* represents the whole spectrum of opinion, all right, but
only on the people it doesn't approve of. But certainly the *Times* is
doing a better job on gay issues than it was ten years ago, don't you
think?

MASS: Yes, especially with regard to the AIDS crisis. After ser-
veral years of what can only be described as malignant neglect, the
Times is finally providing regular, often substantial and multi-fac-
eted coverage. Even as late as 1985, however, Lawrence Altman
could look at me with a straight face (at the international AIDS
conference in Atlanta), when I asked him why the *San Francisco
Chronicle* had had twice as much coverage of AIDS issues with
only half as many cases as New York, and say that the *Times* wasn't
doing more on AIDS "because we're not an advocacy journal."
And we're *still* getting these incredibly stupid, utterly insensitive
editorials saying to the real, legitimate folks, "don't panic, yet,"
because the epidemic is still largely confined to gays and druggies.
Of course, they're still not using the word gay without quotes, and
did you see Christopher Lehmann-Haupt's review of David
Leavitt's new novel, in which he suggests that the old question of
"whether or not homosexual art is inherently limited" is still a
legitimate one? There's been *some* improvement at the *Times*, but,
clearly, we've got a *long* way to go!

DUBERMAN: I think that's the liberal mind-set. They're slow to
accept responsibility for informing the public about a new virus
that's infecting a deviant subculture, but a lot quicker than they are
to accept responsibility for reporting to the public about any other
aspect, especially any affirmative aspect, of life in that subculture.

MASS: Earlier, you said that you had begun collecting the historical
documents that comprise the first part of *About Time* in anticipation
of writing a sexual history of the United States, a fact you don't
discuss in the book's introduction. Why did you abandon this project?

DUBERMAN: For two reasons. First, because I found much more
material than the archival librarians were claiming they had. Yet at
the same time, the material was so fragmentary that it rapidly became obvious to me that it was much too soon to be attempting a

coherent narrative history of sexuality in the U.S.; that such a project would have to await at least one generation of scholarship—a lot of monographic studies, a whole platoon of researchers digging deeply into manuscript collections, etc.

MASS: I understand that John D'Emilio is now working on just such a history.

DUBERMAN: I believe that's so, with Estelle Friedman at Stanford.

[Ed. note: D'Emilio and Freedman are the co-authors of *Intimate Matters: A History of Sexuality in America*, which was published by Harper and Row in 1988. They are interviewed on the subject of their book in *Homosexuality as Behavior and Indentity: Dialogues of the Sexual Revolution—Volume II.*]

I think this is the earliest possible time for such a project, because there has now been that necessary first generation of scholarship. You know, D'Emilio, Jonathan Katz, Esther Newton, Alan Berube, George Chauncey, Lillian Faderman, Lisa Duggan, etc.

MASS: . . . . the scholars you mention in the introduction to *About Time*. In recent years, you've spoken of another cherished ambition, to establish the first official gay studies department in the U.S. Although this goal isn't specifically articulated in either of the Gay Academic Union addresses that are included in *About Time*, I understand that you are now working with other scholars and academics on just such a project.

DUBERMAN: The Center for Lesbian and Gay Studies (CLAGS) is what we've been calling it. Without going into too much detail, the project emerged six months ago coincidentally with a friend of mine, Benno Schmidt, becoming the new president of Yale. Seven years ago, after I had a heart attack, I had already decided that I was going to leave my estate to bettering the lot of gay men and lesbian women, and that indeed had been in my will for a long time. Benno's becoming president of Yale seemed a way of implementing that trust immediately, in the form of a Center, and he encouraged me to proceed. So I then gathered a group of gay and lesbian scholars to prepare a set of proposals. We've been meeting every month or so since.

[Ed. Note: The Center has now shifted its affiliation to the Graduate Center, CUNY, has been formally welcomed there by President Proshansky, and as of 1989 is nearing its fundraising goal.]

MASS: Speaking of sexual history in the United States, I was intrigued by some of your observations in a recent two-part panel discussion in *The Advocate*. At one point, you were quoted as saying the following:

> All the talk about gay men becoming more responsible — because of the epidemic we've supposedly learned how to become more mature human beings who make more meaningful relationships with one another — is bullshit. By its very nature, sex is a wild, uninhibited thing. The way we were relating before AIDS was just fine. We were on the frontier. Larry [Kramer] *always* thought the sexual revolution was wrong, and now he thinks that AIDS has somehow opened our eyes. I disagree totally. I think AIDS has forced us to behave differently than we ideally might want to, but I hope someday to return to the way I used to behave. I hope to be just as wild.

So you think there were no genuine issues of promiscuity or sexual compulsivity before AIDS?
DUBERMAN: First, let me say that those quotes are an extremely edited-down version of an exceedingly heated, five-hour panel discussion. I was trying to make a complicated two part argument that got lost in the editing. I was trying to explain on the one hand why I had chosen celibacy over *safe sex* (because I'd rather not have sex at all than have a rationalized, truncated version of it), and on the other why I continue to defend the sexual revolution in all its original fullness — meaning not just sexual "transgression" but also gender-nonconformity. Nonetheless, essentially, I do believe what the quote suggests I do. Look, you and I have been talking about these issues for years, have we not? I'm asking this out loud, rhetorically: Where does the problem with "promiscuous" behavior arise? Exactly how many partners are too many partners? Exactly what degree of familiarity is necessary with our partners, before we're entitled to say that a sexual exchange is legitimate? I don't think there are or ever could be any set answers to questions like that. Nor am I

persuaded that there's any necessary or clear dividing line that can separate most sexual acts into categories of healthy versus unhealthy.

MASS: So even though we're going through a period of unprecedented knowledge and awareness of the very high risks, currently, of unprecedented numbers and varieties of sexually transmitted diseases (AIDS, herpes, hepatitis, syphilis, gonorrhea, parasites, etc.), these questions are as valid as ever. Is that what you're saying?

DUBERMAN: Yes. I think there's an analogy here with sexual intercourse before the discovery of penicillin. One could have said that we were faced with the legitimate problem of syphilis and that surely, therefore, we should have cut back on the amount of sexual intercourse we were indulging. But because that was a disease that manifestly resulted from heterosexual contact, a lot of scientific work went into finding the necessary prophylactic devices and therapeutic treatments. I think that's where the emphasis should have been and should again be with the AIDS epidemic. I think it's only in a puritanical culture like ours that we say, let's stop having intercourse.

Let's look at what critics said was wrong with us since well before the beginning of the epidemic. One argument was that if you constantly spend your time and energy pursuing anonymous sex, you won't have the resources to find and commit to a "significant other." I never bought that argument and I still don't. I think the impulses that lead one to seek and commit to a "significant other" are often socially induced. Anyway, the very search—so consuming in our psyches—for the "right" person to complete us, to make us whole and happy, is probably itself a mere cultural artifact. I've never seen any convincing evidence that sleeping with a number of different people would get in the way of that search, presuming one wants to undertake the social command to find and commit to a mate in the first place. In fact, I think a number of people have found mates in bathhouses, backroom bars, etc. And people have continued to sustain close relationships over periods of many years, while having other sexual outlets and other sexual partners.

MASS: Of course. That's been well established by a number of studies, most notably by McWhirter and Mattison in *The Male Couple*.

I can't say I believe the desire to find and commit to a mate is always or simply a matter of social command, but I can vouch for much of what you're saying at a personal level. Arnie and I met at the baths five years ago and we remain very committed to each other.

DUBERMAN: Most sex researchers tell us that after roughly three to five years, regardless of the sexual orientation of the couple, erotic zest tends to fade. What most Americans do about that is to give up their sex lives, especially if they're women. (If they're married men, of course, they generally feel entitled to seek outside sexual gratification.) Gay men, especially, have never been willing to give up sex. I think gay men have been able to demonstrate, abundantly and repeatedly, that monogamy and emotional commitment are not necessary preconditions, one for the other, though our monogamously biased culture continues to insist that they are.

MASS: Let's go back to the AIDS epidemic. Even if we're correct that it's impossible to clearly define concepts like sexual promiscuity, compulsivity and excess, would you concede that a number of people in our community—a subset—*were* in fact, by their own admission, habituated to patterns of sexual gratification that knowingly endangered their physical health and sometimes that of others, and that seemed to be inhibiting development and involvement in other areas of their lives?

DUBERMAN: Not without qualification. Sometimes my tendency to overwork becomes so obsessive that I not only neglect sex, but important friendships and even eating. For a time, by my own admission, my life is out of whack—narrowed down and focused on one aspect of living. I don't see anything wrong with that. If the behavior, whether it's overworking, dancing, overeating, undereating, taking drugs or fucking, *persistently* blocks out other areas of potential enjoyment, fulfillment or functioning, then, I would concede, there may be trouble. But I maintain that those in our community who experience such trouble over an extended period of time are a very small number. I likewise suspect that when some claim they are in "trouble," they are reflecting not dysfunction but rather the antisexualism of our culture. They probably felt that the appetite for varied sexual activities with a number of different partners, was in itself sinful or neurotic or abnormal. To me, the most offensive part of this frame of thinking is that those few people who we might be able to agree were genuinely sexually compulsive are being used as a contrivance for devaluing the way most gay men use sex as one tool for exploring themselves and their environment — a contrivance, in other words, for devaluing the sexual revolution in general.

MASS: I can't tell you how rejuvenating it is to hear this reaffirmation of the sexual revolution. In recent years, I've found myself seduced, more often than once, to the viewpoint that we've experienced this gross excess of indulgence in our sexuality that has facilitated the AIDS epidemic, and that sex revolutionaries like you and me didn't provide the kind of right versus wrong leadership that was needed in a time of crisis. Many times, I've wished that I had just gone around screaming bloody murder, mayhem and panic. Although I know that wouldn't have worked, at least I'd be giving the appearance of trying to do everything I could.

DUBERMAN: Look, you were, notably, in the forefront of encouraging gay men to remain sex-affirmative, even while taking the necessary precautions against AIDS, parasites and other STDs. The trouble is that your position, which I share, has been swamped by the latter day sex-phobes, to the point where they have succeeded in making you feel guilty that you ever suggested that there was something affirmative about the sexual revolution.

MASS: Thanks. I needed that! But if the sex-phobes, as you put it, heard what you just said about being sex-affirmative and not regretting the sexual revolution, I think they might say something like this: Well, Duberman, the sex revolutionary who thinks there was no real issue of promiscuity, was one of our so-called leaders who were most silent when the community most needed leadership. What role has Duberman played in helping our community respond to the greatest crisis it has ever known? Where has he been for the last five years?

DUBERMAN: It's simple, Larry. I was physically disabled. For health reasons, I withdrew from nearly all involvement, community and otherwise, well before the epidemic unfolded. Within a year, my mother died after an agonizing and protracted bout with cancer, my lover decided he loved the church more than me, and I ended up in the hospital with a heart attack. My life was in pieces for a while.

MASS: . . . . Marty, I'm not asking you to take this seriously. But I do think that this is the kind of thing that will be used as a weapon against us by the sex-phobes.

DUBERMAN: Some people getting active in the movement, now and for the first time, and who regard the early radical gay movement with contempt, only became active when they could do so moralistically. I mean, they didn't make themselves available in the early days of the gay movement, when the community was attempting to mobilize around life-affirming issues. They were only there when death arrived. Some of them are only in their early thirties, so they would have been too young to have participated earlier.

But there's something else that needs to be said here. No matter what radical protest movement or period of American history you look at, you almost always find that the initial wave of reformers, of protesters, gives way. When I teach the anti-slavery movement, students are constantly saying to me, "Oh, well, you mean to tell me that William Lloyd Garrison really cared about the slaves? No sooner were they freed than he retired and said the job was done." That's a standard accusation against radical protesters. That line of attack comes from people who haven't been around long enough to have any awareness of or sensitivity to the phenomenon of burnout. You can stand on the barricades for just so long without needing to replenish yourself. There are some people—A.J. Muste, Wendell Phillips, Frederick Douglass—who can go on indefinitely in a protest movement. But most of us mere mortals require an occasional retreat. And usually the people who are basically against the initial protest are the ones who will belatedly jump in and say, "Oh, see, they didn't really care about these issues because they disappeared from the front lines, after arguing the issues for a mere decade."

For example, historians of the anti-slavery movement denounced the abolitionists for nearly a century. They called them all kinds of names, like misguided fanatics and neurotics. They also called them "sunshine soldiers," with the implication that they were only in there when the going was to their liking. Here's the point. The fact that they ultimately withdrew from the struggle is used as a way of proving that they never really cared about the struggle in the first place. And if you can devalue the motives of the people who were originally engaged in the struggle, you thereby devalue the struggle itself. And it just so happens that these same historians, who spent one hundred years attacking the motives of the abolitionists, were/ are in fact very conservative men, not at all sure that *anything* could or should have been done about slavery.

MASS: Yes, but I'll bet at least some of the people we're calling sex-phobes do genuinely, altruistically care about our community. Aren't we running the risk of devaluing as sexophobic everybody who was critical of the early gay movement and of the sexual revolution, in much the same way that we may be devaluing as ultraconservative (or implicitly racist) every historian who may have been critical of the abolitionists?

DUBERMAN: We do run that risk and I think that's a needed corrective. But I want to give you an example of the kind of person I'm talking about. I'm thinking of one *littérateur*, who will go nameless, who I wrote to when *Gay Sunshine* was struggling for survival in the early seventies. I had volunteered to write a letter to some wealthy, closeted gays I knew, soliciting support for *Gay Sunshine*. One of those persons, a prominent writer and theater director, is now an "upfront" gay for the first time. But in the early seventies, he responded to my letter by saying he had read the rag and couldn't imagine why I was lending my name to it — and of course he would not support it; on the contrary, he would like to see it cease publication. This man is a multi-millionaire and in his mid-to-late-sixties. He's been gay and rich for a long time and could easily have joined the struggle. But he's only joined now because now he's able — just like any good mainstream heterosexual — to condemn and to counsel "maturity" (which translated means behaving like mainstream heterosexuals). He's saying what America wants to hear about gay people, about gay men especially — that we "abused" sexual freedom, thus bringing down on our heads the retribution of AIDS. So for this *littérateur* to join the struggle now is simply to embrace and proclaim what the straight world has been saying all along about the gay world. To be a sex-phobe now is not to take an outsider position, the way gay-rights people did in the early seventies. It's to take a mainstream position. I certainly don't mean to imply that we can't be critical of ourselves or that everybody who has been engaged in trying to warn the community about AIDS and other STD risks is a sex-phobe. But I do think that this is the essential difference between the people who were active in the early days of the movement and some of those who are currently active. The gay sex-phobe is speaking with the words of the mainstream majority in this country. And for his pains in railing so uncategorically against sexual "promiscuity," the gay sex-phobe, far from being driven to the margin, is being applauded by the mainstream as a responsible citizen; in other words, as the right kind of gay, as an acceptable puritan.

MASS: Why isn't your review of Larry Kramer's novel, *Faggots* included with the other book reviews and selected essays of *About Time*?

DUBERMAN: I left out two or three pieces that were merely negative. We're having enough trouble in the community without reprinting attacks on each other. I think the only negative piece I did include is the review of Al Carmines' *The Faggot*, and then only because I was also able to print the surrounding correspondence which served as a corrective.

MASS: You blasted *The Faggot* as a politically retrograde nightmare of negative stereotypes. And you eloquently defend your position in the accompanying correspondence with Carmines. But the very stylishly campy song, "Disposable Woman," was so wonderful, especially the way the great David Summers sang it when he and Carmines included it in a special cabaret evening they did together at Don't Tell Mama several years ago. David, the recently deceased cofounder of the PWA Coalition and star of the PBS documentary, "Hero Of My Own Life," was the original New Boy in Town in *The Faggot*. Does being politically correct mean we can't have fun?

DUBERMAN: You're askin' *me* that, honey (laughs)!? Me, who overdid everything! Of course, we can have fun putting each other down and on, but not in public during a period when every public appearance counted for so much. There was so little that was saying anything affirmative or balanced or progressive about gay life at that time. On the other hand, I've always been a passionate defender of *Boys in the Band*, which I think was very true to a particular moment in gay life, even though it was a moment of immense self-hatred. Unlike *Boys in the Band*, *The Faggot*, which came five or more years later, was not true to its subject because *that* moment in gay life was also seeing the birth of the gay movement and the surfacing of a more positive self-image. Not that any given artist, like Carmines, is responsible for representing the whole of anything at a given time; he's only responsible for presenting his own perspective. Fair enough. But I found that perspective offensive.

MASS: I'd like to ask you now about one of the most important historical and biographical projects of our time, your forthcoming biography of Paul Robeson. I'm proud that the *Native* will be the first publication anywhere to speak with you about it. I remember when Paul Robeson Jr. first approached you five years ago. At the time, there was supposedly some evidence that both Paul Sr. and his wife had been actively bisexual. Now that you've finished the first draft of your study, were you able to verify or disprove this information?

DUBERMAN: At the very beginning of my research, a highly placed source informed me that Robeson had had an affair with Sergei Eisenstein, the Russian filmmaker. I was startled and pleased, as you can imagine, and eagerly looked forward to being able to confirm that. I've done everything I could to confirm it, including talking with a gay man who lived in Moscow in the 1930s, which was the only time Robeson and Eisenstein had contact with each other. There's absolutely no evidence, finally, to back it up. On the other hand, there's voluminous evidence to confirm the fact that Robeson was a devoted heterosexual. The question of Eslanda (or Essie) Robeson is more problematic. Her son told me that there were love letters from Essie to women in the Robeson Archives that he burnt—supposedly the only things that he destroyed. I've talked to a few people who knew Essie well, who do think that it's possible that, towards the end of her life, anyway, she may have had affairs with women. Much more important, I think, is that both Paul and Essie were not simply tolerant but entirely open-minded about homosexuality. I'll give you an example. In the mid 1920s, when the Robesons went to France for the first time—they were both themselves in their mid-twenties—the first people they looked up were Glenway Wescott and his lover Monroe Wheeler, both of whom are still alive, in their mid-to-late-eighties. They've been lovers for about sixty years and confirm that the Robesons definitely understood that they were gay and that many of their mutual friends were gay. [Ed. Note: Wescott and Wheeler are since deceased.] Gertrude Stein is another example. She and Robeson instantly hit it off.

MASS: Did Paul ever explicitly address the subject of homosexuality?

DUBERMAN: No. But Essie did in her diaries. Regarding a French writer, she wrote that his family couldn't accept him and that she encouraged him to lead his own life regardless. There was nothing wrong with who and what he was. The family would have to adjust. In other words, both Paul and Essie were large people — large in vision, large in their acceptance of a variety of lifestyles and genuinely appreciative of people who were very different from themselves.

MASS: In recent years, you've been working on *Paul Robeson* and *About Time*, alternatively and simultaneously. What kinds of resonances have existed between these projects for you?

DUBERMAN: I guess what binds them together for me is my perspective as an outsider. Because I'm an outsider, I can tune in more readily to other outsiders. In fact, I've just submitted a proposal for a television program. It would be a sort of history of outsiders and would be called *Unofficial Heroes*.

You know, I used to think that I got so involved in black history and black issues, initially, as a sort of screen for protesting my own cause. There may be some truth to that, but my later involvement in the gay movement did not supplant or diminish my interest in black issues. I don't think it's ever really been an either/or proposition, or ever could be. What all this means, then, is that there's a natural coalition that exists between oppressed minorities. This shared experience, of course, has great resonance for me, even though, unlike all blacks and some gays, I've always been able "to pass." I've always been comparatively "presentable" in terms of what our culture has labeled the acceptable model of mainstream looks and behavior.

But I want to say something here about a related issue. I think the current emphasis on having a homosexual identity, which is a fairly recent phenomeon, might come at the expense of a certain complexity and fluidity. In order to talk about our differentness publicly and politically, we seem inescapably to narrow the actual complexity of our personalities and our culture. For example, the way most gay men disdain transvestites, is, I think, really shocking in this regard. Most gay men remain unwilling publicly to include or acknowledge transvestites or transsexuals — indeed, even old-fashioned camp behavior is frowned upon — as part of the full range of our differentness.

MASS: Oh, absolutely! So many among us are like the middle-class blacks who suddenly develop an intolerance for anything too . . . subcultural.

DUBERMAN: Yes, and I think this brings us back full circle to the beginning of the discussion, because one of the ways in which gay people are now, again, being encouraged to pass is to get-their-sexual-act-together. I think that's why the liberals have now taken over the movement. Because, finally, they have a message which they think will make us more acceptable to the mainstream world.

MASS: Liberals?

DUBERMAN: Yes. A liberal tends to emphasize conforming. Liberals believe in the melting pot. Radicals, on the other hand, believe in ethnic, racial, religious and sexual diversity. I think the liberals are seizing this tragic moment in time in order to try to shape gay men up, into what would be a more acceptable image — namely, into people whose sexual pattern is monogamous pair-bonding, into people who have realized the "immaturity" of sexual adventuring and who are now willing to settle down in an "adult" way with one partner. I mean, that's right in the mainstream liberal image. And I think that these are the people who are now lecturing the community: "At least from this terrible tragedy, we have now learned something; we have matured." You hear that constantly, don't you?

MASS: I understand and sympathize with what you're complaining about, but I believe there's a lot of truth to that specific statement. We have learned something from this epidemic and we have grown. I myself have made such statements and don't regret them. For example, I do deeply believe that those who are most comfortable in long-term relationships, and who *may* represent a sizable portion of our community, should be able to legitimize those relationships — legally, socially — if they so wish. Don't you agree?

DUBERMAN: Yes, but I think the AIDS crisis is going to end up legitimizing the most conformist and intolerant elements in our community, and pushing to the margins the most adventuresome, nonconforming elements. I think the gay community is being lectured by its own spokespeople in the direction of adopting mainstream sexual mores.

MASS: While I would reaffirm my belief that some lecturing has been necessary, I deeply share your concern that too much of it introjects the mysogynistic, sex-negative intolerance of mainstream sexual mores. As you point out, we never made much progress with integrating transsexuals, transvestites and drag queens into our community, even though they were the people who were literally on the front lines of the Stonewall Rebellion and the birth of the modern gay liberation movement. This intolerance of gender nonconformity, which is at least as bad as it's ever been, is, I think, a real barometer of where we're at, since gender issues are so fundamentally important to who and what we are.

DUBERMAN: I think it's tragic enough that the AIDS plague is taking so many gay lives. And it will be an additional tragedy if it robs us of our gay specialness. Unfortunately, I think, that's the direction it's taking. I think it will continue to do both because of the sex-phobes in our midst, gay as well as straight.

Index

About Time (Duberman), 223-225,
228-229,236,238
Acquired immune deficiency
syndrome (AIDS), 113-161
civil rights and, 125,146-147,
160-161
etiology and transmission,
114-117,144-146,148-154,
182-183
by blood products, 143-146,
148-149,152-153,156,
157-158
homophobia related to, 117,
122-123,144
medical research regarding,
159-160
opportunistic infections of
Kaposi's sarcoma, 114,126,
128-132,136-142,143
Pneumocystis carinii
pneumonia, 114,120,130,135
prevention, 117-119,147-148
among adolescents, 179-182
by quarantine, 158,183-184
risk-reduction guidelines, 157,
158
"safe sex", 118-119
promiscuity and, 137-138,
140-141,172
Adler, Alfred, 49
Adolescents
homosexual/lesbian
AIDS prevention among,
179-182
gender behavior, 173-174,
186-187

Harvey Milk High School, 167,
184-188
Institute for the Protection of
Lesbian and Gay Youth,
167-182,185
role models, 176-177
sex abuse of, 177-178
social development, 169-172,
175-176
pregnancy, 41,179,180
Age-of-consent laws, 75
Aggression, in childhood sexuality,
41
AIDS. *See* Acquired immune
deficiency syndrome
AIDS Coalition To Unleash Power,
119
AIDS Network, 144-145
Altman, Lawrence, 228
Ambisexuality, 6,34-35
Amebiasis, 113,129-130,133-135,
150
American Academy of Pediatrics,
73,97
American College of Obstetrics and
Gynecology, 97
American Psychiatric Association
Gay Caucus, 8,16-17
homosexuality diagnostic
classification, 9,16,19,55-56,
214,219. *See also Diagnostic
and Statistical Manual-III*
American Psychoanalytic
Association, 53,60
Anal intercourse, 5
Androgyny, 100
Anti-homosexuality laws, 77

Anti-Semitism, 90,192,195,202,208
Apuzzo, Virginia, 144,153
Ashkenazy, Steve, 167,185-187
As Is (Hoffman), 165,181
Association of Lesbian and Gay
     Psychiatrists, 8,168
Athletes, homosexual, 105-112
Averill, Brett, 224,225

Bauman, Robert, 195,207
Beattie, Jack, 226
Beeson, Jack, 189
Behavior modification, 12. *See also*
     Sexual orientation,
     conversion therapy
Bell, Arthur, 123-124,125
   Homosexualties, 5,17,19,71,225
Benjamin, Harry, 221
Berdache, 221
Berkowitz, Richard, 115,118,122
Berube, Alan, 229
Bible, sexuality references of,
     81-83,85
Bieber, Irving, 11,17,28,77
Bilimerence, 34,40
Birth control, 45
Bisexuality
   normality of, 25
   of twins, 216-217
Bisexuals
   father-son relationships, 216-217
   sexual orientation conversion
     therapy, 23,33
Blood donors, homosexuals as,
     143-146,152-153,157-158
Blood products, AIDS transmission
     by, 143-146,152-153,156,
     157-158
Bolsheviks, 194
Boswell, John, 80,83-84,85
Bryant, Anita, 1

Calderone, Mary, 18,29
   interview with, 65-76

Callen, Michael, 115,122
Cameron, Paul, 183-184
Campbell, Robert J., 14
Carmine, Al, 236,237
Cassady, Neal, 227
Catholic Church, homosexuality
     and, 77-86
Caucus of Homosexual-Identified
     Psychiatrists, 8
Cavett, Dick, 25
Center for Lesbian and Gay Studies,
     229-230
Cervical cancer, 62,88,138
Chauncey, George, 229
Chesley, Robert, 165
Children. *See also* Adolescents
   cross-gender activity, 4
     effeminacy of boys, 13,24-25,
       27-28,40,54,216-217
     masculinity of girls, 13,40
   gender identity development, 13,
     24-25,38-39,54
   gender identity disorders,
     213-214,219-220
   homosexual relationships, 73-74.
     See also Man-boy
     relationships
   masturbation, 26
   sex abuse of, 75
   sex education, 63-64,68-71
   sex rehearsal play, 26,31-32,41,
     83,71,72,73,74-75,89
   sexuality of, 70-71,72-73,213
     aggression in, 41
   sexual rights, 54-55
Christianity. *See also* Catholic
     Church
   anti-Semitism of, 90
   homophobia of, 83,84
*Christianity, Social Tolerance and
     Homosexuality* (Boswell),
     80,83-84
Church and the Homosexual, The
     (McNeill), 78,79,83,85
Circumcision, 61-62,77-78,87-104

cancer prevention and, 62,88
hygienic basis of, 75-76,88-90
incest taboo and, 89-90,91
incidence, 87
masturbation and, 88-89,90-91
venereal disease prevention and,
89
Civil rights, of homosexuals, 19-20,
120
AIDS and, 125,146-147,160-161
Bolsheviks' support for, 194
in Germany, 207
Clergy. *See also* Catholic Church;
Christianity
attitudes towards homosexuals, 80
homosexual orientation of, 80,81
CMV. *See* Cytomegalovirus
infection
Cohn, Roy, 195,207
Concentration camps, homosexuals'
treatment in, 197-198
Condom, 45
Conformist, The (film), 194
Coprophilia, 36
Cross-gender behavior, 4,100,173,
219,221. *See also*
Effeminacy, of boys;
Masculinity, of girls
"Cruising", 35-36
Cultural factors
in fantasy, 31-32
in gender identity, 38-39
in sadomasochism, 31
Curran, James, 118,147
Curtis, Charlotte, 227-228
Cytomegalovirus infection (CMV),
128-129,135

Damned, The (film), 194
Dancer From the Dance (Holleran),
121
Decter, Midge, 77,120
*Diagnostic and Statistical
Manual-III,* (DSM-III)
criticism of, 48-49

diagnostic classifications
ego-dystonic homosexuality,
9-10,38,219-220
gender identity of childhood
disorder, 219
homosexuality, 55-56
Diggins, John Patrick, 227
Dignity New York, 78,79,83,168
D'Emilio, John, 162,229
Dolan, Terry, 195,207
Donahue, Phil, 1,25,104,168
Douglas, Ann, 226
Dover, Kenneth, 26
Dragon in the Forest, The (Plant),
189
Duberman, Martin Bauml
About Time, 223-225,228-229,
236,238
interview with, 223-240
Visions of Kerouac, 226-227
Duggan, Lisa, 229
Durbin, Karen, 124-125

Effeminacy, of boys, 13,24-25,
27-28,40,54
Green interview regarding,
213-222
maternal factors in, 216-217
Eicher, Wolf, 39
Eisenstein, Sergei, 237
Endorphins, 44-45
Enlow, Roger, 143,144,153,166
Epstein, Jospeh, 77
Eunuch, 82-83
Exclusivity, sexual, 13-14,25,36,
231-232. *See also*
Pair-bonding

Faderman, Lillian, 229
Faggots (Kramer), 120-122,236-237
Fain, Nathan, 122-123
Family Book About Sexuality, The
(Calderone), 65-66
Family relationships, of

homosexuals and lesbians,
85-86,176
during adolescence, 178
Fantasy
cultural factors in, 31-32
guided, 31
homosexual, 23,30-31
in heterosexual relationships,
30,33-34
political-sexual, 203-204
of power, 202-203
violence in, 5
of wrestlers, 110,111
Fascism, 200-201,203,204
as homosexuality, 207
leather/sex community and, 201,
202,204-206,208-209,
210-212,218
masculinity as, 207-208
Father-son relationships
of bisexuals, 216-217
of homosexuals, 101-103,216-217
Femininity. *See also* Effeminacy, of
boys
of lesbians, 99-100,103
Feminization of American Culture
(Douglas), 226
Fetishism, 36
circumcision and, 93,94,95
Fierstein, Harvey, 74
Fliess, Wilhelm, 94
Flynt, Larry, 43
Fonville, Terry, 144
Freedman, Estelle, 162
Freud, Sigmund, 12,49,81
"archaic" sexual behavior theory
of, 94
homophobia of, 60-61
Friedman, Estelle, 229
Friedman-Kien, Alvin, 118,142,166
interview with, 114,128-132
Fund for Human Dignity, 144

Gamophobia, 14
Gantrell, Nanette, 8

Gay, definition, 99
Gay Activists Alliance, 200
Gay and Lesbian Alliance Against
Defamation, 200
Gay community, 120,121-122
Gay liberation movement, 215-216,
234-236
Gay Male S/M Activists, 204
Gay Men's Health Crisis, 114,
119-120, 122,123,136,157,
164,165,167,182,183
Gay Men's Health Project, 147
Gay Psychiatrists of New York, 168
Gender behavior. *See also*
Effeminacy, of boys;
Masculinity, of girls
of adolescent homosexuals and
lesbians, 173-174,186-187
Gender identity
cultural factors in, 38-39
disorders of, 213-214,219-220
Gender-identity clinic, 40
Gender-reinforcment therapy, 217,
220-221. *See also* Sexual
orientation, conversion
therapy
Genetic factors, in homosexuality,
10,39-40
Germany. *See also* Nazis
homosexual emancipation
movement, 207,210
Giardiasis, 129,134
Ginsberg, Allan, 227
Gittings, Barbara, 179
Goldberg, Irwin, 227
Goldstein, Richard, 125
Gonorrhea, 113,129
Goodman, Walter, 226-227
Gould, Robert, 186
Greece, ancient, 25,26
Greek Homosexuality (Dover), 26
Green, Richard, 11,13,24,25,
214-215,216
interview with, 213-222
"Sissy Boy Syndrome" and the

Development of Homosexuality, 214-215,216
Growing Up Straight (Wyden), 66
Gruendgens, Gustaf, 196-197

Haitians, AIDS transmission by, 148,149-151,156-157
Handley, John, interview with, 105-112
Harvey Milk High School, 167, 184-188
Hatterer, Lawrence, 11,17-18
Hepatitis, 129
Hepatitis B, 113,148,149,151,152, 158,180
  vaccine, 153-154
Herodotus, 92
Herpes simplex virus, 113, 129, 138
Heterosexuality
  ego-dystonic, 38
  as learned behavior, 4,10
Heterosexuals
  homosexual fantasies of, 30,33-34
  homosexual relationships of, 25
  sexual behavior of, 3
Hetrick, Emery, 7-8
  interview with, 168-182
Hill, Carl, 17
Himmler, Heinrich, 190,191,193
Hirschfeld, Magnus, 179, 207,210
Hitler, Adolf, 183-184,190,192,193, 196,201-202,206-207,209
Hobson, Laura, 174-175
Hoffman, William, 165,181
Holleran, Andrew, 121,122
Homolimerence, 30
Homophobia
  towards adolescent homosexuals and lesbians, 168-169
  AIDS-related, 117,122-123,144
  American, 190
  Christian, 83,84
  definition, 14,58
  of homosexuals, 80,209
  Jewish, 85

legal basis of, 77,84,191
Nazi, 189-199
of psychiatrists, 7-15,16-19, 55-56,58-59
of psychoanalysts, 28
Homosexual Behavior: A Modern Reappraisal (Marmor), 19, 55,57-58
"Homosexual conversion", 2. *See also* sexual orientation, conversion therapy
"Homosexual dissatisfaction", 2-3, 6,220
Homosexualities (Bell and Weinberg), 5, 19,71,225
Homosexuality
American Psychiatric Association diagnostic classification, 9, 16,19,55-56,214,219
  biblical references to, 82-83
  biological research regarding, 27-28
  definition, 10-11
  as dysfunction, 1,3,4-5,6,11, 56-57
  ego-dystonic, 9-10,22,38,55-56, 219-220
  as fascism, 207
  genetic factors, 10,39-40
  as learned preference, 2,4,10
  psychiatric research regarding, 14-15
  psychoanalytic theory of, 11-12
  of twins, 216-218
Homosexuality and American Psychiatry: The Politics of Diagnosis (Bayer), 16
Homosexuality in Perspective (Masters and Johnson), 1,2, 3,12,19, 53,54,225
Homosexual relationships. *See also* Marriage, homosexual
  of children, 73-74
  exclusivity in, 13-14,25,36, 231-232

of heterosexuals, 25
intimacy in, 104
Homosexuals
cognitive ability, 15
family relationships, 85-86,176
father-son relationships, 101-103,
216-217
homophobia of, 80,209
as immigrants, 17,50
interactions with lesbians,
100-101,170
masculinity of, 13,99-100,
103-104
narcissism of, 20-21,59-60,94,95
as sex offenders, 126-127
sexual behavior of, 3,53-54
HSV. *See* Herpes simplex virus
Humphreys, Laud, 53-54
Hunter, Joyce, 167
H-Y antigen, 39
Hyperphilia, 35,36
Hypophilia, 36

Identity. *See also* Gender identity
homosexual, 195,238-239
Imagery, erotic. *See also* Fantasy
in children, 31-32
Immigration laws, 17,50
Incest taboo, 42-43
masturbation and, 89-90,91
*Innovations in Psychotherapy with
Homosexuals* (Hetrick and
Terry), 168
Institute for the Protection of
Lesbian and Gay Youth,
167-182,185
International Academy of Sex
Research, 214
Intimacy, in homosexual
relationships, 104
Israel, anti-homosexuality laws, 77

Jaffee, Harold, 158
Jesus Christ, 81,82-83

Jews
homophobia of, 85
homosexual, 77-78
Johnson, Eric, 76
Johnson, Virgina. *See* Masters,
William and Johnson,
Virginia
Joy of Gay Sex, The (Silverstein), 99
Jung, Carl, 49,80-81

Kallman, Franz, 217
Kameny, Frank, 179
Kantrowitz, Arnie, interview with,
200-212
Kaplan, Helen Singer, 17-18,50,72,
77
on gender-identity disturbances,
54
sexual orientation conversion
therapy of, 22,32,174
Kaposi's sarcoma, 114,126,128-132,
135,143
among Haitians, 150
interview with patient, 136-142
Karlen, Arno, 14
Sexuality and Homosexuality, 26
Katz, Jonathan, 229
Kerouac, 226-227
Kessler, David, 8,17
Kinder, Karl, 17
Kirkpatrick, Martha, 20-21
Klare, Rudolf, 191
Kolodny, Robert, 3-6
Kramer, Larry, 115,123,141-142,
153,182-183,230
Faggots, 120-122,236-237
on homosexual leadership, 176,
184
homosexual promiscuity criticism
by, 114,117,118-119,120,
171
The Normal Heart, 118-119,
162-163,164-167,172,181,
182
Krateski, Jim, 8

Krintzman, Donald, interview with, 136-142
Kroening, Vernon, 79
Kung, Hans, 78

Laius complex, 101-102
Laubenstein, Linda, 118,130,163
Lautmann, Ruediger, 198
Law, Liberty and Psychiatry (Szasz), 47,49
Learned behavior
  heterosexuality as, 4,10
  homosexuality as, 2,4,10
Learning
  in erotic imagery, 31-32
  sexual, 70-71
Leather/sex movement, Nazi paraphernalia use by, 201, 202,204-206,208-209, 210-212,218
Leavitt, David, 228
Lehmann-Haupt, Christopher, 228
Lesbians
  femininity of, 99-100,103
  interactions with homosexuals, 100-101,170
  narcissism of, 20-21
  Nazis' treatment of, 191
Levy, Norman, 166
Lilly, Frank, 166
Limerence, 32
  definition, 29,30
  heterosexual, 222
  religious behavior as, 43
  sexual attraction and, 37-38
Lind, Mark, 201-202
Love and Limerence (Tennov), 29, 30
Love and Love Sickness (Money), 29-30,31,35,41
Love object, sexual orientation and, 30
Lynch, Michael, 122

Mailer, Norman, 77
Male Couple, The (McWhirter and Mattidos), 231
Male and Female Homosexuality (Saghir), 34
Malpractice, 21-22,220
Man and Woman, Boy and Girl (Money), 73
Man-boy relationships, 26,101, 169-170
Mann, Erika, 196-197
Mann, Klaus, 196-197
Man to Man: Gay Couples in America (Silverstein), 99,101
Manufacturers of Madness, The (Szasz), 49
Marmor, Judd, 11,22
  on homophobia, 58
  Homosexual Behavior: A Modern Reappraisal, 19,55,57-58
  on homosexuality as dysfunction, 56,57-60
  interview with, 16-28
  Sexual Inversion, 19,55,56-57
Marriage, 81-82
  homosexual, 125,146-147, 160-161,164,172-173
  sexual attraction in, 37-38
Marriage age, 75
Martin, Damien, 8
  interview with, 167-188
Masculinity
  as fascism, 207-208
  of girls, 13,40
  of homosexuals, 13,99-100, 103-104
  sadomasochism and, 195
Masserman, Jules, 17
Masters, William and Johnson, Virginia, 1-6,17,18
  ambisexuality theory of, 34-35
  anti-homosexual bias of, 50-54
  fantasy pattern theory of, 30-31
  Homosexuality in Perspective, 1, 2,3,12,19,53,54

interview with, 1-6
The Pleasure Bond, 13-14
sexual orientation conversion
    therapy, 22-23,32-34,50-52,
    168,174
Masturbation
  by children, 26
  circumcision and, 88-89,90-91
  fetish use in, 36
McNeill, John, interview with,
    77-86
Media, homosexual stereotyping by,
    176-177
Mental health movement, 48
Mental patients, legal rights of,
    49-50
Mephisto (film), 196-197
Mildvan, Donna, 143
  interview with, 114,133-135
Milk, Harvey, 187-188. *See also*
    Harvey Milk High School
Money, John, 18
  interview with, 29-46,113
  Man and Woman, Boy and Girl,
    73
  sex play theory of, 63
  *Traumatic Abuse of the Child at
    Home*, 63
Moore, Paul, 80
Moscone, George, 167
Mother-son relationship, 216-217
Muggia, Franco, 130
Munzer, Jean, 8
Mysogyny, 100
Myth of Mental Illness, The (Szasz),
    64

Nachman, Larry David, 207
Narcissism
  DSM-III diagnostic classification,
    48,49
  of homosexuals, 20-21,59-60,94,
    95
  of lesbians, 20-21

National Gay Health and Education
    Foundation, Inc., 143
National Gay Task Force, 168
Native Americans
  berdache, 221
  swatiska use, 201,202
Nazi paraphernalia/symbolism,
    200-212
  leather/sex movement's use of,
    201,202,204-206,208-209,
    210,212,218
Nazis
  homosexuals as, 193-195. *See
    also* Roehm, Ernst
  homosexuals' persecution by,
    189-199
  lesbians treatment by, 191
Newton, Esther, 229
New York Physicians for Human
    Rights, 114,147
New York Times, editorial policy of,
    225-228
Nichols, Stuart, 8,143
Night Sweat (Chesley), 165
Nonlimerence, 36-37
Normal Heart, The (Kramer),
    118-119, 162-163,164-167,
    172,181,182
North American Man/Boy Love
    Association, 169-170
Nymphomania, 35

Odors, sexual response to, 94
Oedipus complex, 101,102
Ohrenstein, Manfred, 185
Ortleb, Charles, 115

Paige, Karen E., 97-98
Pair-bonding, 13-14,32,225. *See
    also* Limerence
  as addiction, 44
  infant/parent prototype, 42
Paraphilia, 31,33,36,38
  role collusion in, 43-44

Parent-infant relationship, 75
Paulson, Jim, 8
Pederasty, 101
Pedophilia, 75,101
Penis cancer, 62,88
Phimosis, 76,90
Picano, Felice, 224
Pilaga Indians, 73-74
Pillard, Richard C., 18
  interview with, 7-15
  The Wild Boys of Burundi, 7
Pink Triangle: The Nazi War
    Against Homosexuals, The
    (Plant),189-190,194,199
Plant, Richard, 78,206-207,209-210
  The Dragon in the Forest, 189
  interview with, 189-199
  The Pink Triangle: The Nazi War
    Against Homosexuals,
    189-190,194,199
Pleasure Bond, The (Masters and
    Johnson), 13-14
Pneumonia, *Pneumocystis carinii*,
    114,120,134,135
Podhoretz, Norman, 77
Pogrebin, Letty Cottin, 101
Polyiterophilia, 35-36
Pope John Paul II, 79-80
Popham, Paul, 122
Pornography, 101,175
Pregnancy, adolescent, 41-42,180
Prematurity, sex abuse correlation,
    75
Promiscuity, of homosexuals, 35-36
  AIDS transmission and, 114-115,
    116-117,119-120,122,125,
    137-138,140-141, 146,154,
    159,160-161,230-233
  criticism of, 114,117,118-119,
    120,171,160-161,230-233
Prostate cancer, 62,88
Psychiatric Dictionary (Campbell),
    14
Psychiatrists, homophobia of, 7-15,
    16-19,55-56,58-59

Psychoanalysis, future of, 28
Psychoanalysts, homophobia of, 28
Psychoanalytic theory, of
    homosexuality, 11-12
Psychoanalytic therapy, as
    malpractice, 21-22

Quarantine, of homosexuals, 158,
    183-184

Rape, 66
Rapoport, Paul, 122,136,140
Raymond, Janice, 40
Reich, Wilhelm, 113,213
Religion. *See also* specific religions
  homosexuality and, 77-86
Religious behavior, 43,44
  of homosexuals, 80-81
Robeson, Eslanda, 237-238
Robeson, Paul, 223,227,237-238
Robeson, Paul Jr., 237
Robinson, Paul, 83
Roehm, Ernst, 190,192-193,194,
    195,196,206
Role collusion, 43-44
Romkowski, Chiam, 208
Rosenthal, Abe, 77
Rothenberg, David, 224
Rundle, Frank, 8,9,17

Sacerdote, Paul, 44-45
Sadomasochism, 13,101,103
  cultural factors in, 31
  homosexual versus heterosexual,
    27
  Nazi paraphernalia and, 200-212
  role collusion in, 43-44
  in sports, 111-112
"Safe sex", 118-119,230
Saghir, Marcel, 34
St. John, 81
St. Thomas Aquinas, 84
Satyriasis, 35

Schaffner, Bert, 8
Schillebeeckx, Edward, 78
Schmidt, Benno, 229
Schneiderman, David, 125
Schrader, Paul, 78
Schwartz, Mark, 35
Sencer, David, 118,148
  interview with, 156
Senior Action in a Gay
    Environment, 168,177
Sex abuse
  of adolescent homosexuals and
    lesbians, 177-178
  premature birth correlation, 75
Sex By Prescription (Szasz), 50,53,
    55,61,62,63-64,66,68
Sex-change surgery, 40,62-63
Sex education, 63-64,68-71
Sex Information and Education
    Council of the United
    States(SIECUS), 65,67,69
Sex offenders, treatment, 126-127
Sex rehearsal play, 26,31-32,41,63,
    72,73
  intergenerational, 74-75
  as polymorphus perversity, 89
  socialization of, 71
Sexual attraction, limerence and,
    37-38
Sexual behavior
  of heterosexuals, 3
  of homosexuals, 3,53-54
Sexual Excitement (Stoller), 27
Sexual health, 64
Sexual Inversion (Marmor), 19,55,
    56-57
Sexuality
  biblical references to, 81-83
  of children, 41,70-71,72-73,213
Sexuality and Homosexuality
    (Karlen), 26
Sexually-transmitted disease, 231.
    See also specific diseases
  circumcision-related prevention,
    69

epidemics, 113-114
Sexual orientation
  of adolescent homosexuals and
    lesbians, 174
  changes, 70
  childhood determination of, 214
  conversion therapy, 12-13,18,21-22,
    22-25,32-34,50,168,174-175
    for bisexuals, 23,33
  dominant preference in, 34
  etiology, 71-72
  freedom of expression of, 69
  love object and, 30
Sexual Preferences (Bell, Weinberg
    and Hammersmith), 71-72,
    214
Sexual revolution, 45-46,230,233
  sexually-transmitted diseases and,
    113,114
Shapiro, Harvey, 226
Shilts, Randy, 122
Shirer, William L., 194,195
Silverstein, Charles, 18
  interview with, 99-104
*"Sissy Boy Syndrome" and the
    Development of
    Homosexuality* (Green),
    214-215,216
Socarides, Charles, 4,11,14,17,21,
    22,28,227
Sonnabend, Joseph, 114-115,118,
    166
Spiegel, John, 11,17,19
Spirit and the Flesh, The (Williams),
    221
Spitzer, Robert, 48
Sports, homosexuals in, 105-112
Stambolian, George, interview with,
    87-104
Starett, Barbara, 114
Stein, Gertrude, 238
Stein, Terry, 168
Steinman, Wayne, 185
Stereotyping, of homosexuals,
    176-177

Stoller, Robert, 13,28
  Sexual Excitement, 27
Subculture, homosexual, 13,172
Suicide, 179
Summers, David, 236
Swastika, 200-202,204,205,206
Syphilis, 113,120,129,231
Szasz, Thomas, 18
  interview with, 47-64
  Law, Liberty and Psychiatry, 47,
    49
  The Manufacturers of Madness,
    49
  The Myth of Mental Illness, 64
  Sex By Prescription, 50,53,55,61,
    62,63-64

Tennov, Dorothy, 29,30,34,36-37
Therapeutic state, 47-48
Topkis, Gladys, 213
Traitors, The (film), 194-195
Transsexual Empire, The
    (Raymond), 40
Transsexual Phenomenon
    (Benjamin), 221
Transsexuals, 28,39-41,221,239
  sex-change surgery, 40,62-63
Transvestites, 238-239
*Traumatic Abuse of the Child at
    Home* (Money), 63
Twins, homosexual, 216-218

Ulrichs, Karl, 179

Uncircumcised Society of America,
    95
*Under the Rainbow: Growing Up
    Gay* (Kantrowitz), 200

Vachon, Ron, 153
Venereal disease. *See*
    Sexually-transmitted diseases
Vidal, Gore, 77
Violence, in homosexual fantasy, 5
Visions of Kerouac (Duberman),
    226-227
Voeller, Bruce, 20,143,144,215
von Wangenheim, Gustav, 194
von Weizsaecker, Richard, 199

Waggoner, Raymond, 3
Warren, Carol, 19-20
Wescott, Glenway, 237-238
Wheeler, Monroe, 237-238
White, Dan, 49,167
White, Edmund, 122
Wild Boys of Burundi, The (Pillard),
    7
William, Dan, 118,122-123,133,
    135,159,163
  interview with, 143-155
Williams, Walter L., 221
Wilson, Lawrence, 40
Wisel, Elie, 198
Wrestlers
  female, 106-107
  homosexual, 105-112